WINNING
OHIO

WINNING OHIO

THE FINAL 100 DAYS OF THE TRUMP CAMPAIGN AT GROUND ZERO

THOMAS RYAN

Winning Ohio: The final 100 days of the 2016 Trump presidential campaign at ground zero.

Copyright © 2018 by Thomas Ryan

All rights reserved.

Published in the United States by Kenari LLC, located in Columbus, Indiana.

Library of Congress Cataloging-in-Publication Data is available upon request.

Library of Congress Control Number: 2018952733

Paperback ISBN: 978-1-7325757-0-7

Ebook ISBN: 978-1-7325757-1-4

Printed in the United States of America

Cover design by J Caleb Clark

If you would like to retain the author for a speaking engagement, please send a request to contact@winningohio.com.

10 9 8 7 6 5 4 3 2 1

First Edition

NOTABLE CHARACTERS

Trump Organization

Michael Glassner	National Trump Campaign Deputy Director
Katrina Pearson	Trump Campaign National Spokesperson
Kimberly Flanagan	Trump Campaign Midwest Regional Director
Chris Horvath	Trump Director Ohio
Brandon Moffett	Trump Deputy Director Ohio
Kamilah Prince	Trump Deputy Director Advance Team Ohio
Brian Wollet	Trump Regional Director Northeast Ohio
Brenda Johnson	Trump Mahoning County Chair

RNC Victory Campaign

Justin Clarke	RNC Director Ohio
Tony Russo	RNC Deputy Director (Northern Ohio)
Jonathan Schmidt	RNC Deputy Director (Southern Ohio)
Jason Lovett	RNC Northeast Regional Director
Chelsea Callahan	RNC Mahoning County Field Organizer (FO)
Valentina Mancini	RNC Trumbull County FO

Mahoning County Republican Party (MCRP)

Mark Munroe	MCRP Chair
Rose Piper	MCRP Chairwoman
Tracey Winbush	MCRP Vice Chair
Dan Kavanagh	Deputy Director Board of Elections
Matt Harris	Finance Director Board of Elections
Randy Taylor	Associate at Board of Elections
Don Manning	Republican Candidate 59th State House
Corrine Sanderson	Republican Candidate 58th State House
Pamela Alfonsi Durant	Republican Candidate County Treasurer

INTRODUCTION

In 2016, two major shocks changed the global order. First, on 23 June the British people voted to leave the EU and pursue a smaller, more self-interested set of foreign and domestic policies. Then on 8 November Americans who lived in the interior of the country outvoted their coastal compatriots for a similar shakeup of the United States political system.

A new Trump administration faces enormous challenges at home and abroad. Some of these problems are decades or even centuries in the making, and in other cases powers are reasserting themselves in parts of the globe to directly challenge Pax Americana. Just as British voters selected to disengage from Europe, American voters chose to disengage from the world. This act of Americans choosing to put aside the role of global policeman is itself the largest world order transition since the British Empire lost its influence in the shadow of the First World War.

Many analysts would say that the persons who live in flyover states, Indiana and Ohio to name two, did not consider complex domestic and foreign policy issues when they pulled the lever for Donald Trump. I am not sure that I agree. A type of raw populism took hold of the electorate in these states to be certain, but it is also true that intelligent people of diverse professions and interests chose to select Donald Trump for president instead of Hillary Clinton.

- THOMAS RYAN -

The following pages tell a few of the stories of the campaign workers, local candidates, volunteers, media personalities, and most importantly, the voters who made the 2016 election historic. This is a story that I tell through my biases, and I hold to a spirit of truth rather than a factual narrative. In many cases, I wrote characters in the story as composite figures. Some names have been changed. Facts in politics are impossible for mortals anyway.

One final note: campaign workers, volunteers, and candidates experience enormous stressors throughout an election cycle. It is no exaggeration that people die due to this high and sustained level of stress, and although a few volunteers spent days in the hospital due to the manifestations of this stress, thankfully nobody died for campaign reasons in Mahoning County in 2016. The characters willingly endured the trials and stresses of the campaign because they believed in something. Some believed in themselves, some believed in a candidate, still others believed in a movement. Under the leadership of their patient Chair, Mark Munroe, together they almost won Mahoning County, a county with only a 34% Republican base, and as a consequence they won Ohio for the Republicans – and thus they won the White House for Donald Trump.

Money motivates ninety percent of people, and ego almost all of the rest.
    -Unnamed US AFOSI Special Agent

We are all unreliable narrators in our own lives.
        -Anonymous

CHAPTER 1

Wednesday, 20 July 2016, Beaver Township, Ohio

Rose Piper hit the alarm clock. She hit it again and threw it to the ground.

The clock shrieked until she reached down to the floor and turned off the switch. Her head pounded. Rose felt pain in her back as she straightened her body. She walked to the master bathroom, taking small and deliberate steps. Rose pushed the lever in the shower to the far left and cold water rushed from the showerhead. Thirty seconds later, she stepped into the shower, feeling hot water pour over her hair and stream down her face. The heat and moisture opened her breathing passage but did not wash away feelings that were causing her to develop an ulcer.

Worries from the previous night rushed into her mind while water drenched her. The Canfield Fair, the third largest fair in the United States, was going to take place in six weeks, and nothing was ready for the Mahoning County Republican Party tent. *None of the volunteers are working or doing anything!*

Over drinks last night with members of the Canfield Republican Women's Club, the real power behind the Republican movement in Mahoning County, Rose had been unable to get a commitment from any of the ladies to donate money or time. She needed both to adequately prepare for the six days in late August and early September that would bring in thousands of dollars for the Party. She grimaced at the laziness of the people around her. *Why can't they be more like me? Why can't they take pride in their party?* she had thought. *I am seventy-six years old and I work harder than any of these jokers.*

Worse, Tonya Drummond had been showing up to all of the recent Canfield Republican Women's Club events and charming the other women. She *was* volunteering at headquarters, helping the party chair Mark Munroe with his database, entering the names and contact information of donors to the party to one of several Excel spreadsheets.

Quite a few people inside and outside the county had been sending money to the party ever since Donald Trump had started his presidential campaign in the middle of 2015. Tonya had access to these interested Republicans, and she was in a good position to contact them and ask them to support her own ambitions for the position of chairwoman should she decide to challenge Rose's seat in the February 2017 internal Mahoning County Republican Party (MCRP) elections.

And even more gratingly, Tonya had been meeting each person who walked through the doors of the MCRP headquarters and chatting them up in her friendly way. Fifty or more people a day entered the headquarters building located on Market Street in Boardman, a suburb seven miles to the south of Youngstown, to buy Trump signs, hats, or t-shirts, or to see history in the making. Tonya was networking heavily, Rose knew it, and this greatly irritated the current party chairwoman. *I am the chairwoman! Tonya can't take that from me!*

Rose's head was pounding from last night's margaritas. Steam from the shower was helping marginally. *I am too old for this nonsense*, Rose thought. She pushed the lever to the left but it was already at the stop.

Loud, distressed barking, came from somewhere in the house. She grabbed the lever and pushed it to the right to turn off the shower. Without taking the time to dry off she threw on a robe, stepped into rubber sandals, and shuffled out of the bathroom. Her dog continued to bark, and she walked down the hallway and through the main living room towards the back door.

She saw her husband grabbing at her dog, Gigi. "Yaaale, what are you doing?" she said. He flinched. Her raspy voice grated in her husband's ears. Rose saw the dog cowering in the corner and her eyes flashed angrily at her husband.

Yale Piper, an eighty-three-year-old part-time preacher at the Canfield Anglican-Methodist Church and prominent attorney in Mahoning County, was also in a bad mood that morning though he hid his feelings better than his younger wife. He was a man of few words and tended to go straight to action when he thought it necessary. Yale had decided that he needed peace from Gigi's constant yapping, and he was in the process of moving the dog to the car to take it to doggie daycare. He needed some sleep. Rose's dog was not going to spoil a peaceful day.

Rose's anger intensified when she realized what her husband was doing. "Stop that this instant! I told you not to touch my dog!" she said. Her face turned red.

Yale turned away from her and toward the dog. This infuriated Rose even more. "You son of a bitch!" she said, loudly.

She noticed her head no longer hurt. As a nurse, Rose knew the process that was working in her body to cancel out the pain from her hangover. The party chairwoman and adjunct professor of nursing at YSU knew that her endocrine system was filling with adrenaline. There was a limited window to walk away from the situation. She knew that she could de-escalate the scene right then, and she knew that in a moment she would lose control of her actions.

She chose to embrace her rage.

Rose screamed. Yale ignored her. This show of disrespect tripped a chemical process deep inside Rose's nervous system. She began to lose peripheral vision as she focused on the liberties that her second husband was taking with an animal that loved her unconditionally.

Something snapped. Rose turned around and walked away from Yale. But she was not attempting to separate from the situation to cool off. Rather, she shuffled back to the bedroom with purpose. She pushed her lopsided gait as fast as she could.

It was the sudden quietness from his half Italian half German wife, not the shouting, that got Yale's attention. He could sense that something was wrong, very wrong. Yet still he underestimated the strength of Rose's anger. He followed her to the bedroom in a sluggish walk. Decades of fury boiled over in the slow-motion race back to the bedroom between Rose and Yale, with Yale several paces behind Rose.

Rose headed to the elegant nightstand to the left of the master bed. She reached into the top drawer. Furious at how her husband had treated her and Gigi, she pulled out the .38 Special that the two of them kept near their bed to fend off the criminals of South Range. Yale entered the threshold of the bedroom and walked across the doorway of the master bathroom. He saw the flash of the shiny steel revolver and thought, *Now she has gone too far*. He spoke for the first time that morning, "Rose, the dog has to go."

Methodically Rose raised the pistol and squeezed the trigger. The first round exploded in the wooden bathroom door. She squeezed again. This bullet found its mark deep in Yale's calf. The elder statesman crumpled to the ground, screaming in pain, stripped of all dignity. He grabbed at his leg and writhed on the tile floor.

The sound of the gun and the thud of Yale hitting the tile brought the Mahoning County Republican Party Chairwoman back to reality. "Yaaale," she screamed.

CHAPTER 2

Four months earlier, 23 March 2016
Mahoning County Republican Party Headquarters

Chelsea Callahan clicked on Snapchat and uploaded a selfie while sitting in a folding chair at a white plastic table in the MCRP headquarters. She applied a filter that superimposed a cartoon dog ears and nose over her features. She should have laughed, but she did not.

For the past several months in the presidential primary season Chelsea had been volunteering in Youngstown for the Kasich presidential campaign. On March 15th the governor of Ohio had squeaked out a victory in Ohio. Unfortunately for Chelsea, Kasich had lost handily in Mahoning County and the adjacent Northeast Ohio counties, and the Kasich campaign had subsequently ignored her request to be hired on the national campaign team.

The twenty-three-year-old decided to use her frustration to get creative on Twitter. She grabbed her oversized phone and thumbed out a Tweet.

You, Mr. Drumpf, are a disgusting pig, >:>:>

"Aaauuughh!" she screamed. Perry looked up from the front desk at headquarters, and Kate poked her head through the serving window of the kitchen. Chelsea grabbed her head with her hands.

Moments later the Republican candidate sent out a tweet to millions of his followers. The last few words of the Tweet were *Make America Great Again*.

Chelsea typed furiously on her phone.
Like how Hitler made Germany great again?
She pressed the button and replied to Trump putting her own Tweet in front of a global audience.

CHAPTER 3

Friday, 15 July 2016, 115 Days
The Lakes, Columbus, Indiana

A chubby cat clawed at the bedroom door. Boots had black fur with a white underbelly and adorable white highlights on her face. She wanted to see Thomas, and she could not understand why he was still in his room. The sun sent rays through the large upper floor windows, illuminating the feline.

Cocoa, the other cat, heard Boots scratching the carpet at the closed door of Thomas' bedroom suite. The black shorthair that Thomas had rescued as a four-week-old kitten three years earlier trotted up the stairs and across the bridge to the doorway where Boots remained crouched and frustrated. Cocoa bumped Boots with her head and Boots backed up slightly.

Cocoa leapt into the air, and caught the door handle latch with her paw and pulled it down to unlatch the door. Boots stood up and slowly walked into the room, sniffing the floor as she went.

Thomas moaned slightly and rolled over on the Japanese-style floor mat where he slept. Boots walked on the mat and up to his face. She bumped him. "Meep!" she spoke.

Thomas opened his eyes and closed them. He opened them again and reached for his phone.

11:00 am!

- THOMAS RYAN -

Thomas pushed himself up from the mat with his elbows, and then stood and took off his shirt and underwear. The bathroom connected to the bedroom, and he walked in it and pulled on red swim trunks. He grabbed a large thick white towel hanging next to the oversized bathtub and walked out of his room. Boots rubbed against his leg and he leaned down to scratch her head. He shook his own head several times before rubbing his eyes as he walked across the bridge. Out of muscle memory he made it down the stairs, through the living room, past the kitchen, through the kitchen nook, and out the door to the fire pit and patio. He walked through the thick grass, through the line of pine trees, and down thirty steps to the boat landing. After hesitating momentarily, he dove into the water and surfaced in the middle of the canal leading to the lakes. He gasped.

Thirty minutes later, he swam up to the boat landing and climbed out of the water, feeling much better. It was perfect swimming weather in Southern Indiana this Friday morning.

By the time he had walked back up the stairs, through the pine trees, through the backyard, past the enormous grill, past the fire pit, through the patio, and back into the kitchen nook he was humming.

Once inside, he turned on the stove and poured olive oil onto a flat square pan. He broke three eggs on the edge of the pan and turned his attention to prepare the tomatoes, cheese, strawberries, and peaches at the counter. He popped a few almonds into his mouth and walked over to the table, where his phone was resting.

"Hum dee dum," he sang. Boots weaved around his leg. Cocoa sat on the chair by the window and blinked at him.

His phone buzzed. He opened Twitter.

Donald J. Trump
@realDonaldTrump
I am pleased to announce that I have chosen Governor Mike Pence as my Vice Presidential running mate. News conference tomorrow at 11:00 A.M.
10:50 AM – 15 July 2016

Thomas froze.

"Whoa," he said. Each cat turned her head and looked at him. Boots returned to cruising in slow figure eights, and Cocoa rested her head on her front paws.

Thomas was a foreign policy expert with a focus on the Former Soviet Union, energy politics, and the Central Asian region. He knew most of the other experts in his field, and he knew that only a few Central Asian experts were even American citizens, never mind plausible Trump supporters. *Do I have a chance at a policy-making position?* he wondered.

It would take some finagling. Six years earlier, Thomas had run for a state-level political office as a Democrat. He was pro-life, which would help him with the Republicans, and he was pro-labor, which might help him with Trump. Still, he had run for office under the banner of the wrong party. Political operatives took loyalty seriously. Thomas smiled when he thought of how he might conquer the upcoming challenge.

He walked to the stove, plated the eggs and returned to the kitchen nook table. Thomas Ryan stared out the window at his neighbor. Ed Pence kept the lake house ready to use for the entire Pence family, and his brother, the governor, visited often.

Three hours later, Thomas made significant progress in his research into how he might manage to squeeze into the Trump campaign. It was quite late in a presidential campaign to get a job, but he knew how campaigns were run, he knew what needed to be done generally, and he knew he could present an image that made him appear more integrated than he actually was.

By 11:30 pm he had developed a short list of areas that would be key for the general election, including Northeast Ohio. He pulled up a résumé and adjusted it late into the night. At 2:00 am he fired off a slew of emails in his first attempt to reach the senior managers of the Trump-Pence campaign.

CHAPTER 4

Saturday, 23 July 2016, 107 Days
North Lima, Ohio

A Cirrus SR22 revved its engine while sitting parked in the run-up area. It was angled 135 degrees from runway 09 in North Lima, Ohio. The pilot, a local small factory owner, turned his head to the left and to the right and checked each aileron one last time. He looked at the control panel and systematically checked the oil pressure and other gauges. Everything was within operating parameters. He cut the power to idle.

"North Lima traffic, Cirrus November Bravo one-seven-four-two-niner ready for takeoff," he said. He lifted his index finger off the push-to-talk button on the yolk. The pilot again turned his neck dramatically from side to side so that he could visually check for any unannounced air traffic. He lifted his feet from the top half of the foot pedals, releasing the brakes. He advanced the throttle twenty-five percent and entered the active runway.

The pilot lined up the propeller plane with the large numbers painted on the runway and increased the throttle to the limits. Within a few seconds the engine spun up to 2700 RPM, the propeller tips nearly breaking the sound barrier. The aircraft accelerated, pushing the pilot into the leather seat. Fifteen hundred feet down the runway the plane reached rotation speed and the light aircraft lifted off the ground. Feeling he was airborne, the factory owner pulled back on the yoke to gain altitude. Once he crossed the threshold of the runway, he made a hard left turn and looked over his left shoulder at the gentleman's farm below. Tiny people rambled about the green and walked between the large farmhouse and a pavilion kitted out with a professional kitchen.

Dan Kavanagh stood at the outdoor grill and looked up. He saw the plane pass overhead, and then turned his attention back to the chicken. The food needed another ten more minutes, and he checked his watch.

Don Manning spoke up. "Did you ever want to fly?"

There was silence.

"What was that?" Dan asked. He grimaced and reached for the brown bottle sitting on the table beside the grill.

"You know, did you ever want to take pilot lessons?" Don said.

"Nah, not my thing." Dan paused. Then he smirked. "I always wanted to learn to shoot…"

Don had just sipped his beer and tried to hold back his laughter. He failed, spewing a mist of warm foam into the air.

"Where is Rose, anyway?" Don asked, wiping his beard with a paper towel.

"Oh, they took her away," Dan said. He looked at Manning and spoke in a dry tone, "I heard that Rose emptied the chamber and landed two shots near his balls."

Dan expected another laugh, but Don gritted his teeth. "Oh my God!"

The smirk returned. "Are you doing the gun raffle next month?" Dan asked. Don did laugh at this comment, deeply and from his belly.

Two young men walked from the farmhouse to join the two middle-aged men standing next to the oversize grill. Matt Harris and Kyle Morrow worked for Dan at the Board of Elections for Mahoning County, where Dan was the Deputy Director. Matt was chubby and losing his hair, while Kyle was tall and skinny.

The chubby one spoke first and with an irreverent tone, "Dan, are we changing the Party platform on gun rights?" He smiled too widely.

"Hey Matt, glad you could make it." Dan twisted away from his position at the grill and reached out to shake Matt's hand. Dan turned and shook the hand of the tall skinny fellow. "Hi Kyle, how is your dad?" Kyle's dad was John Morrow, the treasurer of the Mahoning County Republican Party (MCRP) and an influential person behind the scenes.

"Matt, Kyle, are you two coming to my gun raffle?" Don asked, his blue Scotch-Irish eyes twinkling. The Republican nominee for the 59th state house laughed again, another one deep from his belly. Matt, Kyle, and finally Dan joined in. Matt gripped his sides and closed his eyes.

CHAPTER 5

Thursday, 28 July 2016, 103 Days
Indiana and Ohio

On Thursday morning Thomas Ryan rented a car and drove east. Political campaigns always needed volunteers to walk doors, to make signs, to do any number of menial tasks, and he was fine with starting at the bottom of the hierarchy. Those with influence would notice him quickly no matter how humble a volunteer task he did, and those same people would look into his background. It would be a race between the nosy, the paranoid, and the ill intentioned, (those who would attempt to shut Thomas out of the campaign), and Thomas' ability to integrate himself into the campaign. Thomas would win the race if could make enough quality connections fast enough.

Mile markers whizzed by. There were many unknown unknowns, as Donald Rumsfeld would have said; however, there were some challenges for which he could anticipate and prepare.

Hi, my name is Thomas and I am from Columbus, Indiana. My family has a lake house next to the Pence family, and although I could not help out in the primary I am here to help Trump win the general campaign. Once Governor Pence was chosen, I cleared my schedule of projects and headed east to Ohio. Also, Indiana will go for Trump so I am here to help in the most important battleground state.

He recited his elevator pitch to passing cars on I-71. *This story is close enough to the truth to be credible,* he thought.

A few minutes past 5:00 pm, Thomas turned the car into the Super 8 parking lot. The hotel was less expensive than most in the Columbus area, and was located about ten miles north of downtown and situated in a marginal area. He checked in, carried his backpack and main bag into the room, and then stretched out on the bed to take a short nap.

Thomas heard buzzing and opened his eyes. Twenty minutes had passed in a blink and he reached with his hands to stop the phone alarm sitting on his chest. He stood up to stretch, then walked outside to the car. He plugged in the address for the Trump campaign headquarters that he had found a few days earlier. It was only a mile away, also located in the bad part of town.

Once there, Thomas saw that an embroidery shop stood where he had hoped to find a bustling hub of volunteers. There was no political literature or any signs of campaign work. He walked to the nearby buildings and looked in the windows of each one. There was nothing that resembled a political campaign office in this area of the capital city of the most important state for the upcoming presidential election. Thomas returned to his car and sat in the driver's seat for a moment to think. *Let's check out downtown, maybe something is there,* he thought. He started the car.

Downtown Columbus looked clean, and he found a parking spot on a main road. He walked to the Franklin County Republican Headquarters and pulled at the front door. It was locked. There were no blinds on the windows so he cupped his hands around his face and peered into the office. Several **Kasich for President** signs rested against the wall, and Kasich handbills and other literature for the sitting Ohio Governor littered the tables and floors.

The Ohio Republican Party here does not support Trump! He knew that Governor Kasich did not support the Republican Candidate, but he was surprised to find no visible support of Trump in the Republican party proper. He walked back to the car and drove to the hotel.

Twenty minutes later, Thomas sat on the edge of the bed and

thought deliberately. He had arranged the room at the hotel for a week, and planned to use it as a base of operations to explore Ohio looking for Trump support.

CHAPTER 6

Saturday, 30 July 2016, 101 Days
Thomas Ryan's Car, I-71

Thomas hit the road vowing to find some evidence somewhere in Ohio of Republicans or Trump campaigners doing something, *anything*, for the presidential campaign. He bumped the cruise control button on the steering wheel with his thumb while driving north on I-71. Cars continued to pass him on the left and right until he reached eighty miles per hour. He plugged in an address of another possible Trump headquarters located in Canton, Ohio.

Canton, Northeast Ohio

Two hours after he had begun his journey from Columbus, Ohio, Thomas passed a used car lot in the town that hosted the Pro Football Hall of Fame. The listed address did not look promising. He drove a little farther north and pulled into a parking lot. He pushed the door open and stepped outside.

The heat and humidity were intense and Thomas felt sweat bead on his forehead during the short walk back south. At the used car lot he looked in every direction while trying to see any sign of a political office that the Internet told him was located here. Two men in a golf cart zipped up to him.

"Can I help you?" the driver said.

"Well, I'm looking for the Trump headquarters and the address I have says it's right here, but clearly that's not the case," he replied. Thomas caught a microexpression of approval from the driver of the golf cart.

"Oh, the headquarters was here, but during the primaries," the man said. He then pointed. "It was in that building back there behind the service center."

Thomas turned and saw the empty building. "Trump's people rented it for a couple months, but they closed it after the vote," the driver said. He meant the primary vote where Kasich had defeated Trump in Ohio.

"Do you know where his headquarters is now?" Thomas asked. He looked at the passenger's face and saw no emotion, and then turned back to the golf cart driver.

"No I don't, but you could try the Republican headquarters of Canton," the golf cart driver said.

"That's what I'll do, thanks for your help today," Thomas said. The two men drove off and a high-pitched whine of the electric motor followed them.

Four miles from the used car lot, Thomas found the Stark County Republican Party headquarters. He leaned his head against the window and cupped his face to peer inside. In contrast to the last six Republican headquarters he had visited earlier in the week this building was full of Trump signs, t-shirts, buttons, bumper stickers, and other paraphernalia. There was a Trump sign-up sheet on a desk.

Yes!

His heart beat faster. There was a number on the door and he called it. No one answered. He sent a text to the number saying that he was available to volunteer.

Next stop, Youngstown.

Along the two-lane road from Canton to Youngstown Thomas saw the beginning of the rolling green hills of Eastern Ohio. He also saw significant rural poverty interspersed among the large farms. Twenty miles outside of Youngstown, he spotted his first Trump sign in the front yard of a small two-story house.

Yes!

Thirty minutes later Thomas pulled into the parking lot of the Mahoning County Republican Party Headquarters building. He walked up to the door and found it locked. There was a white paper taped to the door with a note and an address.

The MCRP HQ has moved as of July 15th. Please find us at Market Street.

Thomas put the address into his phone and drove to the location. No building existed at the address that had been listed on the white paper taped to the old headquarters' front door.

Thomas drove up and down Market Street for an hour. *This is ridiculous,* he thought. He was about ready to leave the Youngstown area and return to his hotel in the center of the state when he saw a giant sign.

Vote Trump/Ground Zero was written in red and blue letters on a whiteboard in front of a small strip mall. *There is the headquarters,* Thomas thought. He drove into the parking lot. Sitting in his car Thomas could see through the large windows that there was even more Trump material here than he had seen at the Stark County headquarters.

There was another car in the parking lot, and someone was inside the building. Thomas walked to the door.

"Can I help you?" a tall lanky man said. His eyes were blank and he stared at the stranger. Thomas was quiet for a couple of seconds and the man continued to stare at him intently.

"Hi, uh, hi, my name is Thomas and I want to volunteer for the Trump campaign. I actually drove here from Columbus today but I'm going to be in the area on business for the next couple weeks and so I want to help out."

The man stared at him.

Thomas stared back at the man, having regained his composure, and then the man in the HQ shifted his facial expression from a hostile countenance to a more neutral one.

"My name is Jason Lovett, and I'm the RNC regional director. Listen, I'll have Chelsea Callahan contact you about volunteering. She is the volunteer coordinator and she will have something for you to do," he said. Jason took out a business card, flipped it over, and used a blue ballpoint pen to write Chelsea's cell phone number on the back. "I hired Chelsea this morning," he said. He gave the card to Thomas.

"Ok, thank you." Thomas thought that he should say something else. "Well, I'll give her a call." He walked away knowing that luck had smiled on him, though he had an uncertain feeling in his gut about Jason Lovett.

Stone Fruit Coffee, Boardman

Chelsea Callahan decided to celebrate her first day as the RNC Victory Campaign Field Organizer for the Trump and Rob Portman campaigns by visiting Stone Fruit Coffee instead of working at the MCRP office. She sipped her six-dollar double Frappuccino and sat at a high table. Downtempo music completed the vibe. She scrolled through Instagram postings, and switched to YouTube meme videos.

Bing

Jason Lovett had texted her about a new volunteer. She ignored the message and started laughing again at the YouTube video showing a cartoon Trump yelling at the moon and wanting to build a wall.

That stupid Drumpf!

Hours later she remembered the message from her boss, and she remembered that she was part of the Trump campaign team in Ohio. She frowned at the thought.

Thomas Ryan's Car

Thomas walked to his car and began the long drive back to Columbus for another night at the hotel. He drove through the town of Medina and found the small city center to be pure Americana in the best way. There was a town square with a gazebo, American flags everywhere, red brick, beautiful buildings, and people walking around holding hands in an old-fashioned way. Ohio had some beautiful parts to it.

He received a text message from Chelsea Callahan.

I can meet you Wednesday at 2 pm.

Thomas responded.

See you then.

The RNC field organizer who worked for Jason Lovett had waited more than three hours to get in touch with him. *Why would she wait until Wednesday to meet with me?* Thomas thought. He continued his drive southwest. *Every hour matters – these staffers are incredibly lackadaisical.* Nevertheless he had a meeting with a Trump staffer, and a meeting at a Republican Headquarters at ground zero in Youngstown, Ohio.

CHAPTER 7

Sunday, 31 July 2016, 100 Days
Ohio Republican Headquarters, Columbus, Ohio

In a red brick building in downtown Columbus stood the headquarters of to the Ohio Republican Party. Mark Munroe, the party chair for Mahoning County, walked down a hall to the main conference room. He was twenty minutes early to the meeting, as he had allowed time for traffic on his drive down from Youngstown. He recognized the party chair from Sandusky and walked over to talk to her.

"Well, the primary numbers in Mahoning County show that Trump has a lot of strength in our part of the state," Mark said.

Susan replied, "Kasich won our county. There is enormous demand for Trump signs, though."

"Same with us, we are selling them at $10 a piece since we have to print them ourselves," Mark said. He did not mention that on average it cost $2.75 to print each sign. Mark was an honest man, and he recognized a good way to fund the county party when he saw one.

Another county party chair arrived, then a Republican Party VIP, and then two more party chairs. Many party officials arrived simultaneously, walking into the room with Matt Borges, the Republican Party State Chair. Walking on the right side of Matt was Chris Horvath, the Trump Campaign Manager for Ohio, and Justin Clarke, the Ohio Victory Campaign Director for the Republican National Committee (RNC).

Walking on Matt's left was a young woman named Veronica. She was a tall twenty-five-year-old dressed in a skirt suit, ready to work her first day as the Trump Campaign Deputy Director for the Millennial Vote.

"Good morning folks, thank you all for coming," Matt Borges said. He explained the rationale and strategy for the dual RNC Victory Campaign and the Trump Campaign that would work together in the upcoming 2016 general campaign.

This is ridiculous, Mark Munroe and several other county party chairs thought. *Politics.*

Matt clicked a button and brought up the next PowerPoint slide. It was about internal Republican Party business. Mark looked around the room. He counted twenty county party chairs sitting at the tables out of a total of eighty-eight county party chairs who held authority throughout the state.

Thomas Ryan's hotel, 10 miles north of Columbus

Thomas peeked out from under the comforter to see a beam of light splitting the curtains in two. He pulled the cover over his head and went back to sleep. Two hours later the steady drone of the air conditioner woke him up for good. He assembled a sandwich from the ingredients packed in the foam cooler, opened the MacBook pro, and checked Twitter.

It was early afternoon when he decided to drive to downtown Columbus and explore.

Thomas Ryan's Car

A motorcycle cop sat on the concrete near the entrance ramp of highway 71. Thomas turned from the surface street onto the ramp. *That was strange,* he thought. *What is he looking for?*

Two minutes later on the highway he saw another motorcycle officer. *End of the month in Ohio!* Thomas chuckled to himself. He was born in Michigan, the only state in the union that had fought a war against another state – Ohio. Yes, historians said that nobody was killed in this conflict, but Michigan historians also emphasized that it *had* been a war. Michiganders maintained the prejudice that Ohio cops were corrupt, especially regarding speeding infraction revenue from out-of-state drivers. Thomas drove past two more cops sitting on their motorbikes under an overpass.

Whomp whomp whomp... "What was that?!" he said. He craned his neck to see the long tail of a helicopter passing a hundred feet overhead. Thomas swiped at his phone and selected the Twitter icon. Twitter reported that Hillary was late to a rally in Columbus. At that very moment, scores of people were fainting in the heat as a second helicopter rushed overhead to give a report to the Secret Service that the route was clear for Hillary's convoy. Thomas drove on, knowing that thirty vehicles were five minutes behind him, flashing blue lights and speeding. He took the exit to the downtown core.

He took a right, left, another left, and brought his vehicle to a stop in a parking spot. He looked out the windshield and saw a large red brick building with white lettering that read, **Ohio Republican Party**.

Thomas walked up to the property and noticed that the parking lot was half full. He peered into one large window and cupped his hands around his face. A young woman noticed a face appear against the window. She exclaimed and pointed. Thomas saw the woman pointing at him and moved his head back. He backed away from the headquarters building, and turned to walk to his car.

Central and Southeastern Ohio

Thomas drove east, leaving Columbus behind and entering the rolling hills of central Ohio. He drove for several hours, first to Athens, the site of Ohio University. He spent an hour walking up and down the city center positioned in the hills. After lunch he drove northeast to Marietta where retirees and college students were enjoying a summer day on the Ohio River. Trump signs were everywhere.

On the return journey, Thomas drove through an Amish village where several horses waited at a hitching post while their owners shopped at the general store. A notice popped up on his phone and

Thomas looked away from the array of horse and buggies. *Trump will be holding a rally in Columbus Monday.* He tried to reserve a ticket using his phone one-handed and almost hit a mailbox.

Hotel Room, Columbus, Ohio

Thomas stood up from the desk, and walked to the window to shut the heavy curtains. He returned to his computer and registered for the Trump event that was to be held tomorrow in Columbus. The event was scheduled for 3:00 pm at the convention center downtown.

He stripped off his clothes and fell asleep on the spongy mattress.

CHAPTER 8

Monday, 1 August 2016, 99 Days
Columbus, Ohio

Thomas took the same path as the previous day, and the same motorcycle cops were installed along the highway. He parked his car downtown and walked to the convention center to the check-in area around 2:00 pm, an hour before the rally was to start. Once inside the center, he noticed blue ropes blocking the path to the ballroom. A hundred or so people stood next to the ropes and talked amongst themselves. Representatives from the convention center arrived and announced that the room was at capacity, and that those who did not have other business at the convention center would have to leave.

Disappointed, Thomas walked outside. Heat and humidity sapped his energy after a few minutes. He saw a line of protesters in the free-speech zone across from the convention center entrance, where college students and their professors dressed up as giant brick walls.

"No wall, no wall!" they shouted in unison.

"Hey, get your Trump hat for $10," a sidewalk vendor said, approaching Thomas. Thomas avoided eye contact and kept walking. Thomas laughed at the wall people protesting, then felt disturbed.

A person brushed up against Thomas and put a printed paper in his hand surreptitiously. It was an anti-Trump pamphlet. The man continued walking and placing these papers in people's hands. *Ah, he is outside of the free-speech zone.*

Cops stood everywhere, at least a hundred. Others rode on horseback or sat in their SUVs. Thomas did not blame the left-wing guy making an act of protest by handing out pamphlets outside of the designated free-speech zone.

Back inside the free speech zone the protesters shouted. "Wall of Trump! Wall of Trump! Wall of Trump!" The protestors used their hands sticking out sideways from the large square costumes to hold up additional anti-wall signs.

"No mas Trump! No mas Trump!" They switched the chant to Spanish. *They are not going win many votes that way*, Thomas thought, this time thinking in Spanish. He walked to his car and drove to the hotel where he drank a liter of water and took a nap.

St. Charles Catholic Church, Boardman, Ohio

Deacon Dan slid the key into the side door and pulled it open. St. Charles, a Catholic megachurch in the heart of Boardman, was normally closed on Mondays and so the hallway was dark. The retired administrator of Mercy Health walked to his office and turned on a light before settling in a nice leather chair. He smiled at the quiet, and he closed his eyes for a minute before getting to work.

Starting in mid-September he would be officiating the Rite of Christian Initiation of Adults (RCIA) for around twenty people who were formally becoming Catholic at the parish. He had run this particular RCIA class for over a decade now, and it was not difficult to organize. The biggest challenge was to verify that the speakers on each topic had noted their responsibilities on their own calendars. He also had to make the photocopies and order the booklets and Bibles that the church gave each catechumen and candidate.

Dan walked over to the coffee machine and poured himself a cup.

"Aaaauuggghhh, oh come on!" he shouted.

A week earlier he had dropped his Ohio State mug and the impact had weakened the handle. The handle had given way, and the mug spilled hot dark liquid over the red and grey shirt of the deacon. He ran to the bathroom to pat down his favorite Ohio State Football jersey with wet paper towels before the coffee set in the synthetic fabric.

Thomas' Hotel Room, Columbus, Ohio

That evening Thomas skimmed Twitter and saw some clips of Trump from a rally that had been held after the Columbus event. This second rally had been held in Harrisburg, Pennsylvania; while in Harrisburg Trump claimed the Fire Marshall at the Columbus rally had limited the seating. In any case, Thomas decided to show up several hours early at a Trump rally from now on.

Maybe, Thomas thought. *Trump might also be unsure of the crowd sizes and so closed things earlier so there would be no empty seats.*

He loaded up Word, edited his résumé again, and looked through his Google Spreadsheet of potential contacts in the Trump campaign. *Ah, the communications director ...* He pasted the résumé and a cover letter into an email. Somehow he had missed that email address last week. With a click he sent off another résumé.

He would spend one more day in Columbus, then set up shop in a new hotel in Youngstown early Wednesday morning.

CHAPTER 9

Wednesday, 3 August 2016, 97 Days
Mahoning County Republican Party (MCRP) Headquarters

Chelsea rolled into the parking lot at 10:30 am. Once parked, she shuffled through the piles of papers and detritus sitting on the front seat to find her purse and work bag. She pushed her way out of her car. Perry looked up to see the short blonde woman move her bags to her other hand and then open the front door to headquarters. Chelsea scowled at Perry and Kate and walked to the conference room in the back. She sat down in the swivel chair and opened her laptop.

She clicked Google Calendar and saw that she was scheduled for an afternoon meeting with Thomas Ryan. "Nope, not doing that," she said aloud. She grabbed her phone and thumbed out a message.

Thomas' Car, I-71

Bing

Thomas changed his view from the farmland and pack of cars on I-71 to the phone on the dashboard. Chelsea Callahan had texted.

I have to cancel our meeting today. I am going to the Rob Portman event.
Thomas responded.
Ok.

"Of course," Thomas said, shaking his head. He had waited until

Wednesday to return to Youngstown from Columbus so that he would not crash the headquarters without having a meeting with a campaign staffer. Time was wasting though. He tried to use his phone one-handed to find out where the Rob Portman fundraising event would be held, but this was not publicized anywhere, and he had too few friends in Ohio to find out this information. *It looks like I will be going to the MCRP HQ anyway.*

Two hours later he made a stop at the same Wendy's in Boardman where he had eaten at on the earlier trip. He ordered the same salad, chicken nuggets, and small Frosty from the same young woman behind the counter. He ate in the same way as before, leaving half of the Frosty in the cup when he dumped his tray into the garbage.

Thomas walked to his car and drove to the MCRP HQ parking lot.

Mahoning County Republican Party (MCRP) Headquarters

Youngstown and the greater Mahoning Valley area had a large population of Catholic and Eastern Orthodox followers due to the ethnic makeup of the region. Southern and Eastern Europeans had immigrated to the region in massive numbers over a hundred years prior for economic reasons. Steel companies welcomed the immigrants as labor for the mills that produced the backbones of skyscrapers in early twentieth century cities and the infrastructure of the nation, such as the Golden Gate Bridge.

South of Mahoning County in Columbiana County was the exception that proved the rule. Pockets of English Quakers, German Anabaptists, Scotch-Irish Presbyterians, and fundamentalists of all ethnic backgrounds contrasted to the Italians, Polish, Slovaks, Hungarians, Ukrainians, Slovenians, and others who were the majority.

Perry and Kate were also exceptions who lived in Columbiana County, and were Anglo-German fundamentalists of some Protestant sect. She wore her long hair pinned up to complement her long denim dress, and he carried religious tracts.

Thomas walked into the MCRP HQ.
Ding-a-ling

His eyes adjusted from the bright sun and he saw an elderly man, slender and wearing a white T-shirt with giant red letters that said **Donald Trump for President** sitting to his right at a large desk near the entrance. The man raised his head from reading an open book that was lying on the desk. Thomas noticed the red lettering sprinkled in the text. *King James Bible*, he thought. "It looks like I'm in the right place!" he said. He looked at the oversized Bible.

No one laughed.

Perry stared at the newcomer from his seat behind the desk. "Can I help you?" he asked.

Thomas stood for a second or two. He noticed a woman to Perry's right, who shared her husband's unwelcoming demeanor. "I am here to volunteer. I met Jason Lovett the other day and told him that I had a work project for a couple of weeks in the area, so during this time I also want to help out with the Trump campaign..." Thomas paused, watched the two faces, and decided to continue. "I am from Columbus, Indiana, Mike Pence's hometown," he said. He had jumbled his partially rehearsed story, but it seemed to make enough sense for Kate.

Perry continued staring at Thomas. He turned his attention to the woman. She spoke, "We love Mike Pence! My name is Kate, like Katie Perry the actor." She meant to say that her husband's name was Perry and her name was Kate. It took her several explanations before Thomas understood.

Perry's eyes never left the newcomer. Thomas turned to his left shoulder to see a woman who was working on some contraption.

"You can help Katesha make buttons if you want." Kate said.

Those were the words Thomas needed to hear to get beyond the front desk.

He jumped into his newly assigned task. What had been a sad little chaotic nothing turned into an industrial operation in a few minutes. Thomas organized the button parts, made a proper workstation for Katesha and her button-making machine, and fed her the materials as she pressed down on the lever to stamp together the buttons. The assembly-line process quickly became too fast for her.

"Would you like to try it?" Katesha asked Thomas.

"Sure!" he replied. He smiled at the elderly Moroccan woman.
Ker-CHUNK
Ker-CHUNK, Ker-CHUNK

After thirty minutes, Katesha walked away to do something else. For the next two hours the machine made a racket every fifteen seconds. Thomas watched the headquarters and listened to the volunteers and visitors from his organized button-making workstation.

Ker-CHUNK
Ding-a-ling

The front door opened and a visitor walked into the MCRP headquarters. Perry stared. "Do you guys have any Trump signs?" asked the man.

Indeed there were many Trump signs in the headquarters building, including about fifty that were leaning against the wall to the right of the large entrance desk. "We sure do," said Perry. "We are asking for $10 apiece, since we printed these signs ourselves. The campaign has not provided us with signs yet."

The man nodded. "OK, I'll take two."

"Would you mind writing your name, address, phone number, and what you bought on this sheet?" Perry pointed to the loose-leaf binder with empty spots for people to write their information. He turned to his right and grabbed two signs while the man filled out information that Tonya would soon enter into the MCRP potential donor database.

The man walked out of the headquarters with his two signs, consisting of a white background and red lettering. *Those are nice-looking signs,* Thomas thought.

Individual men and women, couples, pairs of women, people from Pennsylvania walked through the door, all asking for signs, all paying $10 per sign, and many ordering multiples.

The buttons had several layers that the machine sandwiched together, including a base metal plate, a secondary metal plate, a paper layer with the color printing, and a top thin transparent plastic layer to protect the button. Thomas noticed that he was down to his last few circle paper colored printings. He decided to leave for the day and he arranged his workstation neatly. "Goodbye for now!" he said. He waved to Perry and Kate and walked to his car.

Thomas drove down Market Street a couple of miles to scout out his next hotel location before starting the six-hour drive back to Columbus, Indiana. He had to trade in his rental car for a permanent vehicle.

Traffic sped up once he turned south on I-71. Thomas made a new hypothesis that the Ohio State Highway Patrol controlled the East-West northern route so strictly because there were many interstate travellers that were easy pickings for fines. Drivers refused to go more than a few miles per hour over the speed limit in Northern Ohio. As Thomas made his way to the central and southern parts of Ohio drivers noticeably increased their speed.

A Twitter message alerted Thomas that Paul Manafort had hired all fifty state directors, including the director of Ohio. Thomas thought about what he had experienced in Ohio his first week. *I have witnessed zero work by the Ohio Trump team during my first week here. Only a couple of RNC staffers seem to be doing anything, and even those people are not doing much. No one signed me up to do any volunteering.*

As of August 3rd, 2016, there was no ground game in Ohio for Trump.

Thursday, 4 August 2016, 96 Days
Boston, Massachusetts

Meghan O'Connor felt her phone buzz.

We are trying to get everyone on board to sign this Never Trump national security letter.

She groaned when she read the text of the email.

Her boss, a renowned national security expert and current professor at a university in Cambridge, Massachusetts, had forwarded the text of a letter that stated Trump "lacked the character, values, and experience" to lead the nation in national security areas. The language of the letter got worse as she read.

Yes, I will cosign the letter. Meghan typed out a response.

She had no choice. The Bush and Romney families were aggressively pushing to cut off every avenue of support that Trump might find to help run his campaign, or should he win, to run the government of the United States. The Bush family in particular had close ties with the national security apparatus of the country, that is, those experts who had worked their entire careers in some capacity at the policy level for the US government dealing in foreign policy.

Meghan had worked for George W. Bush as an architect of the second Gulf War rebuilding strategy a decade earlier. She had made it up to the Deputy National Security Advisor rank during that tenure of service. She had ambitions to be a leader in a future Republican administration, perhaps even as the Secretary of State. *Trump can't win*, she thought. She could not afford to do anything else in her career except to obey the whims of the Bush family.

She hit Send.

Thomas' Car, Ohio

Thomas crossed back into Ohio just north of Cincinnati, this time driving a used grey sedan that he had found on Craigslist in Indianapolis. He had returned the rented Nissan for a car manufactured by one of the big three automakers. He had spent one night at the lake house, and was returning to Ohio in the afternoon.

Thomas arrived at the hotel on Market Street in Boardman around 7:00 pm, unpacked, and drove north on Market Street two miles to the MCRP HQ. He walked up to the glass door and noticed all but the back ceiling lights were off.

Headquarters was closed.

Of course, he thought.

CHAPTER 10

Friday, 5 August 2016, 95 Days
Thomas' Hotel

Friday morning was beautiful, if a bit humid for a typical Northeast Ohio summer morning. Thomas ate a peach with cereal and chocolate almond milk, and then ate some almonds. He checked news stories about the election on his laptop before packing his backpack and heading out to the car.

Yesterday he read the sign on the door that said headquarters was open from 10:00 am to 4:00 pm, and so as not to appear too anxious he timed his arrival to be just before 11:00 am.

MCRP Headquarters

Ding-a-ling

"Can I help you?" drawled an overweight man.

There were similarities to Wednesday. However, there was no large King James Bible on the desk, and instead of two tall skinny holy rollers on watch duty there were two short heavy-set people who controlled the entrance door and space.

"Hi, my name is Thomas and I am here to volunteer," Thomas said after taking a deep breath and forcing a smile. He continued, "I am in the area for work for a few weeks, I am from Indiana in Columbus near the Pence family, and I know this area is ground zero." Thomas pointed to the large "Ground Zero" sign that was just outside the window. He stopped talking and there was silence.

"My name is Marq," said the large man at the desk. Marq looked Thomas up and down. He did not like the Pence reference, and in general thought the story was strange.

"Hi, I'm Karen," said a woman. She was standing next to Marq, in Kate's spot from two days prior. Karen had open body language and had a noticeably friendly tone. She thought Thomas was handsome.

"Yesterday Kate had me making buttons," Thomas said. "I am going to make some more." Thomas could tell Marq was about to question him, and Thomas almost certainly would not be able to stand up under any type of rigorous interrogation. He walked to the button-making station that he had set up two days previously. Everything was exactly as he had left it.

Ker-CHUNK

Ker-CHUNK

Every fifteen seconds the sound rang through the HQ.

The remaining button supplies lasted five minutes, so Thomas wandered around the large main room and into the back conference room. He found additional button parts on a shelf and carried them back to his workstation.

A young blonde woman shoved her way through the entrance carrying two bags and a Stone Fruit coffee.

"Hi there!" Karen said.

"Harrumph," Chelsea Callahan mumbled. She scowled, glanced at Thomas at the button-making table, and avoided eye contact while walking to the conference room. She threw the bags on the table and dumped herself on a swivel chair.

Chelsea Callahan, Thomas guessed. This was the RNC Field Organizer who worked for Jason Lovett, the regional field director.

A few minutes later, Thomas walked back to the conference room and introduced himself. He rattled the same spiel for a third time. She stared at him with wide eyes.

"Can you walk doors tomorrow?" she asked immediately.

"I can do any volunteering tasks except make phone calls. I don't like making phone calls but I'm happy to walk doors. I love talking with people face-to-face." Thomas said. He scrunched his forehead slightly as he tried to see any hidden meaning in small facial expressions on Chelsea. *Hypervigilance,* he thought, *maybe it will come in useful.* Chelsea did not react.

"Hi, I'm Chelsea," she responded. Her face was neutral except for her wide eyes. "We have a local candidate that you could walk doors for tomorrow if you want," she said.

"Yes, that's exactly what I want to do. Where do I need to be?"

"Show up here around 10:00 am and I'll introduce you to Don Manning. He's running for the local 59th state house race. Don is working really hard and he'll appreciate the help," Chelsea said.

Thomas turned and walked out of the conference room and back to his button-making workstation in the main room.

Ker-CHUNK

Chelsea asked me to walk for a local candidate, not Trump, Thomas thought.

Marq and Karen were loudly talking. "Hillary needs to be locked up," Marq said with an Ohio River twang.

"She is a witch," Karen added. The two escalated their accusations against the Democratic Nominee for President of the United States.

These two are really pro-Trump, Thomas thought.

People walked into headquarters. Some bought signs, and others stayed and talked to Karen and Marq. None of the other volunteers did any work.

Ker-CHUNK

Ker-CHUNK

Thomas internally recorded the conversations. Much of the talk did not make sense, but he knew that he would recall the conversations when he had learned more about what was happening in the local party, and with this future context what he heard now would be useful. He was in the perfect place to quickly learn about Mahoning County politics. Chelsea stayed back in her conference room.

An hour went by before he ran out of button tops. He walked across the main room to gather more supplies, and shivered as lifeless eyes stared at him. In the front of the MCRP HQ a seven-foot tall metallic bobble-head of Mr. Trump had been printed in some sort of 3D metal printing process and placed front and center in the main room of the headquarters. Local union workers had pooled together their money and bent some rules to print this monstrosity. Someone put a wig on the head, and then a MAGA baseball cap. It did not make the statue better. The bobble-head stared at Thomas while he gathered the button tops from a box.

Conference Room, MCRP HQ

Bzzzzz

"Hello, Brian," Chelsea answered her phone. She leaned back in the swivel chair.

Brian Wollet was the Trump Campaign Regional Director. He was responsible for eleven counties in Northeast Ohio, and he was the counterpart to Jason Lovett, who was the Regional Director for the RNC Victory Campaign, a parallel organization. In 2008, Obama had made a similar parallel organization from the DNC, as Obama did not trust the DNC leaders to do anything but support Hillary. Obama had been correct, and Trump learned from this campaign strategy when he set up his own organization a year earlier.

"Hey Chelsea, listen, I wanted to let you know that I will be stopping by headquarters on Sunday. I'll have some bumper stickers and some signs," Brian said.

"Oh, OK, we are running low on Trump signs. What time will you be here?"

"Around 3:00 pm," Brian answered. He asked how things were going at the MCRP, and he wanted to know the number of doors they were hitting each day.

Chelsea hung up the phone.

Karen overheard parts of the call, enough to know that it was the regional director. "Chelsea, do you have Brian Wollet's number?" Karen asked.

"Why do you ask?" Chelsea said.

"Well, we are running out of the signs and I wanted to let him know," Karen said.

"I told him. Thanks for letting me know," Chelsea said.

Chelsea was guarding the contact information of the Trump organization tightly, Thomas noted. He grabbed his backpack and walked out of the headquarters.

Market Street, Four Miles South of the MCRP HQ

The hotel where Thomas was staying cost too much money to live at for any length of time. He drove by the Davis Motel, which was adjacent to a large truck stop and south of an exit for the toll road I-76. He liked truckers. The motel had good reviews online, and it seemed in decent repair, although the building was old. There was no open prostitution or drug dealing that Thomas could see, although there was a strip club a half-mile to the north. He drove past the motel on Highway 7 one more time.

This will do, he thought.

He drove to Wendy's, got a salad and chicken nuggets, and returned to the headquarters.

MCRP HQ

Ding-a-ling

Thomas looked up from his workstation overflowing with buttons.

"I am supporting Trump and my father was the former Democratic Chair of Mahoning County," a man said. He looked to be in his late twenties and was dressed as a factory worker. "All my friends support Trump too," he said.

"Do you want a sign?" Karen asked, and even as she spoke he thrust a $20 bill into her hand. Karen reached back and grabbed a second Trump sign.

Thomas walked to the storage room, wrestled with an awkward cardboard box that contained fifty wires, and brought the wires to the main area. He returned to the storage room one more time to retrieve a box of the signs themselves. It took about half an hour to put together these fifty Trump signs. There were now eighty Trump signs left, and they were being sold at a high number per day.

Bzzzzz

Thomas saw that he had an email from the State Senate Political Director. There was a position open in the 30th State Senate area to the south of Youngstown.

Ding-a-ling

Mark Munroe, the MCRP Chair, had arrived. He manner was deliberate and polite. "Hi Karen, how is everything going?" he asked.

"We are almost out of signs," she answered.

Mark walked slowly over to where the dark-haired stranger was putting together signs. "Hi there, my name is Mark Munroe, the county chair," he said, addressing Thomas.

Thomas stopped his work assembling the Trump signs and stood up straight. "My name is Thomas," he said. He launched into his spiel, "I am from Columbus, Indiana, and I am here on business for a couple of weeks. Governor Pence is from Columbus originally, and his family has a lake house next to my family's lake house. So, although I couldn't help in the primary for this campaign cycle, as soon as Governor Pence was picked I decided to help out wherever I could, and I ended up here." Thomas' neutral face did not betray his racing heart or the butterflies he felt. His story was *mostly true*.

The party chair is the king of a county, and Thomas knew the impression he made on Mark was important. He had to keep Mark on his side at all costs otherwise all of his efforts would be for nothing.

"Well," Mark said. "Thank you for your help with the signs." He continued in a clear, deliberate manner, "The party paid for these signs, so we are reselling them to people for a small donation. We are waiting for the Trump campaign to deliver a whole bunch, but they have not done so yet."

Mark walked away and Thomas returned to making signs. It was tiring work, and he was sore from punching out 1,500 buttons over two days. He kept his ears open and his mouth closed.

Chelsea left her seat in the conference room and approached Mark. "Brian Wollet called earlier; he is bringing bumper stickers and signs Sunday at 3:00 pm." She continued talking while Thomas made a Google Calendar entry on his phone, *Meeting MCRP HQ 3PM Sunday.*

Bzzzzz

Another email popped up on Thomas' phone. His state representative in Indiana had received his resume and was forwarding it to the Trump campaign. In the email the state representative said that the Indiana Party had ordered 50,000 Trump signs for the state.

Just before 4:00 pm Mark walked over to the active button making workstation. Completed buttons tumbled out of plastic bags that Thomas used to hold them.

"You don't have to do them all!" Mark said. He had a friendly manner, but Thomas could tell that Mark knew that Thomas was hiding his true intentions. These intentions were good, even if Mark might have thought otherwise. Thomas looked around at the 2,500 buttons and realized that in two days he had completed work that Mark had meant to keep volunteers busy for the next three months. Nobody seemed to be buying buttons either; they all bought signs.

Ding-a-ling

The front door saved the awkwardness.

"Hi Mark," Don called out. He was a state representative candidate who was running in the southern half of Mahoning County. Thomas had previously analyzed his race and his chances did not look good.

After walking to the back conference room and briefly talking with Chelsea, Don walked up to Thomas. "Hey, thanks for being willing to walk with me tomorrow. We are meeting up at 9:30 am," he said. Don Manning was charming and had good genes. He looked to be in his mid-forties.

Thomas' Hotel

Thomas continued working on his presentation of the political situation in Ohio, particularly NE Ohio. He sent it to select people on his spreadsheet of likely Trump staffers. He also updated his resume to include that he was "working operations" in Northeast Ohio. He turned out the lights at 1:00 am and fell asleep.

Saturday, 6 August 2016, 94 Days
Thomas' Hotel

A morning sun positioned low in the sky, which had turned from blue to bright, woke Thomas early. The air conditioner had run all night in his hotel room, and today promised to be hotter than yesterday. Thomas got out of bed and surfed the Internet for a while. He had breakfast, changed into a nice shirt and dark hiking pants, and gathered up protein bars, nuts, and apples to put in his backpack.

MCRP HQ

At 9:24 am, he pulled the Ford into a parking spot on the opposite side of the entrance of the MCRP HQ. The parking lot was otherwise empty. Thomas stood next to his car and played with his phone. He leaned against the driver side door.

Chelsea Callahan arrived, her econobox squealing with some sort of belt problem, it sounded like. **Hillary for Prison** and **Rob Portman** stickers proclaimed to any driver following the car her political preferences. Massive quantities of junk filled the interior of the car.

Where are the candidates? Thomas thought. He almost laughed. Today was going to be in the mid to upper 90s by 4:00 pm, it was around 75 degrees now and climbing several degrees each hour. People at their houses would become less receptive to door knockers as the day progressed. *Stay calm...*

Chelsea opened the locked headquarters and walked with her two large bags to the back conference room. She threw them on the table. Thomas sat in the main room at one of the tables near the giant bobble-head and tried to find news about the Ohio political races.

"Thomas, could you come back here?" Chelsea called. Thomas walked to the conference room. She took Thomas' iPhone and downloaded a program called Advantage, the RNC voter database and walking program. This took less than a minute and she clicked away at her keyboard for a few seconds. "You are ready to go!" she said.

Thomas played around with the Advantage app and noticed his phone battery visibly draining. He walked out of the conference room to retrieve his computer and power cords, and returned to the conference room where he took a seat. A high school senior named Caleb walked into headquarters and to the conference room to join Chelsea and Thomas.

"Hillary's people are walking in Boardman today, that's what I heard," said Caleb. Chelsea asked him where he heard this information but Caleb was circumspect on his source.

Don Manning walked up to the conference room; apparently he had arrived shortly after 10:00 am. "Yeah, Hillary was in our neighborhood today," he said.

Then why aren't you guys walking right now?! Thomas maintained a straight face with the utmost effort. He turned his attention to the Advantage app. The questions were ridiculous, and focused on Rob Portman, the US Senate Candidate. Thomas had only been in the area for a few days, yet he had heard no walk-in to the MCRP headquarters refer to Rob Portman, and with good reason. Portman was a traditional conservative Republican who was not so friendly to labor in this blue-collar area.

"Hey Don, I look forward to helping you walk today," Thomas said. "I hope you don't mind, but I don't think I will be asking folks question five," he said referring to the question on the Advantage app that asked if the voter knew who Rob Portman was and if they would commit to vote for him.

"Oh, that's no problem," Don said.

"Listen up," Chelsea said with a loud, clear voice. "The goal for today is 1500 doors." Don nodded his head vigorously. Thomas thought this was a bit strange as there were only four people including the candidate who were knocking doors today. Typically a person could walk about 25 doors per hour in an average American neighborhood; they could do more when houses were tightly packed together and fewer when houses had large yards.

Politicos claimed that volunteers could knock 200 doors a day, and yes, theoretically this was possible in urban environments when working all day during a cool time in October. The four people who were getting ready to knock doors were starting late; it was nearly 11:00 am. The best time to start was just before 10:00 am. Hot and humid weather made the late start today worse for reaching enough doors. Thomas guessed that the four of them combined would not reach 200 doors today. *What is the deal with 1500 doors?* he thought. *Why are we emphasizing Rob Portman while working for the Trump campaign and in an area that largely dislikes the Senator?*

Thomas did not realize the power that Rob Portman wielded within the Republican Party in Ohio. The senator was the most powerful Republican politician, especially since Kasich had lost the primary race for President and was term limited as governor. No politically ambitious person wanted to be seen doing anything other than being completely dedicated to Portman. As an outsider Thomas missed this reality, but it also helped him to see clearly what needed to be done from a strictly strategic point of view for the Trump campaign.

Thomas thought of something else and sent a text message to the Wood County Republican Chair.

Hi Todd, Hillary's people are walking doors today in the Youngstown area.

Thomas' cousin replied immediately.

How are you doing? I will forward this information to the state Republicans.

Information was currency in politics, and even if information was not exactly correct it was valuable to pass along to others who might be able to reciprocate with unique information of their own. Thomas had decided earlier that he was going to try to be a conduit for information in the hope that he would become in the loop as the campaign went on. Todd could forward information to the state party officials and perhaps word would get to them that it was Thomas who had been providing this on the ground intelligence.

There was movement. Don, Chelsea, and a couple of the volunteers stood up and walked to the door of the conference room. Thomas felt goosebumps as he thought they were getting ready to leave to reach the first potential voters.

Alas, a false alarm. Don and Chelsea went out the back door for a smoke break. Thomas felt as if he were a Formula One car that had stalled out on the starting line. He could feel his competitive nature wanting to be unleashed and he used all of his self-control to maintain an outward appearance of calm.

"Hey Thomas, here is a shirt for you to wear," Don said. He held an oversize white T-shirt with *Don Manning for State Representative* on it. Thomas was wearing a collared button-up white-and-blue checked shirt. Thomas took the shirt and did not put it on. He considered putting it on over his dress shirt, but it was hot and humid.

It was 11:42 am and 88 degrees when Don Manning and Thomas Ryan stepped out of Don's Jeep and started walking the neighborhood.

"Hey, I'll take this side," Don said as he walked to the left side of the street. "Do you mind walking on the other side?"

"Sure thing," Thomas said. He looked down at his hands to organize the two pieces of literature. One flier was for Don Manning running for the 59th state house seat and the other, larger, flier was for Rob Portman who was running for re-election to the US Senate. In one hand Thomas held the two piles of literature, and in the other hand he held his phone with the Advantage walking program with the list of voters he was supposed to visit. There were many Strong Democrats listed as SD in the list.

The sun was hot, and Thomas had a large green floppy hat to protect his face from the rays. Don did not have a hat. The first house was an SD, and Thomas led off with a brief introduction that did not follow the Republican HQ instructions.

"Hi, my name is Thomas and I am out walking today for Don Manning. Don is a friend of mine and he is running for a local seat, the 59th state house." Thomas held out the flier and the man in shorts took it, and examined it. "We are also asking folks if they have any local issues," Thomas continued after the slightest pause. He was watching carefully the body language of the person in the doorway.

"No, I don't have any issues, but thanks for stopping by." The man made a friendly gesture holding the flier that seemed to indicate he would read it more carefully.

"Thank you," Thomas replied and turned on his heel to quickly walk back to the driveway, to the street and onto the next house. With his left hand he entered a "maybe" into the phone indicating that the voter might possibly vote for Don. He had not given the man a flier for Rob Portman.

Nobody was home at the next house, and both of these people were listed as SDs, so Thomas wrote, "Sorry I missed you!" on Don Manning's literature and stuffed it in the door. He did not leave a Rob Portman flier. He saw Don walking back from a house and Don seemed to have noticed that only one flier was left at the door. *Great, I don't want to explain to Don why it is not in his interest to affiliate himself with an anti-labor Senator if he is trying to win in an underdog seat.*

Doesn't Thomas know how powerful Rob Portman is in the Party? Don thought as he saw Thomas not putting Portman fliers on doors.

The next house Thomas responded to the chastising look Don had shot at him by giving the woman a Senator Portman flier. She said, "Oh, I don't like him."

Sweat dripped down the nose of Thomas, and Don Manning looked beat red. It was 96 degrees Fahrenheit and the humidity was oppressive. They walked to the jeep. "Hop in!" Don said.

MCRP HQ

Fifteen minutes later the two were back at MCRP HQ having knocked on about one hundred doors in total. That number crept higher as the afternoon went on, and by 3:00 pm Don told anyone who would listen that he had knocked on 200 doors earlier in the day. Chelsea mentioned to several people wandering to her makeshift office in the back conference room that she had "knocked 1500 doors" with her group of volunteers.

A group of high school students walked into the headquarters from the crushing heat and humidity. They had been handing out Rob Portman literature all afternoon. Youth kept them peppy and happy despite the negative response they received continuously at the doors.

A young woman followed the main group into the MCRP HQ and

half-walked, half-danced to the button-making machine. She was tall, blonde, and happy-go-lucky. She smiled and hummed a little song as she made her first button with care and love. She held up the button to her face and showed her friend.

"Francesca, look at what I made!" Rebecca said. Her blue eyes sparkled.

"Look at that, it looks great!" Francesca said. She joined her friend and danced a little, caught up in the joy of a young woman's life.

Rebecca pressed the lever on the button machine slowly and firmly and made another button. She was getting the hang of it, and quickly made a third.

Ding-a-ling

Mark Munroe walked into the headquarters and snapped his head to the white table with the button machine. He grabbed his head with both hands and walked towards the girl. Rebecca looked at her button and began to sing once again.

"Please stop!" Mark said.

Rebecca's eyes got wide. The reaction of the chair to a young girl making buttons seemed out of place.

"Please don't make any more buttons!" Mark said again. He looked desperate. Francesca bowed her head.

Thomas saw this interaction and thought that Mark must have had PTSD from the 2500 buttons that Thomas had made over the previous days. Bags of buttons were scattered everywhere throughout the headquarters building. Thomas realized that he had ruined an entire class of volunteer activity for the next several months in his first three days in Mahoning County.

Thomas walked to the conference room once again. "Does Don have a mailing campaign?" he asked Chelsea.

"No, not that I am aware of," she responded. She didn't look up from her computer.

A short woman walked into the headquarters. "Hi Brenda," Chelsea said. She saw the Mahoning County Trump Chair, Brenda Johnson. Throughout the primary race Brenda had worked hard to assure a Trump victory in the Youngstown area, and due to her hard work she had alienated herself from most of the establishment Republicans in the area who had supported either Kasich or Rubio. Brenda had been showing up to headquarters more recently as the general campaign got underway. People feared her, and for good reason. Decades earlier, the five-foot-tall woman had been a referee for high school football. She did not back down to anybody, and she never had.

Mark left his office and walked to the front door. He stopped and turned back briefly and spoke across the room to Chelsea. "See you Monday," he paused pointedly, "unless you are here tomorrow."

Chelsea immediately replied without emotion, "No."

Thomas saw that Chelsea had missed the subtext of what Mark was saying, or she was being openly confrontational to the chair. Either case was bad. Mark Munroe realized that every hour and every day mattered now until Election Day. *This is a good sign that the chair understands the urgency of the situation.*

Thomas heard gossip coming from the conference room. Justin Clarke, Director of the RNC Victory Campaign, had yelled at the workers, Chelsea included, for not putting forth a good enough effort. Justin had lost his temper and ranted that he and Trump deserved better.

Yep, they sure do, Thomas thought.

Thomas was getting ready to leave headquarters when a man who called himself Jay walked into the office. He said that he had 500 Rob Portman signs.

"Does Senator Portman need any help tomorrow?" Thomas asked Jay after introducing himself.

"Senator Portman doesn't work on Sundays." Jay responded.

Thomas left.

Later that night Thomas saw that there was going to be a Mike Pence event August 10th in Cambridge Ohio, so he registered online for tickets. He then drove around Youngstown to learn the city.

CHAPTER 11

Sunday, 7 August 2016, 93 Days

Early Sunday morning Thomas woke up, showered, and put on his dark gray suit and striped blue tie. He drove north and then east several miles, and turned right to enter a long driveway that passed through a meadow and over a stream to a dome-shaped church in Boardman, Ohio. A hundred years earlier, Ruthenian immigrants travelled to Youngstown from what is now part of Slovakia, and to this day most have kept their Ruthenian Rite Catholic heritage. Vatican II helped preserve the community as the pastoral conference had stripped from the zealous Latin bishop of Cleveland much of his power over non-Latin Catholics in Northeast Ohio.

Thomas walked in the entrance and he heard singing in a language he did not recognize, Old Church Slavonic. He slipped into a seat in the last pew and watched the service. The priests and deacons moved in prescribed steps forward and backward, through the iconostasis and around the altar, mostly hidden from the congregation. One priest swung an incense burner hanging from a chain, and the oscillation spread fragrance throughout the circular nave. Thomas stepped out of the pew and left the church before the service finished. Outside the sun shone brightly, and combined with the heat was enough to persuade him to take off his jacket and tie.

- THOMAS RYAN -

Thomas' Hotel

"Trump cannot win Ohio," Kasich said. He looked at the host and he turned and looked directly at camera two, its blinking red light acting like a beacon to the governor and politician. "I know Ohio and I know Trump has no support among the party faithful." Kasich explained that Trump had offered him the Vice Presidential Candidate slot and that he had turned down the offer. "Trump will lose," he said.

Thomas watched the Meet the Press interview that someone had uploaded to YouTube. Kasich was trending on Twitter for his anti-Trump comments. *This is an opportunity.* Thomas opened an email and began typing.

Countering Kasich's Negativity in Ohio
To: Michael Glassner and other Senior Trump Officials

Hi Michael,

I am currently working in field operations in Ohio for Trump and the Republicans, and I can immediately begin to counteract the Kasich negativity.

Thank you,

Thomas Ryan
Attachment: Résumé

Thomas clicked a button and sent the email that promised a solution to counter Governor Kasich's negativity to seven senior Trump officials who worked out of the Trump headquarters in New York City.

Trump Headquarters, New York, New York

"Interesting…" Michael Glassner said aloud. He skimmed the résumé attached to the email. Michael noticed that Thomas was already in Ohio working operations for several local candidates. *Twenty-five hundred buttons? Do people in Ohio buy buttons?* He saw the bullet point on the résumé and wondered if Ohio people liked buttons so much.

Glassner clicked his mouse and pulled up Amazon. There he found boxes of button parts for sale. With a little typing and two more clicks he ordered four large boxes of button fronts, backs, and plastic liners to be sent to the P.O. Box of the Mahoning County Republican Party. It cost less than $100 out of the national campaign budget and such a goodwill gesture was a great way to build a relationship with local party leadership. *They will love this surprise.*

Michael Glassner turned his thoughts back to the subject of the email. Governor Kasich was bitter since turning down the Vice Presidential Candidate position and was taking his best shot this morning to sink the Trump campaign in Ohio. Glassner picked up the phone to call the leader of the Ohio Trump campaign.

"Hey Chris, I have an interesting fellow for you to take a look at," Michael said.

Columbus Ohio

"Right, right, you're absolutely right," Chris Horvath said. The Ohio Trump Campaign Manager nodded his head and vigorously agreed with the Deputy Campaign Manager of the National Trump Campaign. The call ended.

Brandon Moffett looked at Chris Horvath. Chris looked back at the original Manager of the Trump Campaign for Ohio and rolled his eyes. "Can you set up an interview for Thursday for this Thomas character?" Chris asked.

The recently demoted campaign manager and now Deputy Campaign Manager for Ohio, Brandon Moffett, asked Horvath to forward him Thomas' number.

MCRP HQ

Thomas felt antsy. He got in his car and drove north on Market Street. *There is Mark's car!* He pulled into the parking lot of the candy factory a block north of headquarters and reached for his phone.

"Hello," Mark answered.

"This is Thomas. I have spare time this afternoon. Do you need any help at headquarters?" Thomas asked.

"We sure do. Would you mind assembling some yard signs?" Mark said.

Thomas waited five minutes and then drove his car around to the parking lot of the MCRP. He walked into the building.

Mark was standing, talking to Brian Wollet, the Ohio Trump Campaign Regional Director. Jay from the Rob Portman campaign was adjacent to Brian. Mark, Brian, and Jay were having a stand up meeting. Thomas saw the Trump bumper stickers that Brian had brought to headquarters.

Thomas introduced himself to Brian and to Jay. He then went to the kitchen to grab a knife, opened a second box of signs that Jay had brought in the other day, and combined the first glossy sign with the first wire from a pile of wires leaning against the table.

Jay left a few minutes later, and a half-hour later Brian and Mark prepared to leave.

"You're in charge," Mark told Thomas. "When you leave move this nob here," the Chair demonstrated how to lock the building.

Thomas continued to make signs in the empty building.

Ring

"Hello, this is Thomas," Thomas said.

"Hi, this is Brandon Moffett with the Trump campaign."

There was silence for a second. Brandon continued, "We received your résumé and we want you to come in for an interview.

"Oh, that's great!" Thomas said. "I can drive over to your headquarters even tonight if you give me the address." Thomas had not been able to locate the secret Trump headquarters in Ohio.

"We have a slot available on Thursday for you to interview with Chris Horvath and me," Brandon said.

"Ok, Thursday is fine, but really, I can come over Monday or any day."

"Thursday works best for Chris," Brandon said.

"Well, I'll be there. Thank you for the call," Thomas said.

Thomas felt excited. His Kasich email had worked.

Thomas' Hotel

Thomas decided to write a summary of the work that he had done, and the things that he had observed, and send it to Brandon Moffett.

Mahoning County Republican Headquarters Unofficial Report
To: Brandon Moffett, Deputy Trump Campaign Manager Ohio
Mr. Moffett,

From the end of July to today, this is a summary of what I have observed in the Mahoning County Republican Party Headquarters.

This is my observation and opinion alone and I do not speak for the Mahoning County Republican Headquarters or any of their leadership.

Voter Information

*I walked with the 59th state candidate on Saturday. Out of ~100 doors that we knocked there were four "strong Dems," according to the Republican Party classification system, who had blue Trump signs in their yard.

I experienced no negative words about Trump from anyone of any party at the doors. I did have one Republican lady who did not like Rob Portman.

*One volunteer was conducting a poll through the telephone asking three questions, relating to Obama, Trump/Hillary, and Strickland/Portman. I overheard the volunteer tell another person that zero of the ~50 people he called said that they were voting for Hillary. I am not sure the universe of people that this person called, so I do not know the political makeup of the people polled.

*There are repeated Republican and Democratic walk-in voters who have stories how much they are supporting Trump and how much they dislike Hillary.

Trump Signs and Bumper Stickers

*Republicans and Democrats are visiting the HQ at a steady pace requesting Trump signs.

*Both Republicans and Democrats are visiting from Trumbull, Ashtabula, and

other counties in order to purchase Trump signs.

*On Friday I assembled the last 50 Trump signs out of the original 500 that the county party purchased. The county party is expecting a delivery of Trump signs from the Trump organization on Monday.

*A volunteer brought in anti-Hillary bumper stickers that the volunteers are giving to those guests who request these. People are requesting Trump bumper stickers and the county has run out of their supply.

Thomas Ryan

CHAPTER 12

Monday, 8 August 2016, 92 Days
MCRP HQ

Two elderly men stepped down from each side of a full size white pickup truck. Joe Mazur reached the headquarters door first and shoved it open. Billy Laird followed close behind carrying a new battery for his professional-grade handheld drill.

Joe had been stabbed while working the police beat in Youngstown in the 1970s, and was medically retired. He was a bear of a man, eccentric, and with a keen sense of people. During stressful times he would sing Polish nursery songs that his mother had taught him. Due to his antics, not many understood that he retained those innate and learned abilities that cops and priests have, and that he could make good guesses about people's motives and characters.

The Trump campaign had been a triple win for Joe. First, he loved working with his friend Billy building and painting Trump signs. Billy did most of the building, as he was a retired contractor, and Joe did most of the painting. Second, Joe was making money. Medium-to-large Trump signs were going for $35 to $100. Joe managed to sell one large sign for $200 to a local business owner who wanted everyone driving on Highway 7 to know that this was Trump Country. Third, Joe loved the idea of Trump himself. He read the paper and he hated the elites who were ruining the country in his view. Decades before, these same liberal attitudes had created the environment in which he was attacked in broad daylight by a career criminal.

Joe and Billy walked through the main room in headquarters, through the back hallway, and into the large backroom that had the equipment to build the signs. This backroom also had piles of junk. Sometimes they could find useful items, such as the ten rolls of duct tape that Billy had found the other day.

Billy was older than Joe by a few years. He was whip-smart, and had started a construction company fifty years earlier that he grew into a medium sized business. He had become wealthy during his career due to his intelligence and work ethic. His rough manner made him even more successful in his trade as he fit the stereotype of how people imagined a construction worker should look and talk. More than one businessman had found himself on the short end of a negotiation by underestimating Billy.

A vital part of Billy's success in the trades was his perfectionist nature, but it was a double-edged sword: this nature also gave him anxiety. His wife Ann had been very beautiful in her youth, and she still had the excellent bone structure and presence of a former model. Billy provided the labor for Joe's signs, and he came up with clever ways to make them larger.

In addition to labor for the signs, Billy had built a large part of the headquarters, particularly the kitchen. He and his wife also donated to most of the candidates and to the party itself. They gave thousands of dollars to support conservative causes. Today Billy was not writing checks, but swinging a hammer.

Back in the main room Perry sat at the front desk reading his Bible and selling Trump signs to the many visitors coming in at a steady pace. Perry picked up the phone to call his counterpart in Trumbull County, the county to the north of Mahoning County. "Hey there," he said. "This is Perry from the Mahoning County Republican Party, how is your sign situation up there?" he asked a volunteer on the other end of the phone line.

"We don't have any signs," said the man on the phone. "Maybe after Labor Day we'll get some from the Trump campaign."

Perry hung up the phone and stood up from his chair as another person asked him to purchase a sign. Thomas sat at a plastic table in the middle of the room, and looked up from his computer to watch the transaction.

An hour later, there was a lull in the action. Thomas walked over to count the small number of Trump signs remaining leaning against the wall. There was large pile of Rob Portman signs next to the small pile of Trump signs.

"Thomas, let me give you this tract," Perry said. He pushed a religious pamphlet into Thomas' hands.

Thomas grabbed a chair from under one of the white tables and brought it to the side of the desk. He listened while Perry gave a short talk on his Anabaptist-based religion. "What does the word *logos* mean to you?" Thomas asked. "You know, like in the Gospel of John the first sentence where it talks about the *logos* creating the world," Thomas said.

Perry's eyes got wide. Thomas launched into the same soliloquy that he had heard one time while eating lunch with a stranger at a Divinity School on the east coast.

Fifteen minutes later, Perry tried to ease out of the conversation.

Another hour passed and Mark Munroe showed up to headquarters. He engaged the Trump supporters walking one after another into the main room. "Well, listen, if you wouldn't mind, why don't you take a Rob Portman sign too?" he asked.

"Oh, ok," said the woman. She had purchased a Trump sign and the Party Chair was trying to be a good example for the volunteers to show them that they needed to push the signs of the top Republican official in the state as well as Trump's stuff.

Mark had less luck with the next two people. They were not interested in Portman's signs. One man at least gave an excuse. "I already have a Portman sign," he said. He did not, in fact.

The next man was of Polish ancestry and answered matter-of-factly, "I don't need a Portman sign." Mark scrunched his eyes.

Where are the candidates for local and state office? Thomas thought. He had only met one candidate so far. *Can't these people see the enormous support that Trump is getting? They could be riding on coattails, but they have to do the work!*

Chelsea walked past the white table where Thomas was working on his computer. She avoided looking at him and shut the door to the conference room.

Joe walked from the back room to the main room of headquarters. He intercepted a person who was about to purchase a $10 sign. "Hey, do you want to buy a *real* sign? We are making big ones in the back," he said.

Mark Munroe looked annoyed. Joe led the excited visitor to the Trump sign factory. "Whoa! How much is that one," the visitor said. He pointed to a self-standing ten-foot tall Trump sign with **Ground Zero** painted on both sides.

"That sign is $100, it's great," Joe said. The man told Joe that he wanted it. Joe got Thomas to help load the sign into the bed of the pickup of the visitor.

Mark almost said something to Thomas, but he restrained himself.

There were only forty of the regular-sized Trump signs left. Joe realized that headquarters was almost out of the yard signs and that he would soon have a monopoly on selling his custom signs to the stream of Trump supporters. He began hanging out near the front desk until Mark invited him to return to the back room.

Thomas watched this drama unfold while he added all the Ohio Republican events –candidate fundraisers, county picnics, and monthly county party meetings – to a set of Google Calendars. There were eighty-eight counties in the state, so it was a task that he could repeatedly turn to do should there be a slowdown in other work.

"Well, I'm off to meet the Donald," Mark said loudly. He walked out the door and to his car. There was a fundraiser in Canton this afternoon: Thomas had heard it cost up to $25,000 a plate to attend.

Thomas tried and failed to find out more specific information about the fundraiser, and Chelsea ignored his questions, so he searched Twitter and found the address. He left headquarters a half hour after Mark and made the hour drive to Canton.

It was somewhat of a disappointment as Secret Service agents and county police covered all the entrances. There was no way he could talk his way into the fundraiser at the private golf club. The excessive police presence was interesting to see however, Thomas thought.

Thomas drove back to Youngstown and ate chicken nuggets at Wendy's while sitting in a booth and browsing his phone.

Fifty foreign policy experts renounce Trump. The article under the headline explained that most of the Republican foreign policy experts, many teaching at Harvard University and researching at various think tanks while waiting out the Obama Presidency, said that they would under no circumstances work for Trump.

CHAPTER 13

Tuesday, 9 August 2016, 91 Days
MCRP HQ

"Does Don Manning know how to do a mailing?" Thomas asked Chelsea, who stared at her computer while sitting in a swivel chair in the back conference room.

Manning, the state representative nominee for the 59th district, had just pulled out of the parking lot after stopping by headquarters to place literature at the local candidate table located near the main entrance desk. Don had said hi to each of the volunteers working at headquarters this morning, and spoke to several people at length, especially Chelsea, about how much he was walking each day.

"Unlikely," Chelsea said. She looked at Thomas' face intently. "I like the idea of a mailing," she continued after a pause. She shifted in her seat.

Manning's district was roughly half the county, representing approximately 120,000 people, or about 80,000 voters. It would be a massive undertaking to do a timely and accurate mailing. Don could pay for someone else to do the mailing but that would be expensive: probably $1.15 per letter or $0.70 per large postcard, multiplied by roughly 60,000 households.

Ding-a-ling

"Arrrrrrrr," Joe wailed at the front door. He sounded like a wounded hippo. "Mark took down my sign!" he said. Indeed, yesterday Mark had removed the large ground zero sign that was at the edge of Market Street. The sign did not have the necessary disclaimers on it, and Mark did not want trouble. This was the same sign that Thomas saw that led him to the headquarters building on his first day in Youngstown.

Joe continued with the noisemaking. There was a mixture of animal sounds, yodeling, and plain shouting. Thomas raised his head up to watch the commotion. Perry stared. Kate stopped cleaning the kitchen and stood still, her face like stone.

"*Resumish?*" Joe asked. He spoke to no one in particular. He was loud.

"*Movish po polsku?*" Thomas said. Joe snapped back into reality. Thomas again answered, this time saying that he understood, using Polish words.

"You speak Polish?" Chelsea said. She had walked out of the conference room and was about to leave for Stone Fruit coffee due to the noise when she heard Thomas speak.

"I am off my meds for four days!" Joe said. He was shouting. He realized that Thomas might have been an observer of people just as he was, and he wanted to give an excuse for his animal sounds and yodeling. Joe calmed down and returned to the back room to paint his signs.

Ding

Thomas looked down at his phone and saw a message from Jay Edwards, the young Republican State Representative Nominee in Southeast Ohio. His district covered Athens, a college town, half of Marietta, the historic town on the banks of the Ohio River founded by Revolutionary War veterans, and a large rural area filled with forests and farms. In 2014 the previous Republican nominee had only lost the race by 400 votes out of 54,000 cast. The 94th state house was one of the best chances of a pickup for the Republicans in 2016, and so Thomas had messaged Jay Edwards earlier with documentation showing how the Republicans had a good chance of winning. Thomas had asked how he could help.

We are walking every day, but there is no headquarters except for my living room.

Thomas had an idea to make Gantt charts for the 94th district and other competitive races. This planning tool would help the candidates know when they should do certain things, like do a mailing to potential voters or be prepared to respond to negative attacks. Gantt charts used bars placed across the page to represent how long each task would take to complete, and displayed bars of prerequisite tasks that needed to be done before a candidate could start on a subsequent task.

Earlier Thomas had also texted Martha Yoder of the 64th state district. The 64th district was located north of Mahoning County and included all of Trumbull and Ashtabula Counties. The main city was Warren. There were suburbs with large populations around Warren, and the remaining district was rural. Martha had not responded.

Thomas saw Joe walk into the main room and head to the thermostat control. Kate stepped in front of him. "You do not touch this," she said.

"It's eighty degrees in here!" Joe said. He was sweating from working in the back room.

"NO," Kate said.

Thomas didn't speak even though he agreed with Joe that it was too hot. It wasn't worth antagonizing Kate.

Thomas' Hotel

Thomas prepared a report and sent it to the top ten names on his spreadsheet of likely email addresses of senior Trump campaign officials.

Monday and Tuesday Update from Mahoning County
To: Various Senior Trump and RNC Staff

Below is a summary of what I have observed over the past two days in Eastern Ohio.

Mahoning County

*People continue to come into the Mahoning headquarters in a constant stream to purchase Trump signs. Bumper stickers are also popular.

There are two hardworking local candidates in Mahoning County, the 59th state house candidate Don Manning and the incumbent Judge Shirley Christian. I am assisting the 59th candidate by putting together a mailing plan for him.

The county party is expanding hours as volunteers are increasingly becoming available. This is unofficial as of now.

Anecdote: While I ate lunch at Wendy's, one woman sitting near me talked to her friend about how much she wanted Hillary to be stopped. Another unrelated man walked over to her table and they both discussed their intense dislike for Hillary.

East Ohio State Senate and House Races

The 30th Senate candidate Frank Hoagland has walked doors a great deal in Athens and Marietta in the south of his district. He still needs to walk in Carrollton and Steubenville. This is according to one of his staffers that I talked to this afternoon.

The 94th state house candidate Jay Edwards is walking every day in his district in Athens and half the city of Marietta, according to a conversation I had with him earlier today.

Elsewhere in Ohio

Delaware County - US Senator Rob Portman campaign office will be opening August 20.

There appears to be a conflict among Republicans in Trumbull County. The county chair has sued the state house candidate Martha Yoder in the 64th district. We are seeing Republicans and Trump supporters visit Mahoning County from Trumbull County as the Trumbull office appears to be mostly closed.

CHAPTER 14

Wednesday, 10 August 2016, 90 Days
Piper Residence, Beaver Township

Rose Piper woke up before her alarm, anxious. She could not avoid the party members any longer without risking losing her place coordinating the Canfield Fair. Today she had to show her face at headquarters. Rose forced herself out of bed.

She got up, dressed, skipped breakfast, and climbed into her red car. She turned onto the country road and headed north.

There is that cop again!

Rose reached across to put on her seatbelt. The Mahoning Sheriff's deputy was looking down at his phone and did not see Rose drive by his patrol car while fumbling with her seatbelt. The Chairwoman turned right, and then left onto Market Street. She pulled into the Dunkin' Donuts drive-through window to order a large coffee.

Ten minutes later, she arrived at the parking lot of the MCRP HQ. She noticed a gray car backed into a parking spot with no license plate in the front, signifying that it was from out of state. She opened her car door and walked into the headquarters.

MCRP HQ

Thomas was standing at a white table and working to put together the remaining two hundred and fifty signs from the five hundred that Jay had dropped off a few days prior. No one else had volunteered to assemble the Portman signs due to his establishment Republican positions and the fact that all the unpaid volunteers were at headquarters for Trump alone. This gave Thomas a job, as well as another excuse to hang out at headquarters. He worked much slower on the Portman signs than he had worked on pressing the buttons together and assembling the Trump signs a week earlier.

Rose opened the door and greeted Perry and Kate, who were manning the reception desk. Chelsea was expecting Rose because of a text that the Chairwoman had sent the field organizer while in line at Dunkin' Donuts, and Chelsea walked up to the front desk and welcomed Rose with a hug.

"You look great!" Chelsea said. Rose was wearing a new dress from Dillards. The two of them talked. Rose looked to the middle of the main room and saw a young man with dark hair and broad shoulders standing by a table making signs. He wore dark jeans and a button-up striped blue shirt.

Thomas walked to the kitchen, changed the garbage bag, and hauled out the full bag to the dumpster in the parking lot. He returned to the headquarters building and washed his hands. Rose approached him after he walked back to his sign making station.

"Hi, I'm the chairwoman of the party," She said. She paused to look at him. "Are you twenty-four years old?" she asked.

Thomas laughed. He figured that she was guessing his age low to flatter him. He smiled in a friendly manner to the short woman. "I am Thomas, from Columbus, Indiana."

"I am Rose Piper," she said. Rose returned his smile, and she laughed. Thomas had an open presence about him.

What a nice lady, Thomas thought. Thomas told her that he was attending the Pence rally in Cambridge, Ohio that afternoon. Rose perked up when he told her this.

I have found my way back to the party, Rose thought. *I will guide this young man and he will do my bidding.* She grinned wider. *I am going to stay chairwoman!* Rose walked away to talk to the front desk people.

Thomas stopped making signs and opened his computer. There was an article from the Washington post that said one in five Republicans wanted Trump to drop out of the race. Thomas noticed that they had polled 396 people, and that the article did not specify from where they had polled these people. He speculated that the paper had done the poll with Virginia or DC registered Republicans and then extrapolated the results countrywide. *The propaganda is intense, although the Kool-Aid here is strong too,* he thought.

Thomas browsed through Twitter at the political stories, and Rose shuffled back to his table. "Are you wearing a suit to the rally?" she said, staring at Thomas.

"Yes, it's in the car," Thomas said.

"Good," she said. Her eyes changed from intense to playful. "Let me give you my phone number." She pulled out her phone and exchanged contact information with Thomas. "You know, Chelsea was hired by the RNC, not the Ohio State Party," she said. "Are you looking for a job?"

"Yes," Thomas answered. Rose was perceptive, Thomas noticed.

Ding-a-ling

Two people walked into the headquarters and purchased Trump signs. They followed the pattern of Trump supporters. Nobody took a free Rob Portman sign, but everybody paid $10 to $100 for Trump yard signs.

"I am going to Macy's now," Rose said. Thomas stood until she walked away, then resumed assembling signs.

Ring

Thomas looked down and it was a New York number.

"Hello?" he said.

"Hello, this is Tony Russo, is this Thomas?"

"Yes, how may I help you?"

"Listen, I got your résumé and I want to interview you for a field organizer position," Tony said.

Thomas' heart began to race. With the New York number displaying on the caller ID, he thought this was someone from the Trump headquarters.

"You are way, way overqualified for this position by the way," Tony continued.

"I will definitely do this position, and I could do a lot of good in Ohio," Thomas said. "I actually have an interview with Chris Horvath tomorrow."

"Oh," Tony paused. "I didn't know this. Some wires must have gotten crossed," Tony said. Thomas felt Tony's tone change.

In fact, Tony was not working out of the Manhattan headquarters. He was originally from New York State and he had never changed his mobile number. This cycle, Justin Clarke had hired him to work as the Deputy Director RNC Victory Campaign. He worked out of Columbus, Ohio, one floor below Chris Horvath of the Trump Campaign.

The Trump specific campaign team headed by Chris Horvath took the top floor, and the RNC Victory Campaign headed by Justin Clarke took the bottom floor. The two teams had various levels of cross-coordination. In this instance, Chris did not let anyone besides Brandon Moffett, the Trump Deputy Campaign Manager, know that Thomas was coming in for an interview. Thomas knew none of this at the time, nor did he know how closely Tony Russo, an RNC operative, was supposed to be working with Chris Horvath, a specific Manafort and Trump pick.

"Forgive my ignorance, but what organization are you with?" Thomas asked.

"I am a deputy director on the Victory Team, which is paid for by the RNC. There is a separate Trump Team that Chris Horvath heads up, and we are working closely with him." Tony hung up the phone.

Thomas did not understand the organizational structure of the campaign. His networking skills had meant that he had outrun his ability to learn the byzantine organizational structure of the dual campaigns. He sat down and stared at his computer. Thomas realized that he made a mistake by not aggressively pursuing an interview for the job at that moment.

Cambridge, Ohio, Governor Pence Event

Thomas pulled into the parking lot of the convention center and called

Kevin Schimp. He stepped out of the car and looked for Kevin's black Chevrolet, sweating under his dress shirt.

"Thomas?" Kevin stretched out his hand.

"Here are three hundred pieces of Trump lit," Thomas said. He had nicked the literature made as door hangers from a box of five thousand sitting on a shelf in the conference room at the MCRP HQ.

"Oh, yes, exactly what we need," Kevin said. Thomas could tell that they needed much more than three hundred pieces. "Let me show you the door-walking app we are using."

Thomas realized that it was not the RNC Advantage program, but a separate system.

"This is from O-Rock," Kevin said. He meant the Ohio State House Campaign Committee. "Maybe I can get you into the VIP entrance," Kevin said. The two of them walked to the entrance.

The TSA denied the request, and Thomas emptied his pockets before subjecting himself to the metal detectors, while Kevin walked through a separate door with other VIP staffers. A minute later the two men met inside the large ballroom. A group of candidate staffers and campaign workers were standing and talking.

"My job is done," said a tall skinny fellow. He identified himself as the Southeast Ohio Trump Field Director. This was Brian Wollet's counterpart to the southeast part of the state. "I just have to attend a few fundraisers and kick back," he said. He was in a jovial mood.

Is this why I had to give the Hoagland campaign Trump walking lit, because this guy is not doing his job? Thomas held his tongue and maintained a friendly expression.

A short Black woman walked up to the group. "What are you guys doing?" she said.

"Hey Kamilah, this is Thomas Ryan. He is working for Trump in Youngstown," Kevin turned to Thomas, "This is Kamilah Prince, the hardest-working person on the Trump Campaign." It was true, and Kamilah walked away from the group to continue preparations for Pence's visit. She was another Deputy Director working for Chris Horvath, and she was responsible for arranging the rallies.

Thomas saw Kamilah walk to a bald man in an expensive suit. The man pulled the phone away from his ear. *Trump National Campaign,* Thomas thought.

The music stopped and the local county party chair walked up to the Microphone. "Let's bow our head for prayer," he said. He gave a typical evangelical prayer and emphasized the last few words, "in *Jesus' Name."*

Thomas stood and watched.

The music resumed. Thumping electronic music with a heavy bass beat contrasted with the religious words that the politico had prayed. The crowd went wild.

Two more local Republican candidates approached the podium and gave peppy speeches. The second one was the better speaker and the crowd became frenzied when he introduced the Governor of Indiana. Eight hundred yelled, "Trump! Trump! Trump!" while Pence walked to the stage.

"I am a Christian, Conservative, and Republican, in that order," Pence said. He was interrupted with applause with this first line. He continued.

Thomas expected what happened next, but the press did not. Governor Pence had spent several years of his career as a radio host in Indianapolis, and he spoke in a smooth, gentle manner that caught one unaware with his effortless Southern Indiana charm. One could call it the speech style of a good ol' boy, or more accurately, a father sitting at the dinner table with six kids and mother surrounding him. The kids and young adult children might squabble or say something foolish, and the father would ignore most of it. Then he would tell a story and everyone would turn their attention to him. This is what Pence was like in his speech. He was a patriarch.

CHAPTER 15

Thursday, 11 August 2016, 89 Days
Secret Ohio Trump Headquarters

"You have got to be kidding me!" Thomas said. He pulled his gray sedan into the secret Ohio Trump headquarters that was only a mile away from the first hotel that he stayed at when he arrived in Columbus. It was a nondescript two-story office building that housed an accountant, a psychologist, and the most important state campaign headquarters for the presidential race.

Thomas called Brandon Moffett, and a minute later Brandon walked down the stairs to escort Thomas to the top floor. Brandon and Thomas walked to Chris Horvath's office. In the main room Thomas noticed that the walls were bare. There were a few Trump bumper stickers on a folding table in the central room, but no maps anywhere. There were five or six people doing no discernable work. Chris's office was unfurnished except for a folding table, a chair, and a laptop computer.

"Hi, I'm Chris, thanks for coming in," the state director for Ohio said. He shook Thomas' hand. "I received your résumé from Michael Glassner on Sunday," Chris said.

Thomas said nothing and kept his face completely neutral. He had been driving since 5:30 in the morning and his normally photographic memory was faltering. He tried hard to concentrate while Chris spoke.

"You have a great résumé, but listen, we have just filled our last slot twenty-four hours ago," Chris said. "We have everything under control here in Ohio," Chris continued. Brandon sat in a chair next to Thomas while Chris leaned back in the chair. Chris wore a dark blue polo shirt and khaki pants, and Brandon wore a T-shirt and jeans. Thomas was in a suit.

"OK, I told you that I could even drive out Monday or Sunday evening…" Thomas said. He realized that all of this was planned. *This is why Brandon scheduled the meeting for Thursday.*

They had to interview him because the Deputy Campaign Manager of the National Campaign had strongly suggested that they listen to what Thomas had to say about Governor Kasich. However, Chris did not want an outsider to give him any advice, never mind get in the way and start pulling levers of the campaign. Chris had run the 2010 Rob Portman US Senate race, which he had won, and did not need an upstart weaseling his way into power, no matter his country club connections.

Thomas noticed that the body language of Chris and Brandon changed to unfriendly when he uttered the sentence. He scrabbled to repair the damage and changed tack.

"Well, listen, what I love most is to knock on doors. I am going to go back to Eastern Ohio and knock doors because that is Ground Zero, that is where the race will be won," Thomas said.

"There are a lot of Ground Zeros," Brandon interjected. He did not appreciate Thomas not taking the hint that he should return to Indiana.

"I really appreciate you inviting me here, and I am excited to go back and knock doors," Thomas said. He stood up to leave. Chris's eyes went wide in surprise. The director and deputy director expected either arguing or a detailed field report. Thomas knew there was no use in staying in the office any longer and he would only hurt his relationship with these men if he showed disagreeableness or weakness. He smiled and shook both of their hands, before walking out of the office. A girl arranging the bumper stickers looked at him and smiled as he walked out. *It's the suit. She thinks I'm from New York.* He returned her smile.

Once outside the office, he walked to the neighboring building and stood in the lobby. He called Tony Russo to see if the field organizer position was still open.

"Hi Thomas, what's up?" Tony answered his phone.

"I just got out of the interview with Chris Horvath, and they do not have a spot for me, is your position still open?" Thomas said. He swallowed hard.

"Are you here now…yes? Listen, I am up in Cleveland, but you can do an interview with Jonathan Schmidt. Jonathan is the other deputy director and he and I are considering you for the field organizer position. I filled the position from the other day, but we will be hiring more people soon," Tony said.

Thomas returned to the campaign headquarters, this time one floor lower.

The interview was fast and smooth. "As soon as we have an opening we will hire you," Jonathan promised. Thomas walked to his car and started the long drive back to Youngstown.

Bing

An email from Chris Horvath to Thomas read, "It was nice to talk to you."

This bastard knows he messed up, Thomas thought. *He wanted to demonstrate to me that he had the power, before sending me packing back to Indiana. Instead, he showed me, and he fears that he possibly showed Trump depending on my connections, that he values posturing over winning.*

Thank you for meeting with me as well, Thomas wrote and hit send on his phone. There was no reason not to be polite.

Thomas' Motel

Thomas sat on the bed and watched the swimming events of the Olympics. He pulled up the Trump website on his laptop. He hit refresh for no particular reason. The top of the page showed a new event.

Trump will be visiting Youngstown Monday – Restricted access

"Wow!" he said. He texted Rose Piper first with the news.

I want to go, I have been a Trump supporter longer than anyone! I am also the party chairwoman!! Rose responded in seconds. Thomas realized that he had found out about the Youngstown Trump event before anyone. It was pure luck. He madly texted every number in Northeast Ohio that he had acquired.

Hey Thomas, thanks for the notice! Don Manning responded.

Could you send me Mark Munroe's number? Thomas replied, trying to cash in on the favor that Don owed him for walking in the ninety-six degree humid Ohio heat.

Bing

There it was, he now had the MCRP Chair's mobile number. He texted Mark the news. Thomas knew that Mark would have already known about the Trump visit, but Thomas wanted to demonstrate to him that *he* also knew, and before almost anyone. The chair knew Thomas had had an interview at the Trump headquarters earlier in the day, so he might think that Thomas had an inside connection.

I will look into this news, Chelsea texted. Thomas had scooped the Victory Campaign RNC field organizer.

Thomas texted Kevin Schimp, the campaign manager of the 30th State Senate Republican Candidate, and Hoagland himself, the candidate. He texted Alex, the political director of the Ohio State Senate campaign. *Please keep me in the loop,* Alex texted.

Ask Brandon Moffett or Kamilah Prince for VIP passes, Kevin texted.

Already done, Thomas thought.

CHAPTER 16

Friday, 12 August 2016, 88 Days

Thomas dropped off his clothes and drove out of the dry cleaner's parking lot. He had outsourced the last of his personal tasks. Every minute of each day was now filled with campaign work.

MCRP HQ

Headquarters was packed with people at 10:00 am. The news of Trump's upcoming visit had spread, and volunteers bumped into one another as they angled for a space to fold T-shirts, rearrange bumper stickers on tables, assemble signs, and any other task that they could pretend to do. No one made any buttons. Mark had hidden the machine in his office.

Talk to Jason Lovett about getting a VIP ticket, Tony Russo texted Thomas in response to his email last night, referring to the RNC Victory Campaign Field Director Northeast Ohio, and boss of the two field organizers, Chelsea and Valentina.

Thomas looked at his phone and approached Jason.

"Plan A is to get a ticket through Mark Munroe, and I have a plan B as well," Jason said.

"Thank you for your help," Thomas said. He felt something was off with Jason.

A dark Ford sedan pulled up in front of the headquarters door, and the party chair got out.

Ding-a-ling

Mark walked through the throng of people and to the chair's office where he shut the double doors. He picked up the phone, looked at the list of big money donors for the party, and dialed.

"Hi there, Bill, this is Mark, I am calling to ask if you are interested in attending a Trump event on Monday. It is a very limited audience and I managed to secure you a VIP ticket if you are available. Now, because of the Secret Service you would have to arrive by 11:00 am, and the event will not end until 2:00 pm. I would ask that you be able to remain during the entire event if you wish to take the ticket," Mark said. The first four donors snatched the tickets while the fifth one, an attorney, had a court date and could not attend.

One hour later, Mark ran out of tickets. He kept calling the donors, but changed his message. "Hi Matt, how are you doing on this fine day," Mark said. "Yes, yes, we have a lot of excitement going on at headquarters as you have heard." He paused as the judge on the common pleas bench asked him a question. "Well, I would get you in if I could, but we only received thirty tickets, and we do not have any more available." Mark said.

A tall African-American woman dressed in a skirt and jacket walked into headquarters. She saw an unfamiliar person sitting at one of the white plastic tables and working on a computer, and she walked to him.

"Hi, I am Tracey Winbush, the vice-chair of the party," She said.

"Hi, my name is Thomas. I arrived here from Indiana at the end of July to help on the Trump campaign," Thomas said. He had simplified his introductory speech to new people he met.

Tracey listened carefully and processed his words. "I have been absent the last two weeks because I worked much, much too hard earlier in the campaign," she said. After a few more words she walked to the chair's office where Mark sat, continuing to make phone calls. She sat in a smaller chair and pulled up an Excel spreadsheet.

The steady stream of people coming into headquarters turned into a flood. Nearly every person asked for a ticket at the front desk. That failed, and eighty percent of the people walked to the chair's office to ask Mark for his favor. "This is a limited event, and we do not have any more tickets," he said repeatedly. "They only gave us thirty tickets," he said.

Thomas noted what was happening, and realized that the envy principle was about to be in play. The envy principle states that human beings retaliate or take proactive action against those whom they envy.

Volunteers claiming to be working for Trump for a year would have terrible envy against Thomas should he score a ticket. This would cause additional problems throughout the campaign; still, Thomas thought it was important to make his best effort to get into the event so that it would appear to the campaign staffers and volunteers that he was integrated into the campaign. This mattered, for the right perception now might mean a campaign job, and the right perception later might mean a Plum Book job. The new President would need to hire more than four thousand top-level government officials listed in a federal register commonly called the "Plum Book." He needed good stories from the campaign in the interview process for a policy position at the White House or for a foreign posting in Paris. Thomas thought that his chances to get a ticket and therefore subjecting himself to the envy principle while upping his chances at a later job were about even.

While Thomas thought about the interpersonal political aspects of the Trump ticketing situation, he emailed the Gantt chart that he had created for the 59th state house seat to Don Manning.

Don texted right away.

I love it!

Thomas responded.

If you get any money for a mailing I can organize that for you too.

Thomas opened up reddit.com/r/the_donald and saw pictures of Michael Glassner at the Cambridge Pence event. In every single picture he saw Michael Glassner talking on his phone. *That is Michael Glassner!* he thought, the same person he had seen talking with Kamilah and other staffers at the event.

"Hi Judge, this is Mark," the chair answered his personal cell phone. "I'm sorry Judge, there simply aren't any more tickets left."

So judges are being denied tickets now. Oh, I want one so badly! Thomas thought. He overheard the conversation and he could feel the disappointment of the Judge who called Mark hours too late. Thomas considered whether he should stay at headquarters to try to get one of the tickets, or whether he should leave now to Carrollton to walk for Frank Hoagland. *It's always better to stay at the center if one wants something, the periphery is ignored,* he thought. He felt like a Soviet apparatchik angling for a favor from a politburo member.

Another hour went by, this one was long. Thomas waited at his computer. Jason Lovett walked up to him and leaned close to his ear. "Walk back to the chair's office," he said. He was whispering. Thomas did as he was told.

"What is your name?" Tracey asked. "Spell it for me. And give me your phone number."

"Thomas Ryan, R-Y-A-N" he said.

"This list is going to the Secret Service," Tracey said as she typed his name into an Excel document.

"Thank you," Thomas said. He stood up and walked out of the chair's office and to the white table where his computer sat. He threw it in his backpack and left headquarters before anyone could change their mind.

Carrollton, Ohio

"Hi, my name is Thomas, and Frank and I are out walking today to let you know that he is running for State Senate. Frank is on another street and I can have him come over if you would like to meet him," Thomas said in one breath. He flipped a palm card to the person standing at the door. The lit piece showed a Navy SEAL trident on one side and three standard Republican platform points on the other side.*

"Oh," the man answered. He took the palm card and looked at it. He stared at the trident.

"May I ask, have you heard of Frank?" Thomas asked.

---

* Campaign literature is often referred to as "lit", the common phrase used by candidates and volunteers.

"No, but I will take a look at this."

Thomas thanked the man and left the porch. Frank was walking in Steubenville today, an hour away, but voters were more receptive to a volunteer knocking at their door if they thought the candidate was down the street talking to their neighbor. Thomas had discovered that voters also liked volunteers who were personal friends with a candidate. No one ever asked to meet the candidate to verify either story.

It was clear that no one knew who Frank Hoagland was in Carrollton, and Thomas thought that the same scenario existed in Steubenville and all the cities of the 30th State Senate district. It was good that Frank Hoagland, Kevin Schimp, and Thomas Ryan were all walking this evening.

Ohio's summer humidity increased as the evening progressed. Thomas felt his legs chafe. The sun dipped below the horizon and Thomas drove north back to Boardman.

MCRP HQ

Thomas walked up to the front door of headquarters and pulled. It was locked. He saw Tracey sitting in the same chair facing the computer, as she had been when he had left several hours earlier.

Knock knock

She walked over to let him in. "I have this idea about reaching Black voters," she started. Tracey explained that she had thought about how important it was to reach minority voters in Ohio and other Midwest battleground states where every vote would count.

Thomas listened intently and asked questions.

Thomas is a good listener, Tracey thought.

Tracey is strategic, Thomas thought.

Davis Motel

Thomas sent a report to the Ohio State Senate Political Director about the mood of the voters in Carrollton.

Carrollton Doors Observation
To: Ohio State Senate Political Director

- THOMAS RYAN -

I walked some doors in Carrollton for Hoagland and Kevin today. The people were very friendly and I think most of those I met today will vote for him.

My observation was that the voters I met with today had not heard of Frank Hoagland before.

Thomas

Saturday 13 August 2016

Thomas reached up to feel his left ear. His earplug had fallen out. The air conditioner had run the entire night, and his room at the Davis Motel was cool and dry. Twenty minutes later, he opened the door of his room to a warm and muggy summer morning in Northeast Ohio. He felt well-rested; the bed at his motel room was firm and high quality. Thomas drove past the strip club, past the toll road entrance, past the large gas station at the border of Beaver Township and Boardman, past St. Elizabeth Hospital, and turned into the small strip mall.

MCRP HQ

Crunch, Thomas bit into a locally grown honey crisp apple. It was sweet. He looked down at his phone. *9:00 am.* No one had shown up to headquarters for the big walking day. Thomas stood, leaning on his car, and mused.

I have almost no political capital.

He had managed to secure a VIP ticket to the upcoming Trump visit, but he did not know any of the players in the local or state party, or more importantly, none of these people owed him favors. Presidential campaigns lasted almost two years in America, and the final one hundred days were near the end of the long process. He did not know the main players of the campaign, those who had influence, those who could be safely ignored, and he did not know the narrative that the main players were creating.

The senior staffers had developed their reputations with each other and Trump since the middle of 2015. They had the inside knowledge, the credibility, the favors, and all the ingredients of political cover and political power.

And here I am standing in the parking lot, alone, like a jackass, Thomas thought. He finished eating the core of the apple, apparently useful for preventing cancer, and flipped the stem to the ground.

Apartment in Boardman

Chelsea used a traditional cheap alarm clock in addition to her phone, as the phone alarm was never enough to wake her up. The alarm blared. She grabbed her phone.

9:15 am

"Dammit!" she said.

She forced herself out of bed, threw on a pair of jeans and a T-shirt, and walked bleary-eyed down the stairs and outside to her econobox car. She stopped at Dunkin' Donuts and entered the drive-through to buy a large Frappuccino.

Oh, there is Rose Piper! She saw the red car ahead of her. She grabbed her phone and began texting. Rose responded with saccharine morning greetings.

MCRP HQ

9:34 am

Thomas looked down at his phone again. He had gone into a meditative state, thinking about the campaign. The sun heated the air. It felt like a bath without the water. The day was not yet unpleasant, but it would be soon. By 11:00 am the temperature would surpass 90 degrees according to the WFMJ channel 21 weather forecast.

No one is here, Thomas thought. He fidgeted. *This is the single most important area in Ohio, and the candidates are missing the best time for walking doors.* Heat and humidity combined to make walking doors after midmorning a miserable experience.

Chelsea raced into the parking lot. Thomas noted the time to be 9:54 am, exactly. He was in a bad mood and trying to hide this. Chelsea didn't acknowledge him. She unlocked the front door, carrying the same two large bags as she usually did. She nearly dropped the Frappuccino but managed to catch it, dropping one of the bags in the process. She had a face that could have been cute, Thomas thought, except for her frequent frowns and vulgarity.

Mark arrived. He was the contrast in every way from the field organizer. He greeted Thomas with a smile, and the two men walked into the main room. "Well," Mark said. He spoke with a rasp. "I am feeling a bit ill, so Chelsea, can you be in charge of the office today?" Mark asked.

Clever, Thomas thought. *Mark is avoiding having to turn down hundreds more Party members asking for the special event Trump tickets.* Mark walked out of the building and Perry and Kate walked in. Perry sat at the front desk, put on his reading glasses, and opened his large Bible.

Ding-a-ling

At 10:01, one minute after the official opening time for headquarters, the first non-volunteer arrived. "Hey, I would like a ticket to see Trump," the tall man said. He wore a MAGA hat.

Perry paused before he spoke. "No one is getting any tickets."

"Even we don't have tickets," Kate interjected. Perry looked at her and then back at the hat-wearing man.

"How about a sign?" the man asked.

"Now *that* we can do," Perry said. He turned to the stack of Trump signs behind him and collected the money from the visitor.

Thomas watched the interaction and realized that Perry and Kate had not been put on the list for Monday's Trump rally.

Ding-a-ling

Don Manning and Nicole arrived with two teenage boys.

Poland, Ohio

"You gotta watch your speed around here," Don said. He was going exactly 25 mph on McClurg Road. "The cops are aggressive."

"Mm-hmm," Thomas said.

"I got an invite to the Trump event," Don said. He turned his eyes for a moment to look at Thomas.

"I did too," Thomas said.

"It's a VIP invite," Don continued, not really listening to his passenger.

"Did you receive a call from the Columbus Trump headquarters?" Thomas asked.

"I have already walked this neighborhood in the primary," Don said. He ignored Thomas and changed the subject to the doors that they were going to hit today.

Thomas realized that he had received the same invitation from Mark Munroe as Don had, but that Don was posturing a bit. *Well, everyone is posturing, including me*, Thomas thought. The white SUV made another turn and entered Poland, Ohio.

"Today we are going to walk in Boccieri's neighborhood," Don said. He referred to the Democrat incumbent of the 59th state house district, John Boccieri. Thomas sat stone-faced. Nicole, in the back seat, also remained silent as Don explained about the race.

Don parked the SUV at the side of the neighborhood road and he and Thomas got out. Thomas took one side of the street while Don took another. Both had two sets of literature, Don Manning's palm card and a large Rob Portman flier. Chelsea the RNC representative wanted the two of them to give people Rob Portman literature.

At the first house, the owner was home and answered the door. "Hi, my name is Thomas, and I am out today with my friend Don Manning. He is running for local office and we are introducing him to the neighbors," Thomas said. He felt his spiel becoming natural. Once again there was silence for a second as the person looked at the palm card Thomas shoved into his hands. "Here is information on Rob Portman," Thomas said. He made a split second decision to say the last bit and instantly regretted it.

"Oh, I don't like Portman," the homeowner responded. "I will take a look at this," he said, referring to Don's lit piece.

"Thank you," Thomas said. The door closed in his face. He walked down the driveway and with one hand entered the data into the RNC Advantage app on his iPhone. The next door was three houses down. It always amazed him how few people voted.

At the next house nobody was home. Thomas folded the Manning lit piece and shoved it in the door after writing across it *Sorry I missed you!* Little psychological tricks like this seemed to work.

Don had just finished talking to a person in a driveway, and was walking down the same street when he looked up to see Thomas put the lit piece in the door. *First this guy won't wear my T-shirt, and now he is not dropping off Rob Portman lit? What's going on?* Don wondered.

Slam. Another door shut in Thomas' face. *Well, what do we expect walking to the neighbors of the opposition candidate! What are we doing here?* Thomas was growing annoyed in the ninety-degree heat. He felt sweat dripping off his neck and arms. He walked down another driveway and crossed paths with Don, who looked at him funny. For the rest of the door-knocking, he made a big show of putting Rob Portman lit on the door handles when Don was in sight.

At around 12:30 pm, Thomas flagged down Nicole, who was driving the white SUV. He climbed into the cold and dry cabin. It was a relief.

"Maybe it's better to skip John Boccieri's house," Nicole said.

Thomas laughed.

"Boccieri probably thinks that we don't know what we are doing," she continued.

Yep, Thomas thought. He agreed with her but didn't say anything.

"Hey guys!" Don said. He climbed into the front passenger seat. "Wow, it's hot out there." *What is Thomas' problem? Don thought. Shouldn't he have figured out by now that Portman controls the Republican Party of Ohio?*

MCRP HQ

Thomas was in a foul mood. He washed his face in the bathroom sink and sat in a chair at a white plastic table. He stared into space. He felt dizzy and lethargic. His head hurt. *I am dehydrated,* he realized.

"Hey, Thomas," one of the volunteers said, "the Secret Service is going to move the Trump bobble-head to the Youngstown event on Monday." Thomas did not respond.

Jason Lovett walked into headquarters as Chelsea left. "I have four tickets to the event to give away," Jason said. He spoke loudly and to no one in particular. A volunteer walked up to him and asked him for one of the tickets. "These are reserved for important people," Jason said, smiling.

Thomas saw Brenda walk into headquarters. He got out of his chair and walked over to introduce himself.

"I am Brenda Johnson, the Mahoning County Trump Representative," she said. She held good eye contact.

"My name is Thomas, I am from Indiana," Thomas said. Brenda was scrambling with the upcoming Trump event. She walked to the chair's office.

"I have hit 20,000 doors so far," Jason Lovett said. He was talking loudly again, this time on the phone.

Thomas looked up at Jason and back down at his laptop. Senator Rob Portman was Facebooking today. Facebooking was when politicos pretend that they are doing voter outreach by announcing grand plans on Facebook for everyone to see. In practice the actual work is much less or even nothing than the claims. *We reached 100,000 voters today through phone banking!* The Portman for US Senate page showed enthusiastic workers making calls from the campaign headquarters in the wealthy suburbs north of Columbus, Ohio.

Phone calls never work, Thomas thought.

A young man named Nicholas sat behind Thomas at another white table and hit the dial button. He was using the RNC Advantage phone dialer program that called a likely voter taken from a universe of people who might vote for Rob Portman. "He…hello, My.. my name is Nic..Nicholas," he said. His stammer was so pronounced that the person hung up the phone, and Nicholas hit the button to dial the next person.

This kid has called three hundred people this morning! Thomas realized. It took a few seconds before each voter hung up the phone after Nicholas clicked the button for the app to automatically dial the next number.

Thomas walked up to Nicholas and introduced himself. The two began to talk about philosophy and history. Nicholas was intelligent,

Thomas noticed. "Have you heard about the Jaspers' shift?" Thomas asked.

"No, what's that?" Nicholas said.

"Around the ninth century BCE, the main theme in literature and religion in the ancient world shifted from focusing on the hero to focusing on the wise. Think of the story of Odysseus or Achilles in *The Iliad* and *The Odyssey*. This is the example of the hero, the conqueror. Contrast it with Socrates, Plato, or Aristotle. These philosophers represent the Western version of the Jaspers' shift, and they said that wisdom should be pursued above all else, though Plato and Aristotle disagreed on exactly how one should pursue wisdom and what wisdom specifically was," Thomas said. He was using his teaching voice. "In the fifteenth century CE, the Jaspers' shift reversed with the fall of Constantinople. The Ottomans effectively ended the Silk Road, prompting the Portuguese and Spanish to begin the age of exploration and globalism. Columbus, Magellan, and all the other explorers brought hero worship back into primacy over wisdom."

"Interesting," Nicholas said. He smiled at Thomas after thinking for a moment. "I like the hero."

I like the wisdom, Thomas thought. He scrunched his eyes.

Sunday, 14 August 2016, 86 Days

No lights on, door is locked. The MCRP headquarters was closed. Thomas walked to his car and decided to drive around the area looking at churches. He turned left on McClurg Road and then left again at South Avenue. A mile or so north he saw Infant Jesus of Prague Byzantine Catholic Church, where the choir sang multi-tonal Slavonic songs.

A few minutes later, he passed another church that looked to be Eastern Orthodox, but again, this was another Eastern Rite Catholic Church. It was Ukrainian.

On Highway 224, the main road that connected Canfield with Poland he saw a giant church with a large wooden steeple that reminded him of his time living in Poland. This was St. Charles parish of Boardman, the largest parish in the Youngstown metropolitan area.

More than eight thousand Catholics were registered at St. Charles, and a significant minority attended one of the several masses offered each weekend.

This is a result of the mass immigration for the steel jobs a hundred years ago, he thought. Many Eastern Europeans had joined Italians to immigrate to Youngstown over a century earlier, and until the 1960s had lived in small ethnic enclaves organized throughout the city. St. Charles was built after this time, during the White Flight to the suburbs. Although many of the churches had been rebuilt within the last fifty years, Thomas could see the remnants of Ruthenian, Ukrianian, and Polish communities.

The next church was called St. Maron's of the Maronite Rite of the Catholic Church, formed by Lebanese settlers. Down the road was a Romanian Byzantine Rite Catholic Church. *Aren't Romanians Orthodox?* he wondered.

At 10:00 am Thomas drove past the MCRP HQ on Market Street and saw Mark Munroe's car in the parking lot. He continued to explore the area for a while longer to not appear *too* eager.

His mind drifted. *Chris Horvath and his staff are doing an excellent job of organizing the rallies. Kamilah? Was that her name?* he thought. There had been tremendous energy at the Governor Pence rally, and Pence had shaken the hands of about five hundred out of the eight hundred people who attended. The rally had also garnered local media attention as well.

At 2:00 pm, Thomas was back in his motel room reading on his computer.

Bing
Tracey texted Thomas.
Can you meet today at headquarters?
Thomas texted back.
I'll be there in 15 minutes.

MCRP HQ

"The urban voter is vital this election," Tracey said. She sat at the chair's desk and Thomas sat facing her at the side of the desk. "Republicans don't know how to reach these voters."

Thomas felt something staring at him and he turned to his left. The giant Trump bobble-head gazed at him. "Is that thing going to the Trump event Monday?" he asked.

Tracey laughed. "Oh no, the Secret Service nixed that plan," she said.

Thomas regained focus. "Ohio went for Obama because of the African-American vote," he said.

Tracey nodded. "Trump needs a Black person on the campaign," she continued. "I have some ideas on how to reach this urban voting block. Maybe you could help me write a memo or something. I already have some ideas written down." She pulled out two pieces of paper on which she had outlined strategies for reaching inner-city voters. Addressing crime was at the top of the list.

Thomas took the paper and read the outline. "Let me think about this," he said.

Bing

Thomas looked at his email.

Trump – Youngstown Event Special Instructions

Special Instructions for Policy Speech by U.S. Presidential Candidate Donald J. Trump
Venue: Youngstown State University, Kilcawley Center (1 University Plaza, Youngstown, OH 44505)
Parking: "Far West Campus," Parking Lot #M70 (previously #M24)
Arrival Time and Registration: Please arrive early for security screening. Doors open at 12:00 PM, and you should anticipate lines. Please stop at the registration table located outside of the Kilcawley Center to pick up your ticket. Photo ID is required.
Doors Open: 12:00 PM
…

Thomas felt exhilaration. He stopped reading the email from the Ohio Trump Campaign and looked at Tracey. "I just got my Foreign Policy Speech ticket," he said.

"That's great!" she said. "By the way, have you had a good meal yet here in Youngstown? Where have you been eating?" she asked.

Thomas didn't answer.

"There is some really great food here. I'm going to take you out to eat tonight," Tracey said.

Thomas hesitated. He didn't want to owe Tracey a favor, but he also could not risk her ire by rebuffing her. "That sounds great," he said.

Tracey and Thomas walked out to her luxury SUV and drove to Field Grille.

"Wow, you weren't kidding," Thomas said. He took another bite of his pork chop. "This is delicious."

"Didn't I tell you?"

Thomas was wondering how he was going to stop Tracey from paying for his meal.

"What do you hope to get out of this campaign?" Tracey asked. Thomas didn't answer directly.

"Hi Tracey!" a man walked up to the table. Tracey knew him from the Board of Elections and introduced him to Thomas. After a moment of small talk, he walked away from the table and went to the bar.

"Bob is a great guy. I work with him at the Board of Elections. He is a Democrat, but he's all right." Tracey said.

A few minutes later, the waitress walked over to the table. "I wanted to let you know that a man has taken care of your bill tonight," she said.

Yes! Thomas rejoiced.

Tracey scrambled. She left the table to find Bob but her colleague had already left, spoiling her plan to have Thomas indebted to her.

An hour later, Tracey and Thomas returned to the MCRP HQ. Mark was inside in his office. "What are you two doing?" he asked. He made an effort to sound like he was joking, but clearly he was not. Tracey filled him in on the dinner.

"We are getting calls from Cleveland," Mark said. He changed the subject to tomorrow's event. "There are only a total of 350 seats and thousands of people, mostly donors, have asked for tickets."

CHAPTER 17

Monday, 15 August 2016, 85 Days
MCRP HQ

In some fundamentalist sects, the pastors place a great deal of importance on wifely submission to her husband. Followers of this doctrine often manifest an exaggerated appearance of this behavior; for example, the wife will wear clothing of extreme modesty while the husband will perform acts of cartoonish chivalry. Yet, it is often the case that gratuitous demonstrations of these principles are contrarian indicators. Many times, the woman controls the man completely in such relationships.

Kate likewise controlled every aspect of Perry's life, not that one could see this power dynamic from her dress. She woke him up in the morning at 6:00 am sharp for a joint prayer session. She fixed his breakfast and told him to eat his egg whites. She forbade her husband from tasting the yolks or bacon bits. She prohibited Perry from putting sugar into his coffee or eating any foodstuff made from processed flour.

At the MCRP headquarters building, Kate's audience increased. She had issued a command to the women of the Party to refrain from using any perfume or scented body wash. This morning, a well-heeled member of the Canfield Women's Club had not heard of Kate's order prohibiting scents, or had ignored it. Sarah was in her mid-forties and had stopped by the headquarters to talk to Mark before returning to her job as a Vice President at St. Elizabeth Hospital across the street. She decided to go to the restroom before visiting Mark.

Kate was waiting for her outside of the door of the single-person toilet. "Oh, hi, my name is Kate. Listen, we don't allow perfume in headquarters."

"Excuse me?" the woman said.

"Would you mind washing it off?" Kate continued.

The woman turned on her heel and walked back down the hallway to the main room, and then to the chair's office where she talked to him about the financial support the Canfield Women's Club was going to provide to the MCRP.

"By the way, who is Kate?" she asked Mark.

Thomas walked into headquarters and passed the executive as she walked out of the building. She flashed a smile to the young man in a dark gray suit and striped blue tie.

Ding-a-ling

Joe had not wanted to miss the action or his ticket, and had moved the sign making operation from the back room to the main room. People walked around the white tables and gawked at the huge signs on which he was stenciling lettering.

"Mark, where is my ticket?" Joe asked. "I have been working harder for Trump than anyone!" He was getting agitated.

"You are on a list, Joe." Mark reassured the former Youngstown cop.

Thomas took a seat at a plastic table facing the entrance desk, and watched people stream in and out of headquarters, taking Trump signs with them on their way out. Not many were buying one of the 2,500 buttons that filled overflowing plastic bags sitting on the floor behind the counter.

Kate walked over to Thomas. "How many days have you been volunteering here?" she asked.

Thomas recognized her tone as hostile. "Every day," he answered. He did not raise his eyes from the computer.

Mark walked over to Thomas and asked him something. Thomas stood up and talked to Mark for a minute while several of the other volunteers watched. "Do you see that reporter talking to Rose?" Mark asked. He turned to face M.L. Schultze of NPR. "Can you go over and watch things?"

"Yes, of course," Thomas said. He approached Rose Piper and the reporter. Rose was rambling.

"Hi, my name is Thomas and I am a volunteer here," he said. The reporter looked away from Rose and up at him. She had an attractive face that was relaxed and friendly.

"I'm M.L. Schultze from NPR," she said. She pointed to a recording device in her other hand. "Do you mind doing a short interview for me?" she asked. Rose stopped talking and stood next to Thomas.

"Not at all," he answered.

"Would you state your name and spell it out for my records?" She held up her recorder. Thomas did. "How are you helping out the Trump campaign?" she asked.

"I am mainly knocking on doors," Thomas said.

"There has been some controversy over Trump's treatment of women. Have you found people at the doors concerned about this or other behavior of the candidate?" She asked.

Thomas recognized the trap. "Well, I have talked to people of all political backgrounds at the doors – we are targeting Democrats as well as Republicans in the area – and people are most concerned with trade policy. Specifically, people feel that they or their family members have lost jobs due to unfair trade practices by other countries and due to a lack of action by American officials to protect them," Thomas said.

Rose spoke up to give the chairwoman's official response to the question as soon as Thomas stopped talking. She borrowed a few of his key phrases including saying, "trade policies," twice.

M.L. Schultze smiled. *This is no volunteer.* She asked a few other questions and Thomas gave similar answers, staying carefully on message of trade policy and jobs, and simply ignoring questions of social policy or alleged candidate behavior. Rose would jump in whenever Thomas finished to give the official local party stance, using Thomas' key phrases.

Schultze clicked the recorder and lowered it. "Thank you so much," she said. She shook Thomas' hand. Thomas turned to walk away and Rose followed him.

Ding-a-ling

A man walked into headquarters visibly angry. "My sign was stolen last night and I want another one to replace it," he said. He spoke aggressively to Perry. Kate was in the kitchen. Thomas looked out the window and saw the man's new Cadillac STS.

Perry paused before he spoke, and the veins on the angry man popped out higher. "The signs are $10," Perry said.

What is he doing, Thomas thought.

Within two exchanges the man escalated his words. "I will never vote for Trump! Trump is just as corrupt as everyone else...he just wants to make money on the presidential race!" The man said. He walked out of the room, slamming the door as he left the building. Perry stared at him, and Kate walked up to the front desk.

Thomas got out of his seat and quickly chased the man down outside. He caught up with him as he was getting in his car. "What's the problem?" Thomas asked.

"You people are all corrupt," the man said. "I donated $100 to the party and you still want to charge me for a sign."

It became obvious to Thomas that at least two things were taking place here. First, this was a greedy old man who had an anger problem and a lack of ability to communicate clearly. Second, the volunteers needed to be trained to de-escalate situations and give someone a sign if the visitors were causing a row. This man probably recognized that someone, whether Trump or the local party, was making a lot of money selling these two-dollar signs for ten dollars. The man drove off aggressively. Thomas walked into the headquarters building.

"Perry, if someone gets angry, just give them a sign. That particular man had already donated $100, so it was no problem just to give him one," Thomas said.

Immediately Kate got into Thomas' face. "Who do you think you are? You do not tell us what to do!"

Thomas was shocked at the aggressiveness. Kate looked like a Rottweiler straining against a chain. He managed to keep a neutral face. "It is more important to keep people happy than to make money," he said.

"You are a guest here! You do not tell us what to do!" Kate said forcefully. Perry looked away and down at the floor.

Thomas was not one to back down. "Listen, the man already gave $100 to the party and it does not hurt to give him a sign," Thomas replied. He felt several people staring at the front desk. He offered an olive branch that might save Kate's face. "However, he should not have gotten angry while inside."

"Everyone must pay. We are not giving away signs," Kate said.

Thomas walked away and sat at his table with his MacBook Pro. Perry and Kate walked to the kitchen and Perry whispered to his wife.

A few minutes later Kate walked next to Thomas and apologized. "It was obvious that the man was angry and nothing could have been done to calm the situation," Thomas said. "By the way, I received my ticket from the RNC: the national party, not the local party," he said. This seemed to calm Kate and confirmed what her husband had told her in the kitchen, that Thomas had come from Washington DC to work on the campaign. Thomas was not, in fact, from Washington DC, and he had no idea how he had gotten a ticket to the Foreign Policy Speech.

YSU Building

"Hi Don, great to see you here," Thomas said. Don Manning nearly jumped in surprise at the sound of Thomas' voice. Don turned to face Thomas and his eyes were wide. He had not expected the outsider to have a ticket. He shook Thomas' hand.

The hallway was packed with the Party VIPs. Someone pushed Thomas and he bumped into a tall woman. She did not turn from her position facing almost away from him. Thomas noticed that she wore a lanyard. "Excuse me, are you Ivanka?" he asked.

She laughed, "No, but I wear her clothes." Now she turned to engage. "I'm Victoria, the millennial director for the Trump Campaign," she said. She smiled and lithely made her way through the crowd to the entrance guarded by Secret Service agents.

Soon enough Thomas and the others passed the check-in station and the security check. He used the bathroom, and while washing his hands he overheard someone say the name "Randy." There was a middle-aged fellow standing next to him at the sink. "Are you Randy Law?" he asked.

"Sure am," the man said. He was gruff.

"My name is Thomas Ryan, I am helping in Mahoning County quite a bit. I am from Indiana near where the Pence family lives. Can I give you my number in case I can help you somehow?" he gave his sales pitch to the Trumbull County Chair. The two exchanged numbers.

The press pen in the back of the room contained plastic tables and another platform, this one for at least ten professional video cameras. Two reporters sat at their computers typing up copy, and a few cameramen adjusted the settings on their equipment. Someone had left the pen gate open, and at least twenty other press members meandered throughout the hall, looking for interview targets. Thomas purposely stood in the way of several, but each reporter ignored him and approached Trump supporters who looked disheveled or outlandishly dressed. *Joe is talking with* The New York Times. Thomas saw the New York photojournalist holding a recording device up to Joe.

Thomas found a seat, but resumed walking around the hall after only a few minutes. He had too much nervous energy, and he used it to meet as many Republican donors as possible. An hour later he found another seat near the rear of the hall next to the owner and COO of a small factory.

"What do you think of Trump's chances?" the owner asked.

Thomas responded with an analysis of the race, as he perceived it. "Trump has an eighty percent chance of winning," Thomas said. "I have been knocking on a lot of doors, and most people I talk to support Trump. Rob Portman may not be popular here, but I have contacts in other parts of Ohio and Portman is popular in those areas, and I don't see Portman voters doing anything else but holding their nose and voting for Trump. There is no way an establishment Republican voter will allow the Clintons back in the White House." Thomas delved in some numbers, explaining the primary race in Youngstown, and how it pointed to a Trump victory.

The factory owner was impressed. "Say, would you mind coming to the Warren Rotary Club to give a lunchtime speech? We have speakers each week during our lunch and I think you could give an interesting one," the owner said.

Thomas thought for a moment. "That would be fun," he said. The factory owner said someone would get in touch with him to arrange everything.

"Can you get us a couple of Trump hats?" the COO asked.

"Sure, stop by headquarters after this and I'll get you a couple," Thomas said. He thought that businessmen like these might be his plan B. That is, should Trump not win, he could work at one of their companies. He liked the area.

Thomas looked at Twitter. One news organization was reporting a poor turnout for the Trump event.

Fake news! he thought. *Which one of you bastards just wrote this?* Thomas stared at the press pen knowing that a light from the heavens would not in fact illuminate the guilty party. Pounding music revved up the crowd. Rudy Giuliani stood behind the heavy curtain waiting to make a surprise entrance. Behind him was Governor Mike Pence, and waiting patiently behind both men was the Candidate.

MCRP HQ

"Can I have the hats for free?" Frank asked. The COO of Berk Enterprises pointed at two MAGA hats. He drove a hard bargain.

"I..I'm so sorry, but they are $15 a piece," Nicholas said. He had returned to headquarters after the speech and was manning the front desk while making phone calls to potential Rob Portman voters.

"I can give you two for $20," Thomas said. He stepped between the college freshman and the Republican Party financial backer.

"Wh..what? No, these hats are $15 a piece."

Thomas was annoyed at the interruption from Nicholas. "It's okay, Nicholas, these guys are big donors to the party, right?" Thomas said.

He walked next to Frank. "Are you going to be the bad guy?" he asked the Young Republican member.

Nicholas shot Thomas a dirty look. "I gu...guess I'll have to be the bad guy," he said.

"Here," Thomas gave Frank the two red hats and took the twenty-dollar bill that he held out.

"Oh yeah!" Frank said. He and Thomas walked outside where Frank lit up a cigarette. "That was something else today, wasn't it?" Frank said. Thomas nodded.

Nicholas called Chelsea to complain about Thomas breaking the rules. Chelsea in turn called Jason Lovett to say that there had been an incident at headquarters with Thomas and Nicholas and a customer. Jason grinned and wrote up an incident report.

Carrollton, Ohio

By 6:30 pm, Thomas arrived to the small town an hour southwest of Youngstown. The town was on a hill, and the evening was hot and humid. Thomas sweated through his clothes. He noticed the Hoagland lit in his hands had become soggy.

"Hi, my name is Thomas and I am out walking with my friend Frank Hoagland, who is running for local office," he said. He flipped the Navy Seal's lit into the hand of the man at the door. The man studied the picture of Frank.

"By the way, how do you feel about the presidential race, if you don't mind me asking?" Thomas asked.

"At this house, we support Trump," he said. "I'll take a look at your friend."

Thomas walked back to the center of town and stopped at the Dairy Queen for chicken fingers. His crotch hurt from his jeans rubbing his legs. It was too hot. *This is the last time I walk doors without a candidate,* he thought. In fact, Hoagland and Kevin were in two separate small towns in the 30th state senate district also walking doors in the heat and humidity.

An hour later Thomas drove by the MCRP HQ. The lights were off and the doors locked.

Davis Motel

Youngstown and Eastern Ohio Observations August 12-15
To: Senior Trump Staff and Senior Victory Campaign Staff,

Here are observations that I have noted while I continue to volunteer in Eastern Ohio.

Trump Invite-Only Event Youngstown

*People I talked to at the invite-only event in Youngstown were very receptive of Trump's speech.

*The Trump visit energized all the local candidates and the party in general in Mahoning County.

*Many, many people say that they want Trump to return to the Youngstown area and hold a large rally.

Eastern Ohio

*People continue to drive to Mahoning County Republican HQ from several surrounding counties and even Pennsylvania (one couple today) to purchase Trump signs and other paraphernalia. There are six Trump signs left out of the original 500 county buy.

*Most people, Republicans and Democrats alike, continue to be very positive towards Trump at the doors in Mahoning County and to the south in Carroll County.

*Victoria of the Trump campaign led a team of 5 or 6 college republicans in Mahoning County to make calls to voters after the Trump speaking event.

*A group of three democratic ladies walked into the Mahoning County Republican Party HQ on August 13 to purchase Trump buttons. They said they were scared to say publicly that they supported Trump. Furthermore, they stated that they supported several down-ticket Republican candidates.

Overheard

*Overheard August 12 at Panera while at lunch: A woman told her friend to "be careful what you write on Facebook and what you say regarding Trump and Hillary." The lady discussed with her friend some harassing behavior that she had experienced voicing her support for Trump.

*One volunteer who had walked in the Cleveland area reported that some Democratic voters in Cleveland were not as receptive to Trump as the voters have been in Eastern Ohio.

*A contact in socially conservative Northwestern Ohio was surprised at the high demand for Trump signs at the Republican Party tent at the local fair. People have said that they like Trump's value of speaking truthfully and they like his hard work ethic.

Thomas Ryan

CHAPTER 18

Tuesday, 16 August 2016, 84 Days
Trump Visits the Valley

M.L Schultze typed out a title and the first draft of her report on the Trump visit to Youngstown. She did not include any of the quotes from Thomas, but she did learn that according to him voters at the doors did not seem to mind past indiscretions that the media were reporting with gusto. *Does the indifferent attitude stretch to the traditional religious right voter?* She thought. It did make sense that in Youngstown jobs, or more specifically the lack of jobs would be the most important issue. She was less sure that the West Michigan Calvinist voter or the Pennsylvania traditional Catholic family homeschooling their children in the mountains would maintain a steadfast support of Trump.

Dunkin' Donuts

Ding

Rose looked at her phone. She was in line at the Dunkin' Donuts drive-through, and Chelsea Callahan had texted her.

Who is this Thomas Ryan guy? How did he get a ticket to the Trump event yesterday?

Rose shook her head as she typed out a response. *He is a friend of the Pence family and a good guy.* "Millennials," she said. Sometimes they exasperated her. *How do millenials know so little?!*

Honk honk

Rose looked up and saw that she was holding up the line.

MCRP HQ

Ringggg

"Hello, this is Thomas," Thomas picked up his iPhone.

"Hi Thomas, this is Susan from the Warren Chapter Rotary Club. We would like you to come and speak at one of our meetings," Susan said.

Thomas and Susan chatted for a moment. "I'd love to, OK, bye bye." Thomas finished the call. He grinned. This type of connection with the local business owner community was exactly what he had hoped to achieve as a plan B. *I wouldn't mind staying here and working for a local company*, Thomas thought, *Who needs DC?*

Thomas looked up and saw Chelsea walking out the door. "I am off to Columbus for Wednesday, Thursday, and Friday training," Chelsea said to the volunteers.

Thomas realized that this was the official campaign kickoff most likely. That is, the Ohio Republican Party was gearing up for the Trump and Portman general election campaign effort. He resumed memorizing the local candidates and elected officials in Ohio that were listed in a spreadsheet. Last week, one of his relatives had compiled the list for him. Knowing this type of information always came in handy, and had proven useful at the Trump Foreign Policy Speech.

"Thomas," Rose Piper had walked up to his table without him realizing it. "Thomas, Chelsea is only twenty-three years old," she said. "That Jason Lovett," she muttered. "I wish you had his job." She stopped. "Chelsea is immature," she said.

"Everyone is immature when they are young," Thomas said. He wasn't hearing what Rose was trying to tell him, namely that Jason and Chelsea were spreading rumors about him. Rose walked away to go to the kitchen.

Thomas walked to the back room to help Joe put together a large sign. "The New York Times interviewed me for twenty minutes yesterday!" Joe said.

Of course they did, Thomas thought. Thomas' lack of reaction did not spoil Joe's mood. Joe was working even harder than usual today building the signs, and Thomas realized that the candidate visits fired up the volunteers in addition to all the other good they did.

"Hold this piece," Joe said. He nailed a baseboard to another large *Vote Trump Save America* sign.

6:00 pm Meeting in Headquarters

Chelsea walked into headquarters wearing a dress and jacket. Jason Lovett, Valentina from Trumbull County, Mark Munroe, Tracey Winbush, and Dan Kavanagh along with a few other local party officials, gathered around two white plastic tables that had been pushed together.

"Folks, thanks for coming in this evening to the Mahoning County RNC Kickoff Meeting," Jason Lovett said. He talked about the organizational structure of the RNC Victory Campaign based out of Columbus, Ohio, and he explained that it was separate from the Trump organization. Jason continued to talk about the number of doors that he had already knocked for Rob Portman and the fundraising parties and other events that his team had been coordinating. He stopped looking at his notes and postured about his importance using anecdotes. "Be assured, all of us are working for one goal," he said.

Sure, whatever, Dan Kavanagh thought. He took a drink from a beer bottle that he'd added whisky to. *This guy needs to shut the hell up so I can leave.* Kavanagh had little respect for Jason Lovett, the outsider from Virginia who had made enemies four years earlier while working for Mitt Romney. *God knows why he is here in Youngstown.* Dan gave a crooked smile to the group.

Jason paused for a moment. "Do any of you know who Thomas Ryan is?" he asked. He looked around the tables. Everyone stopped their daydreaming and paid attention. No one answered. "This guy shows up out of nowhere and starts causing problems," Jason said.

"Problems, what problems?" Mark Munroe asked. "What do you mean?"

"Just yesterday, for example, Thomas took advantage of the disabled kid, what's his name, Nicholas? He tried to bully Nicholas to get free hats for some people," Jason said.

"Well....I have only seen him be helpful. He walked for Don Manning, he takes out the trash every day...." Mark said. Mark tried to find the good in people, and never said a bad word about anyone.

Jason was not getting the reaction that he wanted. Mark had spoiled his attempt to influence the table against Thomas. "He's a spy," Jason Lovett said abruptly. He did not offer any evidence.

Dan Kavanagh saw that Mark supported Thomas and so he chimed in, "If Thomas is a spy, send ten of him. That guy works hard." Dan's smile bent upwards on the left side ever so slightly. He loved making Jason look like a clown.

Tracey listened to everything and stayed silent. The meeting ended and the attendees filtered out of headquarters after several sidebar conversations.

Thirty minutes later, Tracey called Thomas. "Hey Thomas, I wanted to ask you, I noticed some tension between you and Nicholas, is everything all right?" Tracey asked.

"Everything is great," Thomas said.

Tracey pushed with her questioning and Thomas mentioned the hat incident. "Are you at the office?" he asked. They decided to meet. At a few minutes past 8:00 pm, Thomas drove up to headquarters.

"Listen, Nicholas has poor judgment," Tracey said. "Yesterday you negotiated a discount to the donors when they wanted the hats. Everyone knows you are really smart," Tracey paused. "Still, some people are saying, 'Thomas is wearing a blue shirt, is he a spy?'"

Thomas blinked. He realized that Tracey was telling him that both Nicholas and Don Manning had complained about him. Don did not appreciate that Thomas did not wear Don's T-shirt on the walking day.

For another time in his short stay in Youngstown, Tracey told him in a deniable way, using analogies and metaphors, the rumors that were circulating that could cause him trouble. *She is the smartest one of the bunch*, Thomas thought.

Wednesday, 17 August 2016, 83 Days
MCRP HQ

Ding-a-ling

"Jason Lovett is horrible!" Rose said. She walked into headquarters in a terrible mood. Earlier this morning Jason had ordered Chelsea to drive to Akron to pick him up from his house and drive them both to Columbus for the kickoff meeting. Chelsea became upset at this assignment and had texted Rose the details, where Rose had seen the details while at Dunkin' Donuts.

Thomas texted Chelsea to ask for a walking list. This was a test to see if she was avoiding him while in Columbus, Ohio for training. He wanted a record that he had asked for doors to knock so that it would be her responsibility should he not meet voters today.

Joe walked into the main room sweaty from work. He headed to the thermostat next to the chair's office. "Don't turn on the air conditioning!" Kate said. Joe did anyway. Thomas felt the tension rise.

Nicholas walked into headquarters and made a point to say hello to everyone in an excessively polite manner. He avoided talking to Thomas. Nicholas walked to a chair at one of the plastic white tables and put his phone on the desk. He called the first person using the RNC dialer app, and started the script. As had happened the other day, each person hung up on him after a few seconds when it became clear that he had trouble articulating clearly.

What is the point of all of this? Nicholas kept calling in spite of the hangups. Thomas no longer believed the story that this was a disabled but determined young man who would accomplish his goals through gumption and hard work no matter how big an obstacle the world put in his path. *He is getting credit by call, not by any type of effectiveness evaluation,* Thomas realized. *That sneaky guy!*

Nicholas, Chelsea Callahan, Jason Lovett, Tony Russo, Justin Clarke, and Rob Portman all claimed responsibility for these repeated hang-ups that counted as voter contacts. There was an inverted pyramid of completed voter contacts that began with a stuttering kid making phone calls in the MCRP headquarters and ended with each politico exaggerating the number and taking full credit for the effort. The Ohio Victory Campaign was leading the nation in completed voter contacts, and it all started in Youngstown with Nicholas.

Victory Campaign HQ

Tony Russo addressed the crowd of field organizers. "We will be walking for Rob Portman for now," he said. Chelsea smiled.

She leaned to her friend Valentina and told a dirty joke about the younger Deputy Director, Jonathan Schmidt. They both broke out laughing, and several members of the class turned to look. Chelsea grabbed her phone and thumbed a text to Thomas Ryan. *Are you going to walk doors today?*

Thomas responded.
I need Don's lit.

MCRP HQ

Bing

A text from Kevin Schimp popped on the screen.

Hi Thomas, Frank needs your help for a call-in town hall tonight – can you do it?

Thomas picked up the phone and called Kevin. "Hi Thomas, we need a few volunteers to prime the pump, so to speak. Could you ask one of the questions? I have already prepared the questions that we need, so you would just follow the script," Kevin said.

"Sure thing," Thomas said. He hung up the phone.

Ding-a-ling

Brenda Johnson walked in the main room and up to Thomas. "A bunch of international press will be here next week," she said.

Bing

Thomas looked down at his phone to see that Chelsea had texted back.

You can walk with Portman lit.

Thomas shook his head. This would only spoil doors for Don Manning. He sent a reply.

Could you get an OK from Don Manning since this could spoil his doors if I don't bring his lit along.

Once a voter started to receive lit from one candidate they became increasingly less receptive and even hostile to the next candidate to approach them. That was why it was almost never too early to walk doors in a campaign, and why neighborhoods could get burned out within a month or more ahead of Election Day.

Chelsea waited a moment, then texted.

He is OK with it.

She called my bluff, Thomas thought. Minimum door counts each day mattered to the RNC and the Victory Campaign, but not to voter outreach effectiveness. He should not have thought otherwise, Thomas realized.

Poland, Ohio

A drop of rain formed out of the humidity in the air and fell on Thomas' shoulder. *Yes!* he thought. He texted Chelsea that it was raining, and promptly drove back to headquarters. The previous hour of door-knocking had been useful, as he continued to find a pro-Trump response in Poland. People liked Trump, but they were unsure of his foreign policy speech. Several people told Thomas that they liked Trump because he was not a politician.

MCRP HQ

Thomas walked up to Tracey at headquarters. "Did you hear Trump's Michigan speech?" he asked. "It's what we talked about with the inner city."

Tracey nodded.

"Do you mind if I used the chair's office for a bit?" Thomas asked the vice chair of the county party. "I have to help a candidate with a phone-based town hall."

"Sure, go ahead," Tracey said.

Thomas walked to the chair's office and shut the double glass doors.

Hoagland Town Hall

"OK, we are ready for our first question. Go ahead caller from Steubenville," the host of the phone-in town hall said. Fortunately one of Hoagland's campaign volunteers had corrected Thomas' pronunciation of Steubenville while they prepared for the town hall. He had been pronouncing the city's name using a precise German accent rather than using the Ohio accent that ignored the first letter "e".

Thomas took a breath and said the script from memory. "Hi, my name is Thomas. I'm a soldier on terminal leave here in Steubenville. What is Mr. Hoagland going to do to help Veterans or Veterans Affairs in Ohio?" Thomas said. He stumbled a bit on his script. The slip-up made him sound nervous and added credibility to the performance in front of the three thousand listeners.

"Thanks for the question, Thomas," Frank answered. He ran through the answer like a bull charging a matador.

The next question was also a preplanned one, and Thomas stayed on the line to hear it. Frank answered it in the same aggressive way. *This guy only has one speed!*

Another caller spoke, this time in a feminine voice. "Hi, my name is Amy and I would like to know how you are addressing the *garbled* issue in the *garbled* school?" she asked.

Frank thought that this was preplanned question number three. It wasn't. The state senate candidate talked about active-shooter drills, the importance of engaging the enemy swiftly and decisively, and his Navy Seal training. The woman who had asked about the kindergarten reading program gasped.

Davis Motel

Report on Eastern Ohio and Michigan August 16-17

- WINNING OHIO -

To: Senior Trump Staff and Senior Staff Victory Campaign

There are a few observations from August 16-17 below.

At the Doors in Eastern Ohio

*Today two people asked whether I supported Trump when I knocked on their door to talk about Rob Portman and a local candidate. They were Trump supporters.

*The mood is turning even more towards Trump for voters in Eastern Ohio. One voter mentioned the Wisconsin "law and order" speech as something he liked.

Overheard

*More than one voter whom Mahoning party volunteers reached by telephone in the past two days has requested another Trump visit to the Youngstown area. These voters openly requested another visit during the standard poll questions.

A Tale from Michigan, another Battleground State

*Today a man on a journey somewhere east who drove from Michigan walked into the Mahoning County Party HQ and wanted a sign, a Trump hat, and other paraphernalia. He said that in Michigan it is impossible to find any Trump "swag" as every hat, bumper sticker, sign, shirt, etc. is immediately grabbed by someone.

Follow-up from Invite-Only Youngstown Trump Event

*I ran into an "influential" Trumbull county party member in the hallway of the Trump event on Monday, and this person said based on a gut feeling combined with experience Trumbull County should do well for Trump and all Republicans running this year.

Apparently if the "local internal party conflict" can be managed by someone, there is a good chance to have an unusually high crossover vote for Republicans in all races in Trumbull county.

Thomas

The Ohio State Senate Political Director responded to the report within minutes, asking for details on the local internal party conflict in Trumbull County. Thomas punched his name into the iPhone and called him.

Thursday, 18 August 2016, 82 Days
MCRP HQ

We forecast that Trump would take 42% of the national vote and Hillary Clinton would take 43% of the national vote. The polling error is +/- 3%. –LA Times

Thomas grinned while reading the article. The *LA Times* was one of the more conservative national papers, it was true, but this was great news. The Drudge Report linked to the article.

"Joe, get that paint out of here!" yelled a woman at the front desk. Thomas could not see who it was through the crowd of people surrounding the entrance, all wanting to purchase Trump signs. Mark had ordered volunteers to insist that each person take a free Rob Portman sign along with their Trump sign purchase, but most people simply refused. Not many people were buying buttons, either, though they were purchasing MAGA hats.

Joe had started using a new paint on his gigantic Trump signs. It smelled terrible and was most likely toxic. He had moved his painting operation to the main room from the back room. Billy was not at headquarters today, perhaps that was the reason that Joe did not stay in the back room. He wanted company. No one else wanted to breathe in the noxious vapors, however.

Thomas saw that Joe finished a sign and left it on the plastic table to dry. The former police officer moved to the next table and resumed painting. Thomas walked over to the finished sign and carried it to the back room where it could dry.

The smell from the paint made it hard for Thomas to concentrate, so he clicked away from the draft version of his next report. He decided to check the Trump website before indulging in random web surfing. *Another rally!* He texted the news to about fifty people in two minutes. He had gotten lucky for a second time.

Randy Law texted him back.

Hey, this is confidential.

The information was not confidential as of a few minutes prior, but Randy had only heard about the rally from the Trump campaign. Once again, Thomas had appeared to have information that was closely guarded.

Jonathan Schmidt, Deputy Director of the Victory Campaign, an RNC employee responsible for all the southern counties in Ohio texted Thomas.

I just found out myself.

Thomas got up to stretch his legs. He walked to the kitchen to grab some water, and saw a man standing by the kitchen counter holding a bottle. The man looked to be in his mid-forties. He had brown hair and brown eyes, and was just under six feet tall. He was handsome, but with a strange smile. The man wore a polo shirt and khaki Dockers with brown shoes.

"Hi, my name is Thomas. I am from Columbus, Indiana," Thomas said.

"Yes, yes, I know," Dan Kavanagh said. "Dan Kavanagh," he said. He furrowed his eyes and looked at Thomas closely.

"Are you one of the officers?" Thomas asked.

"Yeah, I'm on the executive committee and I help Mark out a lot around here. I'm the director at the board of elections, and for another month or so I will be helping out the Party, but then I have to stay away when the vote gets closer." Dan said. "It's for the appearance of impartiality." He explained that each Party chose half the workers to staff the Board of Elections.

"Our building is the old hospital of Youngstown on Oak Hill," he said. "The morgue is in our building…" he finished, his brows still furrowed. He was trying to read Thomas. "Listen, I have a meeting with Mark, but nice to meet you."

"Nice to meet you as well," Thomas said. He shook Dan Kavanagh's hand, and noted that this guy was important.

Ding-a-ling

"Don't you leave!" Tracey ordered Thomas. She saw him in the kitchen talking to Kavanagh. The other night Thomas had snuck out of the building before she could stop him. She checked in with Mark and Dan and walked over to the white plastic table where Thomas sat with his computer. "Some higher-ups have been contacting me about the plan to reach African-American voters," She said.

"Trump already used some of your ideas," Thomas replied. He referred to the speech Trump gave the night of the foreign policy speech in Youngstown.

"Yes, I know. I would like you to work with me to make a presentation we can send to the campaign headquarters," Tracey said.

"Absolutely," Thomas said.

Wendy's in Boardman

Thomas walked into Wendy's and saw two familiar faces. The young woman behind the cash register smiled, and the disabled college freshman waiting for his food order frowned. Thomas turned to the girl and ordered.

A moment later Nicholas approached him. "H…h…hi Thomas," Nicholas said. "Wh…wh…what are you doing at headquarters?" he asked.

"Working hard everyday," Thomas said. He had a neutral face.

Nicholas tried a different tack. "Are you making any phone calls?"

Thomas laughed. "Oh, I don't do phone calls," he said. The Party leaders had ignored Nicholas after he had complained about Thomas giving discounts on MAGA hats to large Republican donors. He was attempting to get information from Thomas to use against him in an attempt to bully him out of headquarters or at least reduce his growing influence.

"Wasn't the Trump visit exciting?" Thomas asked. He gave Nicholas a big smile. It was his turn in line and he turned away from Nicholas to order his chicken nuggets and small frosty.

Davis Motel

Thomas lay on the bed and turned on the TV. A tall woman in a bikini jumped and spiked the ball across the sand court. The American woman attempted to dig the ball for her teammate to return, but she couldn't reach the ball before it hit the ground. People in the stands dressed in green stood and cheered.

Thomas remembered eight years earlier when President Bush had walked out to the sand courts in Beijing and slapped the bum of the same woman. It was on that day that Putin had called the President and warned him to remove twelve hundred US Special Forces soldiers from Georgia within twenty-four hours. These were soldiers who were training the Georgian Army in the Caucasus as part of a larger initiative to spread the influence of the United States around the world. Once President Bush made it off the court and to a room to hear Putin's notice and give his own orders, he did the only thing that he could do. He was using too many resources fighting the insurgents in Iraq. A few hours later many large transport planes descended into the airspace of the Former Soviet Union Republic of Georgia.

There was another spike, another dive, and another lost point for the Americans. For the first time in decades, the US Women's beach volleyball team did not win a gold medal at the Olympics.

CHAPTER 19

Friday, 19 August 2016, 81 Days
MCRP HQ

Industrial engineers are wary of what they call "the bullwhip effect," and they learn to take expensive measures in supply chain management to avoid the phenomenon. To put it simply, the bullwhip effect represents the oversupply of inventory that companies accumulate when moving down the supply chain. The oversupply is mostly due to incomplete information and a lack of understanding of customer demand cycles, and employees ordering too much material based on an erroneous perceived shortage of a product.

Mark Munroe carried two boxes of button supplies from his car trunk to the storage room in headquarters. There were 2,500 buttons sitting in bags around headquarters, and four additional boxes of button parts had arrived at the Post Office addressed to the MCRP. For some reason, the Trump campaign had sent materials for another 5,000 buttons.

It was at the Boardman Post Office where Mark had almost lost his cool. The government bureaucrat had forced him to take possession of the boxes, and Mark's WASP upbringing prevented him from tossing the four boxes in the dumpster in the parking lot. Headquarters volunteers sold one button a day on average, so this button supply would last...*twelve years*. Thomas watched Mark return to his car and bring in two more boxes of button parts, remembering a case study on the bullwhip effect.

Jason Lovett walked over to the white table. "Thomas, could you come outside for a minute?" Jason asked. Thomas followed Jason out the door to the parking lot. "I expect you to be walking 150 doors a day," Jason Lovett said. The harsh tone surprised Thomas.

He waited a second to respond and looked at Jason's face to see if he could learn anything from the body language. "That's not likely to happen," he said.

Jason physically reacted. "Excuse me?"

"Well, get me a candidate and I will happily walk with him," Thomas said. It was always much more effective to hit doors with a candidate, and Thomas was not happy that none of the local candidates except Don Manning were walking doors. "Or get me a field organizer position." Thomas said.

"That's what a field organizer does everyday. Before Chelsea was hired she volunteered for me every day hitting 150 doors," Jason replied.

Probably not, Thomas thought. "Jason, there are only one hundred pieces of lit at headquarters right now," Thomas said. "Besides, I am working for several other candidates in other areas. For example, I am working for Frank Hoagland in the 30th state senate race."

"I don't give a shit about the 30th state senate race," Jason replied.

"Tony Russo does, though, and he fully supports what I am doing," Thomas said. He was not backing down in the face of Jason's aggressive posture.

Jason had flinched a second time. "You talk to Tony?" he asked.

"Yeah," Thomas said. "I have to go." He walked to his car.

In the car Thomas called Tony Russo. "Let me cut you off," Tony said. "We want to hire you and we will as soon as we get permission. By the way, I really appreciate your updates, please, keep sending them," Tony said. Indeed these updates were useful to the entire RNC/Trump staff, as Kimberly Flanagan referred to them in her senior staff meetings.

Thomas returned from lunch and saw Jason Lovett sitting in his car, talking on the phone. Jason was calling every person he could think of at the Victory Campaign and in the leadership of the surrounding counties to tell each one that Thomas Ryan was a Democratic spy.

Two hours later, Jason returned to the headquarters main room. He walked up to Thomas who was sitting at a table and working on his computer. "How's everything going?" he said.

"It's going great," Thomas said. He didn't look up from the screen.

"Well, I have to go to Stark County," Jason said.

"I'll be working for the candidates here," Thomas said.

"You are a candidate too," Jason said. He smiled.

"That's right, I ran for political office several years ago," Thomas said.

"I know you did," Jason said. He walked away.

Thomas stood up when Jason left the building. He felt anxious. He walked to the kitchen and saw that someone had left a box of signs leaning against the counter. The signs were for a judge in the common pleas court, the highest court in Ohio other than the state appeals system. These signs were a different design, but not difficult to assemble. The judge walked into headquarters and saw him working. She introduced herself and thanked him. *At least I will never have to serve jury duty,* Thomas thought.

Valentina walked to the kitchen and passed by the judge and Thomas. "How is Ashtabula County going?" he asked. The field organizer walked by him as if he wasn't there. The judge gave Thomas a strange look.

Saturday, 20 August 2016, 80 Days
Dunkin' Donuts Boardman

Thomas turned his gray car into the Dunkin' Donuts parking lot on Market Street. He walked in the store and stood in line behind the late-morning customers. *Need coffee,* he thought.

"Can I help you, hun?" the woman at the cash register asked.

Thomas looked down at the note from Rose. "Twelve glazed donuts and twelve donut holes, please," he said. He yawned and did not cover it in time.

Three minutes later, he walked out of the coffee shop and through the drizzle to his car carrying two boxes and a paper cup. He put the car in gear.

There is one of Joe's signs! Thomas noted a very large *Crossover Vote Trump* sign in someone's yard.

MCRP HQ

Ding-a-ling

Thomas walked in to a packed house. He walked to the conference room hoping to avoid the crowd for a few minutes.

"Hi Thomas, we are electing officers for the Young Republicans," Matt Harris said. The finance director of the Board of Elections welcomed Thomas to the conference room where nine college students gathered.

"Uh-huh," Thomas said. He stood in the corner near the door and Matt Harris led the process for the Mahoning County Chapter of Young Republicans to elect a chair, vice chair, treasurer, and secretary. One young woman stood up and gave a stump speech on why she should be chair. Her friend spoke next and gave a worse speech, so the members voted for the first girl for chair and the second girl for vice chair. The meeting broke up shortly thereafter, and the two young women, with newly endowed authority, meandered to the local TV reporter to explain their thoughts on life to a Mahoning Valley audience.

Thomas followed the crowd out of the conference room. He felt less irritable now compared to twenty minutes earlier as the caffeine stimulated his nervous system.

Mark Munroe walked up to him. "Well…Thomas, do you mind giving an interview with the TV news?" Mark asked. Mark and Thomas looked across the main room at the new Young Republican leaders struggling in the interaction with the WFMJ channel 21 reporter.

"Sure thing," said Thomas.

He walked to the reporter. There was a large camera mounted high on a tripod and she stood on her tiptoes in an attempt to push the camera lower. Her cameraman had wandered off somewhere and he had left the camera at his height.

"I will get this in a minute," Lindsay said, half to herself and half to Thomas. She noticed he stood tall, with his back straight. He was not unfriendly, but he had a presence about him.

"Hi, my name is Thomas, and Mark told me you were looking for volunteers to interview," Thomas said.

The mechanism finally gave way, and Lindsay shoved the camera down to a height where she could control it. She shook Thomas' hand. "I am Lindsay McCoy. I want to interview a volunteer and hear how the campaign is going. Are you willing to do that?"

"Yeah, I can do that," Thomas said. He kept his face neutral.

Lindsay laughed. "I'm short, and I left my heels in the car," she said. She had to reposition the camera higher to get a good angle on her new volunteer. Thomas felt his heart race.

"Have you found a profile of a Trump supporter?" she asked.

"We are finding that all types of people are supporting Trump – engineers, trade people, working people," Thomas said. This was the clip that made the news.

"Attention, everybody," Mark Munroe said. He stood at the podium that was connected to a PA system. "I want to welcome all of you here today to the Mahoning County Republican Party Headquarters for our kickoff Saturday." Mark spoke in a loud and articulate manner. "Today we are going to knock doors for our many great local candidates, state candidates, and federal candidates." Mark made eye contact with a member of the crowd. "The average Republican turnout for Mahoning County is around 35-36%. During the election of 1980, Ronald Reagan made the high-water mark by winning 40% of the vote." Mark paused. "This year is something special. During the primary election, we had over 6,000 registered Democrat voters cross over to vote in the Republican primary. I think that for the first time ever, Mahoning County will go for a Republican candidate." Mark was talking louder and slower now. "We will win Mahoning County for Trump, and as a result Trump will win Ohio. By winning Ohio, Trump will win the White House."

Every volunteer and candidate cheered and applauded Mark. Thomas felt goosebumps. Lindsay and the local *Vindicator* newspaper reporter turned and looked at each other. Their eyes were wide.

Doors, Poland, Ohio

Don Manning could not walk doors today, so Thomas went alone to the doors in a former working-class neighborhood. The doors were close together and he made good time. He talked to around fifty people before he stopped. All but two of the voters openly announced their support to Trump.

MCRP HQ

"Thomas, I need you to man the front desk this afternoon." Thomas looked down and left to see Rose Piper tugging at his shirt. "Yes, we need someone like you at the desk today since it is so busy," she continued. Thomas believed there was another motive.

Rose slapped down a piece of paper with dates and times. "Put your name down on the times you can volunteer to work at the tent for the Canfield Fair," she said. She used her nurse's voice to give the order.

Thomas thought that acting slowly might save him. He picked up the paper and examined the names already written in the boxes. Rose slammed the paper down.

"Write your name!" she ordered. "Here is a pen."

He wrote his name down in one square.

"Here, here, and here," she pointed to three other spaces that were on open slots on other days. "When people come in, have them sign up to volunteer for the fair." She changed the subject. "Jason Lovett is stealing food," she said.

Thomas was happy to have an excuse not to walk more doors, and he leaned back in the leather chair at the front desk.

Jason Lovett walked into headquarters and turned his head so as not to look at Thomas. He hurried to the conference room. The glass door was open and Chelsea welcomed him. "We hit two thousand doors today," Chelsea said.

Trumbull County

A few hours later Thomas left headquarters and drove north to Trumbull

County, the adjacent county to Mahoning. Working-class neighborhoods surrounded dilapidated steel mills. In 1986, a Korean company had begun demolishing the blast furnaces, the heart of the operations, at this particular stretch of land in the flats next to the Mahoning River, after they purchased the closed mills for pennies on the dollar. It had appeared to many residents in Northeast Ohio and western Pennsylvania that foreigners wanted to prevent Americans from ever again being self sufficient in producing the basic building block of civilization. Only the steel ingot processing buildings remained, weathered by several decades of neglect.

Yard after yard displayed Trump signs. Some signs were blue and red; the owners had ordered them directly from the Trump campaign or Chinese vendors making and selling pirated copies on Amazon. Thomas noticed several of the white Trump signs that the MCRP were selling at a profit. These signs looked the best of all, he thought.

In two hours driving the streets of Trumbull County he saw zero Hillary signs.

Beaver Township

"Yaaale, there is Thomas!" Rose screeched. She saw Thomas explaining to Lindsay McCoy which voters were supporting Trump. "Yale, come here now!" she said. He walked to the living room from the kitchen.

Davis Motel

Unofficial Door Report from Eastern Ohio August 18-20
To: Senior Staff Trump Campaign and Senior Staff Victory Campaign

Below are a few observations the last three days.

Mahoning County

*There is a ~lot~ of motivation in Mahoning county. This morning the chair gave a rousing speech where he predicted that Mahoning County would vote for Trump. The Republican base is estimated at 36%.

- THOMAS RYAN -

*A crossover democrat is volunteering for Trump, and a local volunteer is making humongous Trump signs in addition to all the other activities that are taking place. It is a zoo here in the best sense of the word.

*In the past seven days at least five different reporters have visited the county party headquarters.

At the Doors

*The Saturday Trump Kick-off followed the arrival of Trump literature on Friday

*In Mahoning County, two separate democrats in a wealthy neighborhood stated to me that they did not like either candidate, but will pull the lever for Trump as Hillary is "too radical" in the context of the next President replacing Supreme Court Justices and upholding 2nd Amendment rights.

There is indication that wealthier democratic voters may vote in a similar fashion to their middle class democratic neighbors, that is they will vote for Trump, even if motivating factors are distinct.

*An enthusiastic group of Trumbull County Young Republicans drove down to Mahoning County to knock doors Saturday morning.

*On Friday in Poland, Ohio, one older voter listed as strong democrat told me he had changed his party to Republican. He encouraged me to read about the dangers of liberalism.

*There were several rain delays walking doors Friday - when I did manage to get to people they remain positive about Trump, and do not show signs of getting tired of election activity.

*There are increasingly positive comments and body language tells from voters.

Southeast Ohio

*In the 30th state senate race, voters are beginning to recognize Frank Hoagland at the doors, and they are also reacting positively to Trump.

- WINNING OHIO -

Northeast Ohio

*I drove through a large part of Trumbull County this evening and counted five Trump signs and zero Hillary signs. Two of the Trump signs appeared to be purchased from Mahoning County Republican Headquarters.

Overheard

*People in Mahoning County are excited about Trump's Monday rally an hour away in Akron. Some will attend.

*One person said it would be "amazing" if Trump would come and personally knock a few doors in Eastern Ohio.

Thomas Ryan

Thomas hit send and grinned. He was the "one person" who thought Trump should knock doors with him in Eastern Ohio.

CHAPTER 20

Sunday, 21 August 2016, 79 Days

Praise Him... praise Him...

A young man standing on the right side of the choir leaned down and strummed a solo on his guitar. Thomas looked to his left at the full auditorium. Movement caught his eye. Two rows in front of him a thirty-four-year-old woman gyrated her hips to the music. She wore yoga pants. Thomas looked away and gripped the back of the pew in front of him. His knuckles turned white.

He left mass early and walked to his car. Thomas drove by headquarters on Sunday midday on his way to lunch. It was closed.

Kevin Schimp texted him.

Hey Thomas, can you come down to Toronto and walk with me this afternoon, say 4 or 5pm?

Thomas replied.

Sure. How about 5pm?

He pulled up Google Maps on his phone to see where Toronto was located. It was on the Ohio River about an hour south of Youngstown. Thomas felt tired, and he returned to the Davis motel where he took a nap.

Thirty minutes later, he put on lightweight hiking trousers and a red short-sleeve shirt. He made another drive to headquarters. There were cars parked near the building.

MCRP HQ

A disorganized mailing is one of the most frustrating events in the life of a politico. Multiple take-charge volunteers, usually elderly women, repeat tasks, negate earlier steps in the process unknowingly, and generally take the resources of twelve people to do a job that two people can do faster.

The mailing for the local Republican county treasurer candidate was the opposite. Thomas smiled at the three plastic tables arranged in one long row, with an elderly woman sitting calmly at each station. There was the compiling station, the folding station, the stuffing station, and the stamp-moistening station, to name a few. He saw that the crew was using an efficient batch system to transfer the work to the next stage of the process. Three batches of materials were at the folding station, and he took a seat there to reduce the backlog.

"Hi, my name is Mary," an Italian woman said to Thomas. He introduced himself.

"I have to go to the hospital later today to see my husband," she said. "He is in surgery for his heart." She explained that her husband was suffering from heart problems and the doctors at St. Elizabeth had been trying to heal him, unsuccessfully so far.

Thomas looked down.

An hour and a half later he finished folding the last piece of mail. He wished the candidate good luck and walked out the door.

Toronto, Ohio

Kevin waved to Thomas in the parking lot of the Family Dollar. The volunteer got out of his car and climbed into the passenger seat of Kevin's Chevy. They drove north on the grid pattern streets of Toronto. Kevin parked the car and the two men walked to the doors of the tightly packed houses, heading in a generally southern direction.

The late afternoon was hot, but the reception at the doors was cool. Several people did mention that they had heard of Frank Hoagland. Thomas and Kevin saturated the dense city with Trump door hangers and Hoagland palm cards.

I'm out of lit, Thomas texted Kevin. A moment later Kevin drove up to the side of the street and Thomas once again got into the car.

"Four hundred doors!" Thomas said. "Not bad at all."

Kevin was the best campaign manager a candidate could ask for, and he was combining cost effective phone-based town halls with lit drops and candidate door-knocking to effectively introduce his candidate to three hundred thousand people in the state senate district.

Back at the parking lot of the Family Dollar, Thomas returned to his car and ate the apple that he had left on the front seat. On the drive back to Youngstown, he saw a tugboat using one of the massive lock systems to travel upstream on the Ohio River. He pulled the car over and watched the process.

Monday, 22 August 2016, 78 Days
MCRP HQ

"I don't know how to get volunteers for Trumbull County," Valentina said to Chelsea. "It's so hard!" she said.

Thomas kept his head down to ignore the two millenials and worked the large button press. There were thousands of small buttons but not yet an oversupply of large buttons. Joe had brought in a button-making apparatus for the large buttons that he had found in the back room.

Ding-a-ling

Rose Piper walked into headquarters and over to Thomas. "We are going to C's for breakfast this morning," she said.

"What is C's?" Thomas asked.

"You will ride with me." Rose ignored his question and walked to the conference room.

She opened the glass door. "Chelsea, Valentina, I want you to come to breakfast. You millennials never eat enough."

Thomas overheard Rose talking to the two young women in the conference room. *That's a blatant lie,* he thought. Chelsea was a good thirty pounds overweight, and Valentina was obese.

"You millenials need to learn to eat a good breakfast," Rose continued.

"Uhh, we have to work," Valentina said. Chelsea knew better than to interrupt Rose.

"Git, git out of your seat and go," Rose started hitting Valentina with a rolled-up newspaper. The two RNC Field organizers submitted and walked from the conference room to the parking lot. They made it to the door of Chelsea's car.

"Thomas, you are riding with me," Rose said, repeating her earlier order.

Thomas witnessed the beating and walked outside to the passenger side of the red Volkswagen. It was unlocked, so he climbed in and waited. He witnessed Rose thrash Valentina one more time for moving too slowly.

Rose grunted and put herself in the pilot seat of her car. The seat was positioned all the way forward, and the chairwoman wrapped herself around the steering wheel.

Bing, bing, bing

"That will go away in a minute," she said. A warning chime vainly reminded her to use the seatbelt. "Chelsea is really young, she is a millennial," Rose said. "You are older, I can tell, you work hard."

Rose made a jerking motion to grab her seatbelt. Another county sheriff's deputy waited in the parking lot near the stoplight ahead.

"Do you believe in angels?" Rose asked.

The question made Thomas raise his guard. He wasn't sure how to answer. "Sure, I believe in angels," he said.

"I believe in them too. My husband Yale and I attend the Methodist Church in Canfield along with Jim Tressel," she said. She was referring to the former football coach of Ohio State University and the current President of Youngstown State University.

"Tonya is trying to take my seat as chairwoman. The elections for the Party are next year."

Thomas listened, trying to figure out what she was talking about. Rose jumped around subjects occasionally, and Thomas did not have enough local political party knowledge to follow all her monologues.

"Are you married?" Rose asked.

C's Restaurant, North Lima

Chelsea and Valentina ordered hearty portions. Thomas attempted to order two eggs, but Rose would not have it. "He'll get what they're having," she said, pointing at the two girls.

"Thomas, you seem to know what you are doing in a campaign, don't you?" Rose asked. She didn't wait for an answer. "How old are you, Chelsea? Twenty-two? Aren't you in your thirties, Thomas?"

Chelsea and Valentina were making faces at each other and texting on their phones.

The food came, and Rose gave up trying to convince the two field organizers that Thomas should replace Jason Lovett as regional director. She was frustrated. Thomas would be a better boss than Jason, couldn't the girls see that? Rose had Thomas wrapped around her finger, *so if he had the RNC job that would be good for the local party too*, she thought.

Rose's Car, Sharrott Road

Thomas and Rose returned to the red car and drove west before turning north on Sharrott road.

"I live one street over, in Beaver Township, but it's also Canfield Township," Rose said. Thomas did not understand.

"See that farm to the right?" Rose pointed. "That is the Moretti farm. They are an Italian family. Dan Kavanagh married into the Morettis, and they have six kids."

Thomas was trying to take it all in. "Are you Italian?" He asked.

"I am half Italian and half German."

"I am half German and half Irish," Thomas offered. "The Italian explains your fashion sense," Thomas said. Something ever so slight in his tone indicated he was not taking his words seriously. It was the Irish charm.

Rose laughed, "This is a really nice place to live. You should think about settling down." Rose said. She had the directness of a grandmother.

"I have eight kids, you know, and three of them are lawyers like my husband. Maybe you could become a lawyer?" Rose said.

"Maybe," Thomas said.
She wants me to marry one of her granddaughters, he thought.

Mahoning County Court

At 3:00 pm a short deputy sheriff opened the door from the judges chambers. "All rise!" she called. The judge's stature contrasted with the petite frame of the bailiff. Rose and the others in the courtroom stood for the Judge entering the Mahoning County Court of Common Pleas. He handed down her sentence and pounded the gavel.

Parole and probation, Rose wiped her brow with relief. "Yes your honor, I have given up my firearms, and I have no interest in owning another gun ever again," she affirmed.

She had helped arrange the judge's fundraiser when he ran for office in 2014. The judge knew that the police had confiscated the pistol and were not going to return it to Rose in any case. Yale Piper guided his wife out of the courtroom. The sheriff's deputy reached out to steady him as he stumbled.

MCRP HQ

Thomas saw Mark walking over to the white plastic table where Thomas was working on his computer. He had expected this for some time and took a deep breath to calm himself. Thomas stood up as Mark reached him.

"Thomas," Mark paused and motioned with his hands. "What are you doing here? Weren't you supposed to be in the area for a week because of work?"

Thomas knew that his next words would determine whether he could remain at the MCRP headquarters.

"I am a neighbor of the Pence family," he said.

"Yes, you've said this," Mark said.

"Once Pence was picked as the Vice Presidential candidate I reached out to the campaign and decided to come to Ohio. I asked permission from Chris Horvath, the head of the Trump campaign in Ohio. This was especially important, because about ten years ago I ran as a Democratic candidate for a state office seat. Chris gave me permission to volunteer in the state," Thomas said. He was glad that he had had the meeting with Chris a few days earlier. *Maybe the absolute truth is not completely necessary*, Thomas thought. He saw Mark soften his look.

"Currently, I am working for Tony Russo, the Deputy Director of the Ohio Trump Campaign. I am sending reports to him about what I see at this headquarters and elsewhere in Ohio so the campaign can get an outside observer's perspective. I can give you Tony's number if you like. He has asked me to continue doing this and he has told me that it is helping the national campaign."

Thomas took a breath. "The other day I stepped on Jason Lovett's toes, and I know that some people are wondering about me," he continued.

Thomas pulled up a picture of the lake house and the Pence house. The Pence house had a Trump sign on the lawn. "These signs are illegal if they are placed in the yard more than thirty days before an election. My mother is the inspector general of the homeowners' association and she is giving the Pence family a pass," Thomas said.

Mark laughed heartily. The humor was unexpected. "Your mother is the IG?"

Mark walked away and Thomas sat down. He had to stand up again as his heart was pounding.

Once outside Mark called Tony Russo to verify Thomas' claims. They were true.

Trump Rally in Akron

"Lock her up! Lock her up! Lock her up!" eight thousand people chanted. They stood on their feet, pumping their fists, screaming at the top of their lungs. Thomas felt a surge of energy throughout his body.

A graduate student waited until the crowd noise died out and held up a sign that had a slogan against Trump. The man shouted something that no one could hear except those within a few feet radius.

"Booooo, booooo," the crowd yelled.

"Out, out, out!" the woman next to Thomas shouted. She held her hands around her mouth. He joined in haranguing the disrupter.

"Go home to mommy," Trump said. The crowd roared.

Thomas felt as though he was on the downslope of the tallest rollercoaster at Cedar Point, an amusement park two hours away. He and everyone else at the rally except the Secret Service and the Press screamed. "Trump, Trump, Trump!"

He felt buzzing. Thomas looked at his phone and saw his twitter feed pop up. The national news reported that Chelsea Callahan had been openly anti-Trump on her social media in the primary elections. Justin Clarke, the director of the RNC Ohio Victory Campaign had hired her anyway. Chris Horvath, the director of the Ohio Trump Campaign had approved.

CHAPTER 21

Tuesday, 23 August 2016, 77 Days
Victory Campaign

Jonathan Schmidt stepped out of Tony Russo's office. They had discussed the issue of where to place Thomas Ryan in the state once they extended an offer to him. He was doing so much work in the northeast and southeast parts of the state, that it seemed obvious to leave him there. However, the regional director Jason Lovett hated him, and his reports painted a negative picture. Thomas was not a people person, he caused trouble constantly, and he had nearly gotten in a fight with a couple of volunteers over some Trump hats, apparently. Jonathan sighed. It was best to remove him from the most important county of the country.

MCRP HQ

Chelsea circled part of a wealthy neighborhood on the map displayed by the RNC Advantage program. She moved her finger on the touchpad and clicked *create walking list*. Large yards meant lots of walking and few doors. *Let's see Boston Boy brag about doing doors on this map!*

Valentina walked into the conference room jingling her car keys. "Let's go get something to eat," she said.

"As long as we go to Stone Fruit first," Chelsea said.

- THOMAS RYAN -

Doors, Poland, Ohio

Thomas walked about ten doors before heading to his car. No one was home and these lawns were an acre each. The driveways were curvy and long. The doctors and professors in this neighborhood used the fenceless dog control system, and at the last address a dog had rounded the rear of the house, barreling full speed at Thomas. He had seen pure hatred in the eyes of the pit-bull mix before he turned and booked it across the neighbor's lawn, dropping several pieces of Trump lit in the process.

Chelsea is sabotaging me. Thomas stood with his hands on his knees, panting.

He remembered his psychiatric professor. "You must trust people to act in their interests," he had said.

What is her interest?

To sabotage Trump.

MCRP HQ

"Did you hear about what Rose did to Yale?" Dan asked. He and Chelsea stood outside the back door of headquarters and smoked.

"She shot him," Chelsea said. She looked at the candy factory a few hundred yards away.

Dan glanced at her, "I heard that she emptied the chamber and hit him twice," he said. Chelsea didn't respond.

"What do you know about that Ryan guy? The one from Indiana," Dan inquired.

"He has had two cars and three different license plates," Chelsea said. "He takes out the trash every day." She paused. "Jason Lovett hates him, but Mark likes him. Rose likes him too, for some reason."

Dan joined her watching the candy factory. A big box truck pulled out from the bay full of chocolate bars and caramel bites.

Inside headquarters, Thomas sat at the front desk. He saw Dan Kavanagh walk from the back hall to the kitchen. He stood up to walk back and talk with him.

Ding-a-ling

A young woman walked into headquarters and almost bumped into Thomas.

Thomas turned his attention to the girl. "How can I help you?" he asked.

"Hi, I'm Katherine, Dan's daughter." She said.

"Dan Kavanagh?" Thomas asked. He raised his eyebrows. He didn't think Dan was old enough to have a daughter this age. He introduced himself. Katherine touched her hair.

The eyes of the other volunteers watched Katherine and Thomas at the front entryway. Katherine noticed the attention from the others. "Can you tell me where the recycling bin is?" she asked.

Thomas waited a beat before he answered. "You are in the wrong headquarters, Katherine," Thomas said. His voice was slow and clear. Marq, Karen, and three other volunteers laughed. Thomas lowered his voice after making the joke at the attractive young woman's expense. "Are you in high school?" he asked.

"No, I'm a sophomore at YSU," she said. She had an accent, somehow halfway between that of a Youngstown and Pittsburgh accent. She talked quickly and dropped the endings from some of her words.

"Oh, what are you studying?" Thomas asked.

"English, I like it a lot," Katherine answered. She tilted her head. Thomas noticed her pupils dilated.

"Mm-hmm, well, nice to meet you," Thomas said. He walked away.

Dan stood in the kitchen observing the interaction. He walked up to the front desk where Katherine told him some business about the Moretti farm.

Davis Motel

Unofficial Report Eastern Ohio August 21-23
To: Senior Staff Trump Campaign and Senior Staff Victory Campaign

Below I give a few observations that I have made over August 21-23.

- THOMAS RYAN -

Mahoning County

*The first local candidate mailing was sent out Monday - 1500 pieces.

*I talked with unique voter class at the doors today, Democratic or Independent voters who did *not* vote in the primary election. A significant percentage had a positive reaction toward Trump, although there was also some negative reaction. I have not yet visited a sufficient number of this voter profile for concrete conclusions.

Southern Ohio

*Relatives vacationed in Marietta and Southern Ohio over the weekend. They reported seeing many Trump signs and no Hillary signs. There was an exception with one Hillary sign at the democratic headquarters in Marietta. This Hillary sign was from her 2008 campaign.

*People at the doors in Toronto, Ohio were mostly neutral towards Trump. There was not overt hostility to Trump even with a solidly democratic voter walking list.

Akron Trump Rally

*The energy was incredible and Trump gave his best speech yet.

Thomas Ryan

Wednesday, 24 August 2016, 76 Days
Back Room

Billy put oversized hearing protection on his head and pressed the saw down on the lumber. The noise was loud. Joe walked up to him and Billy waved him a way. Fifteen minutes later he had cut the first four hundred bricks.

Joe ran the vacuum over the wood that was cut into brick size pieces, and over the workstation. He opened a can of red paint and used a roller to complete the job of making red bricks for the Trump Wall.

Thomas and Chelsea walked to the back hall to see the drying bricks. "What is this I hear about Rose?" Thomas asked.

Chelsea's eyes became wide. "One day a month ago Rose just stopped showing up to headquarters," Chelsea said. "We read in the paper the next day that she had shot her husband.

"Wait, Rose shot her husband?" Thomas asked.

Chelsea held up two fingers. "Twice."

Thomas didn't know what to say. "What happened then?"

"No one knows, except she showed up again shortly after you arrived," Chelsea said.

MCRP HQ

Thomas thought he would get a snack in the kitchen while the bricks were drying. He walked up to the refrigerator and saw a sign.

Jason Lovett!

Stop stealing beer and alcohol.

We know you are doing it.

STOP IT!

"What is this?" Thomas said aloud. He opened the door and grabbed several cheese cubes and sausage bites from a platter. He closed the door. *What is going on here?* Thomas pulled out his phone and took a picture of the sign. He grabbed the sign and ripped it down from the refrigerator. He walked to the front desk in the main room.

"Sign this," Dan Kavanagh stood next to the front desk with a red brick and a felt tipped marker. The volunteers were signing bricks with their name or a message to "prime" the Trump Wall with a few starter bricks.

Thomas did not want to sign the brick and he set the pen down on the table. He knew that the media would soon film the wall and the bricks. Kavanagh picked up the pen and shoved it in Thomas' personal space. "Sign it," he said. Dan Kavanagh laughed.

Thomas signed the brick and Kavanagh put it with the other twelve bricks in a triangle shape at the base of the wall.

Mark walked into headquarters. "The media is about to arrive," he said. "From Australia." He looked excited. His phone rang and he answered it.

"That was from DC," Mark said. "Word is getting out about Youngstown." He looked at Thomas. "We had over 6,000 Democrats cross over in the primary to vote for Trump. Typically we have 14,000 or 15,000 votes in a Republican presidential primary, and this year there were 36,000 Republican ballots."

Kavanagh nodded along while Mark was explaining the election results to Thomas. "There were 15,000 Republicans who voted who have not voted in at least two election cycles and another 6,000 Democrats who crossed over," Dan Kavanagh said.

Chelsea and Valentina walked past Mark, Dan, and Thomas and pushed the front door. "We are going to get food," they said in unison.

"I need you guys to be working!" Mark said.

"Do you need me to do fake calls for the cameras?" Thomas asked. He referred to the Australian reporters that were about to arrive.

"There is a lot of fake work being done around here," Mark said. He lowered his voice. "Keep an eye on Joe for me, Thomas."

Joe walked into the main room as Mark spoke.

The TV crew from Australia arrived and Perry walked up to the cameraman to give him a religious tract. The crewman did not know what to do while he was carrying the heavy equipment. The reporter talked with Mark and the cameraman set up the camera next to the wall with the twelve primer bricks.

Thomas cringed. He did not want his name to be on a brick and broadcast on international news.

Kavanagh joined the two field organizers and walked out the front door. Thomas saw his opportunity and walked up to the cameraman. Thomas grabbed his brick and walked away from the wall as the reporter returned to the wall with Mark by his side. Thomas put the brick in his backpack.

It was nearly 6:00 pm and Thomas gathered his things to leave headquarters. Jason Lovett arrived and walked to the back of the main room. He opened his computer and said, "Dead Puppies."

"Dead Jason," Chelsea said.

Thomas walked for the front door and left headquarters disturbed by the exchange.

Thursday, 25 August 2016, 75 Days
Davis Motel

"Are you staying another week?" asked the man. He was the other brother who owned a share of the motel.

"If you don't mind. Your beds are really nice here, I want you to know," Thomas said. It wasn't flattery. The thirty-dollar-a-night rooms had a firmer mattress than some rooms Thomas had stayed at that charged ten times the price.

"I heard you're working on the campaign?" the brother asked. "My brother's a huge Trump supporter. I'm a Democrat, but it is interesting to have a person from the campaign staying here."

"Yep, I sure am," said Thomas. He was not in fact working on the campaign, rather he was volunteering.

The two men had a conversation and then Thomas left for headquarters.

MCRP HQ

"Should we burgle Brenda's house?" Thomas asked. A group of volunteers and Rose Piper gathered around him. He told them that Brenda Johnson, the Mahoning County Trump Coordinator, had one thousand additional Trump signs stored at her house. She was in Florida or travelling somewhere that was not Youngstown.

Rose has a police record so she can't take part in any plan, Thomas thought.

Marq thought it might be a good idea. "We only have two days left worth of signs," he said. "They are selling like hotcakes."

A new intern, Sara was standing in the group. Thomas introduced himself to her. She was a tiny woman who looked like a deer standing in the headlights.

"Thomas, you didn't put the volunteers in alphabetical order!" Rose said. She had tasked Thomas to make a list of the Canfield Fair volunteers so that someone could call them to tell them to come and pick up their complimentary tickets. "Come here," she said.

Thomas humored her and followed her to a white table. "Didn't you ever make a list in school? You have to put names in order!" she said. She shook her head and laughed.

Chelsea and Valentina arrived back to headquarters carrying sacks of food. They motioned for Sara to join them, and the three of them walked to the conference room where Caleb was sitting. Valentina closed the door.

Inside the conference room Chelsea addressed the new Republican intern from YSU. "Beware of Thomas," Chelsea said. Sara officially worked for Valentina, but Chelsea felt comfortable bossing her around too. "He's a spy. He ran for office as a Democrat."

"Why is he here?" Sara asked.

"I don't know. Mark is letting him stay for now, I guess," Chelsea shrugged.

In the main room, Thomas rearranged the names on the volunteer list. Visitors walked into the headquarters and bought bricks. Most bought the five-dollar red bricks while a few bought the twenty-dollar gold bricks. Each person smiled when they pressed the brick loaded with glue on the Trump Wall.

Mark Munroe had stumbled onto a moneymaker by selling Trump signs out of headquarters two months earlier. Dan Kavanagh had started a goldmine by coming up with the Trump Wall idea. He had supported Rubio in the Republican primary but saw the Trump wave sweeping over the valley. The funny thing was that he detested everything about Trump.

Dinner with Dan, Tracey, and Mark at Los Gallos

Dan finished chewing a bite of the chicken enchilada. "What's this about Thomas being a spy?" he asked Tracey and Mark.

"He's not. In fact, I heard today that the RNC is hiring him," Mark said. "I got a call from Columbus yesterday, and they were doing some sort of vetting on him. They wanted to know what he had been up to around here."

"I like Thomas," Tracey said. She looked at Dan closely.

Chelsea Kenney's Apartment

"OK, last thing, guys," Justin Clarke said. He had one more topic for the nightly Victory Campaign conference call. "We are going to be onboarding additional field organizers September first. Let me run down a list of your new colleagues."

"....Thomas Ryan, Chad Thomson...."

Oh Shit! Chelsea caught Thomas' name. It was completely unexpected. *What is Jason Lovett smoking? Why has he been bad-mouthing Thomas this entire time?*

While still on the conference call she thumbed out a text.

We need to talk.

CHAPTER 22

Friday, 26 August 2016, 74 Days
MCRP HQ

A German woman opened the front door. Rose was in the kitchen making cookies and Thomas was in the back making bricks. "Halo?" the reporter said. She spoke loudly, as she didn't see anyone in the main room.

Thomas lifted the paintbrush from a brick and turned his head. *That's a German speaking English.* He walked down the hall into the main room and saw Rose approaching the reporter.

"Can we speak in German?" Thomas asked, in German.

Annette smiled, "Your accent is good!" Germans did not give fake compliments.

"I'm the chairwoman of the party," Rose interrupted.

Annette asked her a question and Rose rambled. Rose mentioned the Canfield Fair starting in a few days. "What does 'Canfield Fair' mean?" the reporter asked. She turned to Thomas. The next question was directed at him. "How important is this area to Donald Trump?" she asked.

Rose interrupted. "This area is so important, and we are having the Canfield Fair soon, and..."

"Excuse me, I am talking to Thomas," Annette said. She turned her body away from Rose.

She doesn't realize that Rose shoots people! Thomas thought. He grimaced even though he recognized that normal German behavior. This reporter was being polite according to her customs. Thomas saw Rose's face turning red. She clenched her tiny fists, which were out of the line of sight of the reporter.

Thomas motioned Annette to walk with him. "We will win Mahoning, carry Ohio, and go to the White House," he said. He copied Mark Munroe's line exactly from the earlier kickoff Saturday. Annette followed Thomas and they walked to the brick kiln in the hall connecting the main room with the back room. "Here is where we make the big signs," Thomas said.

Annette and Thomas talked for twenty minutes, and the two traded contact information. The reporter left headquarters to find the closed steel mills about which she had read.

Rose walked up to Thomas. "I didn't like that woman," Rose said. "You have to redo the checklist for volunteers. This time, handwrite it."

Thomas ignored her.

Bing

There was a text from Kevin Schimp.

Hey Thomas, could you bring more Trump lit with you down to Carrollton?

Thomas walked to the conference room and snagged a few hundred pieces of Trump lit from a box that held several thousand pieces. *So the Southeast director still isn't doing his job*, he thought. Thomas remembered how at the Pence event the Southeast director had claimed his job was basically done and easy.

Ring

Tony Russo called Thomas to let him know that they were looking to hire him, and that they needed to "vet" him a few more days. Thomas told Tony that he had also been offered a job in Wood County as well. As soon as the words left his lips he realized he had made a mistake.

"You mean you were offered a job from your cousin?" Tony said. Tony realized that he had solved the problem of where to put Thomas in the campaign.

Carrollton, Ohio

"Hi Thomas, thanks for coming down," Kevin said. He grabbed the Trump walking cards that Thomas handed to him.

"Listen, we can walk on either side," Kevin pulled up the map on his phone. "There are two neighborhoods that I would like to do."

"Sounds good," Thomas said. The two men walked to doors on opposite sides of the street. In a little under two hours they knocked on an additional two hundred doors for Frank Hoagland.

MCRP HQ

"Another two hundred doors on the books!" Thomas said. Several volunteers looked up at him as he walked into headquarters bragging on his doors. Thomas had planned this line at the forty-fifth minute into the drive back north. He walked to the conference room.

"I got your text. What did you want to talk about?" Thomas asked.

"I think we got off on the wrong foot," Chelsea said.

"I understand the situation," Thomas said. He was about to elaborate on Jason Lovett when Rose interrupted him. She had seen him enter the front door and had caught up to him from her spot in the kitchen.

"You need to talk to Dan Kavanagh about volunteering for the Republican Picnic tomorrow," she said. "I wouldn't say no." Rose was still in a bad mood from the German reporter incident earlier in the day.

Los Gallos

Thomas had time before the first football game of the season to eat a sit-down meal at the Mexican restaurant a mile south of headquarters. He was surprised when the server brought out a coleslaw dish to accompany the tortilla chips. This was a direct result of the Eastern European influence on the area; he remembered how much coleslaw the Polish people ate when he lived an hour west of Warsaw.

South Range Legacy Football Stadium

The television series *Friday Night Lights* introduced the world to the place of honor that Americans who live in Texas put on high school football. The rambunctious crowd at the South Range Raiders football game told Thomas that Ohio was not far behind in adoring the sport. He had misunderstood the directions from Dan and had missed most of the opening night pageantry. Yet the part that he had seen resembled choreography more attuned to collegiate or professional athletic contests.

The drum core set the mood for the players and fans. *Ratatat-tat-tat-tat-ratatatat*. Young men lined up for the coin toss. South Range lost and would be the first to kick the ball in the gladiator contest. The marching band walked off the field to the beat of the drum core. The beat livened the already festive atmosphere.

There were home and visitor stands. To the right of the home grandstand there was a large sloped hill, and people were sitting on the slope on blankets and lawn. Many people had coolers, and although alcohol was officially prohibited, it was obvious that the thermoses did not contain hot cocoa on the eighty-degree night. Thomas wandered through the crowd sitting on the slope.

"Hi Joe!" he said. He saw the ex-cop who painted signs at headquarters.

"Lookee-here," Joe replied. He squinted his eyes momentarily. "The boys should have a good team this year, although the front line is too young, we lost a lot of seniors last year." He said. He continued to explain the tactical problems of the team.

"Do you have anyone out there?" Thomas asked.

"No," Joe said. He shook his head.

Thomas realized that there were several thousand people at the stadium. The entire North Lima and South Range rural population had come to the game, regardless of having a child on the field or in the high school.

"This is my granddaughter, Alexis," Joe said. A girl about five years old went running by Thomas and her grandfather. She stopped and stared for a second at the man talking to her grandfather.

"I'm Alexis," she said.

"Nice to meet you, I'm Thomas," he replied.

Alexis laughed and ran down the grass hill. A young boy chased after her, and they ran through the crowd toward the end of the field forty yards away.

Crash, the Raiders had gotten the ball from a punt, and then on the second play the quarterback fumbled the ball. A linebacker picked it up and ran for a touchdown. The score was 0-7, Raiders. The visiting crowd cheered.

At halftime Thomas found Dan Kavanagh on the visitor side of the field. He was talking to several men and a few of the players' mothers. One man was grilling hamburgers and cheeseburgers on an old steel cylinder grill.

A man walked up to Dan Kavanagh with a fistful of money. "I want $50 on the gun raffle tomorrow," he said.

"Give it to Thomas," Dan Kavanagh said. He wanted to show Thomas that the people of South Range trusted Dan and those who Dan said were trustworthy.

Ok, Thomas thought. He took the money and put it in his pocket.

"The burgers are $3.50, and they're delicious," Dan said.

Thomas asked the man standing at the grill for one and went to the visitor concession stand to pay for it.

"The guys probably won't win tonight, the front line is too small. It's a rebuilding year," Dan said. He repeated many of the same points as Joe. Thomas didn't understand Dan much better. *Are these guys on the coaches' conference calls?*

"They'll win," Thomas said. He saw Dan's expression. The Raiders were down 14-0 at halftime. "I was watching them in the first half and the defense is really good. The points are from turnovers. The turnovers are from nerves. They have so much energy and are having trouble controlling it. This energy will burn off in the second half and their training will take over." Thomas didn't know football but he knew teamwork and psychology.

"We'll see," Kavanagh said.

Thomas asked Kavanagh about the football team and South Range.

He might as well learn something else new. A man in his late eighties walked up the hill. Dan waved him over.

"This is my dad, Jim," Dan said.

Thomas introduced himself to Jim and Dan walked away. Jim and Thomas talked, and Thomas found out that Jim had been a football coach for thirty years during his tenure as a teacher. The two of them left the grill and walked down the visitor grass hill to be close to the sideline. They watched most of the second half of the game leaning against the chain-link fence. Jim explained the plays.

Around the start of the third quarter, Jim gave Thomas a religious tract. "Do you believe in Jesus?" Jim asked.

Thomas looked at it. "You're Lutheran?"

"I go to a good Lutheran church, not one of the liberal ones," Jim answered.

"My parents are Lutheran. I go to St Charles," he said, referring to the Catholic Church he had attended once.

The Raiders scored again, this time taking the lead. From across the field the home stands erupted in loud cheers. Cheerleaders threw each other high in the air. "I told Dan that we would win tonight! The guys are really working well together," Thomas said.

"The front line is too small, they're only tenth graders," said Jim. He liked Thomas, but this guy from Indiana didn't know football.

Fifteen minutes later, the South Range Raiders' record stood at 1-0.

CHAPTER 23

Saturday, 27 August 2016, 73 Days
Shriners Club, South Range Road

At 7:45 am Thomas arrived and was the second car in the parking lot of the Shriners Club. Dan Kavanagh arrived after him driving an old black GMC SUV with a crack in the windshield. Matt Harris, Kyle Morrow, and a couple of other guys from the Board of Elections turned off of South Range Road and onto the long road back to the pavilion.

Kavanagh unlocked a series of padlocks and opened the large pavilion in the back of the property. The guys unloaded supplies from the cars. It was extremely humid, and promised to be a hot day. Earlier in the morning, fog had covered the ground and had hidden the dips in the terrain, but now the sun was burning away the remaining wisps.

Thomas carried another box of canned beer to the outdoor bar. He returned to the back of the SUV and looked for other drinks. There were soft drinks to complement the alcohol. *Where is the water?*

Thomas had brought two bottles of water and two sports drinks with him. He had already drunk the contents of two of the bottles. *What are the other volunteers who are setting up for the picnic going to drink? What am I going to drink?*

A Sparkle grocery store was two miles away according to Siri, and he drove there, and bought $50 worth of water and Gatorade. When he came back to the pavilion the temperature was well past ninety degrees. With one exception, the other guys stuck with beer.

At 10:00 am Dan walked up to Thomas. "Hey, do you want to go with me to get some cooking utensils?" He said.

"Sure," Thomas replied. He knew that Dan as an influential leader of the MCRP was evaluating him and he welcomed it. He followed Dan to the black SUV.

Dan started the vehicle and pulled onto South Range Road. "This baby gets twelve and a half miles per gallon," he said. He did not use his seatbelt. "It's a piece of shit, but it works," Dan continued. This negativity surprised Thomas. Kavanagh went on to explain that his other car was in the shop and he had to drive this car for the time being.

"You can't find a safer car," Thomas said.

Kavanagh turned left on Sharrott Road and drove past the small airport, down a hill, and turned right at the dirt road to the Moretti farm.

Moretti Farm

"My in-laws own all of this property," Kavanagh said. The gravel crunched beneath the tires as Dan drove the GMC up to a farmhouse sitting a thousand feet from the road. He turned the vehicle around and stopped the engine.

Thomas heard a dog bark. "That's Rudy," Kavanagh said. He stepped out of the black SUV and Thomas did the same. Rudy ran up to Thomas, who crouched down in a baseball catcher's stance. The dog sniffed his hand and knew that this man was friendly. Thomas caught Kavanagh looking at him and the dog.

A few minutes later Thomas and Kavanagh walked toward the greenhouse where Mr. Moretti grew vegetables. "I had over 1,000 people at my wedding, and I didn't pay a dime," he said.

Thomas thought he caught an expression, just for a fraction of a second. Maybe it was the crooked smile. Maybe the eyes did not quite match the face, but if it had happened it was quick, and he couldn't remember exactly what he saw. *This guy might want to prove himself...maybe he feels emasculated by his father-in-law who owns the property,* Thomas thought.

The two men walked into the farmhouse. Mrs. Moretti smiled widely at Thomas while she worked in the kitchen. Mr. Moretti and Dan talked for a moment, and Thomas felt the discussion was veering into personal territory so he walked outside and called Rudy. He threw a stick and the dog retrieved it. Once again he felt Dan Kavanagh's eyes on him, but he did not turn around to look.

Thomas saw a blue crossover vehicle kick up dirt on the gravel road leading to the farmhouse. It came closer and he saw a woman with long curly black hair, waving and laughing. Thomas waved back. He looked to his right and noticed that Dan had come outside. Kavanagh must have heard the tires crunch against the crushed stones. The Italian woman and heiress to the estate pulled up to the German-Irish men.

"Oh, I thought you were Katherine," Thomas said.

She laughed. "Hi, my name is Melanie," she smiled broadly.

"My name is Thomas, I am from Indiana," Thomas said.

Melanie talked to her husband about something and once again Thomas stepped away and played with the dog. Melanie walked inside the house and her father stepped outside.

Mr. Moretti led Thomas and Dan to the pavilion and the attached professional kitchen fifty yards east of the house. He and Dan talked about the utensils that Dan might find useful for the picnic today.

Dan and Thomas climbed into the black SUV and drove back to the Shriners Pavilion a mile to the southwest. Thomas carried two large ladles. "My brother-in-law runs the Georgetown," Kavanagh said. "It's a catering company."

Shriners Pavilion

"Thomas, sit here," Rose said. She pointed to the wooden picnic table at the front of the pavilion facing the parking lot. She gave Thomas a roll of tickets. "These are for the raffle." Rose sat to his left with the cashbox.

A man walked up to the table and set down a handgun next to the roll of tickets. *That's a Glock 19!* Thomas felt unsure how he should act. His gut told him to walk away. While he struggled with his inner dialogue, a red Cadillac STS pulled into the parking lot. Thomas noticed Rose locking onto the car like a phased array acquisition radar system.

"Guard the gun, I have to talk to the judge," she said. "I won him his reelection."

"Uhhh," Thomas said.

The judge parked his car and stepped outside. He opened the back door of the car and leaned inside to retrieve a chocolate cake that his wife had made last night. She had baked the cake as a contribution to the Chinese auction to raise money for the MCRP. He straightened his back and held the cake near his chest. The judge looked up at the blue sky and saw puffs of white clouds. It was hot but he enjoyed the heat. He whistled and walked at a cheerful pace, heading to the bar located at the front of the pavilion and to his right. The judge had a spring in his step.

"Judddgeee, judddgeee," Rose said. She spoke too soon and painted the enemy bomber. He heard the warning chirp in his earpiece that signaled an interceptor had found him and was preparing to launch as soon as her missiles were in range. Rose was yelling now. She walked towards him.

The judge turned his head to the left, and then he snapped it back to the right with a look of recognition and pain. He changed his course to the right, to reach the bar directly, and he quickened his pace by taking long strides. His smile and song were gone. The Foxbat MiG-25 pilot used her left hand to throttle up her engines to maximum recommend power. The interceptor jet moved on a course to confront the B-1 Lancer, a bomber trying to reach his target and release his kinetic ordinance of cake. The judge reached his goal first, and placed the cake on the countertop. He turned on his heel. The B-1 was lighter now and the pilot pushed the control stick down to enter a shallow dive. The bomber accelerated through the sound barrier. Rose had played the angle well and had a chance to catch him on the return journey. The wrathful pilot hyper cycled her engines, ignoring Moscow Center's instructions. This gave her a speed in excess of Mach 3.2, but only momentarily before her engines destroyed themselves. The judge broke into a jog. Rose tried to do the same but her legs failed.

The judge slammed his door and did a reverse J maneuver with his Cadillac to exit the parking lot. *It's been a long time since I've seen one of those,* Thomas thought. Rose stopped, and walked back to the table where Thomas had observed the entire cake delivery sequence and the failed intercept attempt. He held the roll of tickets.

"That was the judge who sentenced me," she said. "He wouldn't have his job except for me."

Thomas looked pointedly at the firearm lying on the table in front of him.

He stood up and walked to the back of the pavilion where Dan Kavanagh and the Board of Elections crew were preparing to barbeque chicken. On his way back he passed by a young woman with dark hair that reached to her lower back. "Hi Katherine!" he said. He realized that the hair was too curly, and her face was different. She looked older. This wasn't Katherine.

"I'm Kayla," the girl said. Thomas introduced himself and continued walking to go help her father.

A half hour later Thomas walked to the front tables, and this time he saw Melanie and a young boy standing by the Trump Wall. It was half filled with red and gold bricks. Melanie waved him over and introduced him to her youngest son.

"How old are you?" he asked.

"I'm ten," Christian said. Thomas walked back to the kitchen carrying the rags he needed. Kayla followed Thomas with her eyes.

Three hours later, the heat was intense. The pavilion offered shade from the sun but the humidity felt oppressive. Thomas thought that his senses were dulling. "Folks, it's the time you've been waiting for. Get your tickets ready for the handgun raffle!" a voice announced on the PA system. Everyone formed a line. Thomas could not figure out what was happening.

He noticed an old man who he had not met earlier in the day. This man had a large smile and stood in the center of the pavilion. The man moved to the gun raffle line.

"Hi, my name is Thomas, and I'm helping out the Trump campaign," he said. He looked at the man who grinned even wider.

"Hello, my name is Yale Piper."

- THOMAS RYAN -

Afternoon, Shriners Pavilion

Thomas saw the reporter and cameraman following Brenda Johnson again. The two Guardian reporters had arrived early in the day, and after about 11:00 am they stopped interviewing anyone but the Trump County Chair.

Why is the cameraman holding the camera low? Thomas noticed that the reporter, Brenda Johnson, and the cameraman were sitting at a picnic table, and the cameraman held the camera just off the floor with the lens pointed at Brenda. Thomas walked over and the reporter sensed an intruder.

"Brenda, do you mind if we take a little walk?" the reporter asked. The three walked away from Thomas.

This repeated itself for several times, where Thomas would sidle close to the discussion between the three people, and the reporter would glance to the side and see him coming, and at his gesture the three people would move again. Finally, Thomas trapped them against the bar.

"Hi, my name is Paul," the reporter said. Thomas introduced himself and they traded phone numbers. Thomas assured him that he would send him information as he found it. Reporters were always happy to have an inside source.

"I heard that some democrats were crossing over, but I didn't believe it until I came here to Youngstown," the Guardian New York Bureau Chief said. "Would you excuse us for a minute?" Paul said. The three of them walked away from Thomas for a fifth time.

The cameraman kept the camera rolling, and by late afternoon the *Guardian* had nearly six hours of video footage of Brenda Johnson talking on all manner of topics.

Before sunset, a series of state officials gave stump speeches to the remaining crowd. A former state senator was the fourth official to speak and she thanked God and praised the people of Ohio as a precursor to her speech. Thomas heard giggling and he turned to see Matt Harris trying to contain laughter. Dan Kavanagh had grabbed hold of the plug for the PA system. With a sharp movement, he yanked the cord out of the socket, silencing the politician. Mark Munroe used the momentary technical difficulty to step in and ask folks to help clean up the picnic tables. Thomas stayed until 11:00 pm hauling trash bags to the dumpster.

Davis Motel

Unofficial Update Eastern Ohio August 24-26
To: Senior Staff Trump and Senior Staff Victory Campaign

Below are a few observations over the past few days.

Mahoning and Trumbull Counties

*Trumbull County Republican Party HQ now has Trump yard signs, apparently purchased by the County Party.

*Two guys from Pennsylvania stopped by the Mahoning County Republican Party HQ to request yard signs. They said that there were more Trump yard signs displayed at neighborhood houses in Pennsylvania than any recent past Republican candidate.

*A German reporter from ZDF, the prestigious public TV channel in Germany, stopped by Mahoning County Republican Party HQ this morning. Rumors are that several additional international and national media reporters will come to Mahoning in the next week or two.

*The New York Times published an article this morning on Mahoning County and on the significant Trump support coming from the area.

At the Doors

*Data gathering test at the doors:

There is enormous support in Mahoning County for Trump from Republicans and from democrats/independents who voted "Republican" in the primary. We tested out a hypothesis of democrats/independents who *did not vote* in the primary. So far it appears ~20% of registered democrats who did not vote in *the primary election support Trump, while the other 80% were noncommittal. There was no overt support for Hillary among this group of voters.*

Additionally, a very high percentage of African-American voters did not vote in the primary election we are discovering. Past data does show African-Americans vote less often in the primary in most cases, so more data-gathering and analysis needs to be done to determine if the findings are significant.

Southeast Ohio

*Frank Hoagland of the 30th state senate seat is getting better name recognition at the doors in Toronto, Ohio.

Thomas Ryan

Sunday, 28 August 2016, 72 Days

St. Charles

Blessedly, the music stopped. There was a brief moment of silence while the Deacon clad in a long white robe and sash walked to the podium. "For those who wish to join the Catholic Church the next RCIA class will start September 18. Please contact the church office or me this week to sign up.

Boom tish boom tish

The drummer brought his wrists down sharply and thumped his foot in time. A cute girl made a dipping movement with her body and plucked at the bass guitar.

Thomas left the auditorium and made a hasty exit to his car parked in the Walmart-sized lot.

MCRP HQ

Mark and Rose were at headquarters. "The guys are all at the Canfield Fairgrounds building the floor for the Republican tent," Rose said. "You should go help them," she told Thomas.

"Get ready for hell week," Mark said.

Thomas walked back to this car and drove to the fairgrounds.

Canfield Fair

Thomas drove through the maze of roads at the Canfield Fair and parked his car. He grabbed a large brim hat, work gloves, an apple, and a bottle of water, and walked for a half mile until he found the lot leased by the MRCP.

Dan Kavanagh and several young men were already there, and working on building the floor frame. Thomas stood by Dan, who bent over and swung a hammer, pounding a nail to attach two pieces of lumber. "I had to do my Sunday obligation," Thomas said. He was not Catholic but he wanted to feel out if Dan was. Thomas figured Dan was, as his dad was Lutheran and he had married into a Catholic Italian family. Most people were Catholic in the Mahoning Valley.

"St. Dominic's is really quick – in and out in fifty minutes," Dan said.

"Why don't we see you there?" one young guy asked.

"I had a 'disagreement' with the priest," Dan said. Everyone laughed.

Thomas grabbed the top of a large wooden frame while one young man hammered the wood. They were trying to salvage the good pieces of wood on this old frame, and that meant tearing down the old frame before rebuilding a new one. Kyle grabbed the wood where Thomas did and nearly fell over backward when he lost his grip. *Why does this guy keep getting in the way?*

"There are too many people here," Dan said. He kept hammering at the floor made up of a combination of old and new boards.

CHAPTER 24

Monday, 29 August 2016, 71 Days
MCRP HQ

"Well, just because he has a majority in the polls doesn't mean that he will win," Chelsea said, into the phone.

What the hell... Thomas overheard Chelsea discussing the Trump poll with a friend.

Thomas worked on Mark Munroe's mailing project with three other older women volunteers. "Oh no, this won't do," a woman whom Thomas did not recognize walked up to the mailing operation.

"Who are you?" Thomas asked.

"I am a professor at YSU, my name is Phyllis," she replied. Thomas' facial reaction remained neutral. "Here, move this letter like this," Phyllis said. She grabbed the top letter and put it underneath the response card.

"Mark specifically wanted the mailing to be in this order. Should I call him?" Thomas asked.

Phyllis grabbed another set of the five papers for the mailing and rearranged them. She instructed one of the elderly women to follow her lead. Thomas sent a text to Mark.

Crazy woman attempting to change your mailing.

I am almost to HQ, Mark texted.

Thomas said nothing more and re-arranged each set of papers back to the original order. Phyllis interpreted his silence as obedience, and she stuck her jaw out when the other volunteers did as she said. Using her most condescending grandmotherly voice she decided to push her advantage. "Dear," she said to the handsome young man, "would you go make us some coffee?" Phyllis's next tactic was to use the principle of chivalry against Thomas.

"Why don't you make a pot?" Thomas said. He saw Phyllis's face twist into ugliness.

Ding-a-ling

Mark walked in. "What's going on here?" he asked, in a friendly way. He said a kind word to each of the volunteers. Phyllis slithered to the front desk and the mailing procedure returned to normal.

Thomas had a bad feeling. Phyllis was dangerous and manipulative, and when he typed her name in the YSU search engine he discovered that she had no employment of any capacity as a professor or administrative staffer at the college.

Phyllis spoke again from across the room, "Maybe Thomas will help take these envelopes to the post office."

"Oh, no, that's not going to happen." Thomas said. He was forceful. *This is going to be a problem.*

Joe walked into the main room with his granddaughter, Alexis. She ran to the podium and pushed it, nearly knocking it over. She jumped on the stage and off the stage before running full speed across the room to the kitchen. Thomas felt something fly by his ear. He followed a blur bouncing around the room. Alexis had thrown a rubber Super Ball with all of her might. The ball crashed through a set of half-completed letters and startled two volunteers.

Thomas walked over to the five-year-old. He knelt down to her level. "Hi Alexis," he said.

She stopped running and looked at him. She stood tall, "Hi, Thomas!" She remembered him from the football game.

"Do you want to be my intern?"

"What's an intern?" Alexis asked.

"It means that you would work for me in the campaign stuff. There is a lot of work to do, and I could use your help."

"Ok!" Alexis answered. The two old lady volunteers saw this interaction and chuckled. They thought that Thomas was humoring the young girl to stop the rubber ball projectiles from hurtling through the mailing workspace.

"Come here for a minute." Thomas walked with Alexis skipping behind him. They went to the candidate table that was pushed against the wall, sitting between the kitchen serving window and the front desk. The table was covered in papers and used paper cups and plates. "I would like you to clean the table. When you are finished cleaning the table please line the candidates' lit up, like this," Thomas said. He walked over to the front desk and grabbed a few Don Manning walking lit pieces and laid them neatly on the table. "There are the other candidates lit pieces over there," Thomas pointed to the front desk. "Do you understand?" he asked.

"Yes!" Alexis said. She grabbed three paper cups, and ran to the kitchen garbage can to throw them away. With a jump she smashed the paper cups down into the bin. Thomas walked back to the mailing table.

He watched Alexis run back and forth from the table to the garbage can throwing away the papers and cleaning up the table. He smiled and turned his attention to the two women volunteers, talking with them while keeping an eye on Alexis.

Three other people watched this interaction closely. Joe saw for the second time Thomas taking an interest in his granddaughter, and Joe saw how Thomas had put the little girl to work, how he had channeled her energy to become the fourth most productive member of the MCRP HQ volunteer crew after Joe himself, Billy, and Thomas.

Phyllis also sensed that Thomas was a good man. This made her furious. She watched with cold eyes as the little girl put her energy to a useful purpose. Nicholas noticed Alexis, and he had witnessed Thomas telling her what she should do. Nicholas exchanged glances with Phyllis, and walked over to the table where the little girl was doing her internship assignment.

"Hey Alexis, what are you doing?" Nicholas asked.

"I am the intern," Alexis said. "I am cleaning the table."

"You don't have to clean the table," Nicholas said. "Why don't you go play?"

"I want to," Alexis said. She was strong willed.

"Why don't you–" Nicholas started to say.

"What are you telling my intern?" Thomas interrupted Nicholas. He had seen the interaction from the mailing table and was now standing tall over Nicholas and Alexis. "I asked her to clean the table."

"*You* should clean the table," Nicholas said.

"No, this is a job for my intern," Thomas replied.

Nicholas snorted and hobbled away. He flashed Thomas a dirty look.

Thomas returned his attention to the young girl. "Alexis, when you are done here could you go over to my spot and help the women with the mailing?" Thomas asked as an officer asks an enlisted sailor, giving an order in the form of a polite question.

"Yes sir!" Alexis doubled her speed to clean the table and display the candidates' literature neatly.

Thomas' phone rang and he walked outside to the parking lot. Tony Russo, the Deputy Director of the Victory Campaign offered him a field organizer position in Wood County, Northwest Ohio.

It had taken six weeks of hard work and maneuvering to receive this phone call. Thomas said he would take the job.

Thomas walked back inside and sat at his computer. Jason Lovett walked over to him. "Congratulations on your new job," Jason said.

"You know more than I do I'm sure," Thomas said. He flattered Jason.

Jason nodded, "I've known for sometime but I couldn't say anything."

Thomas could not keep up the charade of ignorance and stared at Jason without saying anything else.

"I wasn't sure when it was going to happen," Jason said. He thought for a second that he could paper over the earlier hostility, but he noticed Thomas was not relaxed. Jason changed his own expression from friendly to neutral. He walked to the desk and picked up his bag, and then walked to the front door. At the front door Jason stopped and started laughing loudly.

Something about the laughter triggered Thomas. "Why are you laughing?" Thomas asked.

"Oh, its nothing…it's just…Tyler. You'll do fine," Jason laughed again and walked to his car.

Thomas felt a tingling sensation up his back, and he saw red in his eyes. Something was wrong.

Victory Campaign Nightly Conference Call

"Listen up everybody, we have a special guest to start the conference call tonight, our Midwest Regional Director Kimberly Flanagan," Justin Clark said.

"Thanks, Justin," Kimberly said. She sounded like an executive VP from a large public corporation. "I want to begin by saying that the Victory Campaign has dedicated a lot of effort to Northeast Ohio, the ground zero of this election campaign. Thanks to our efforts there, we are getting preliminary polling data that shows Mahoning County will break all records for Republican turnout."

Kimberly looked down at her pile of unofficial reports that she had received from Thomas Ryan. She took credit for almost everything good that he had reported, giving a few scraps of credit to her underling, Ohio Director Justin Clarke. He groveled before her ladyship on the conference call line. She left the call.

Chelsea fumed. She texted Rose, *I am the one who has done so much work for Trump in Mahoning and Kimberly took all the credit!*

Tuesday, 30 August 2016, 70 Days
MCRP HQ Parking Lot

Today was the Canfield Fair setup day. Thomas was getting ready to leave the MCRP for the third time and travel the five miles West to the fairgrounds, his car filled with materials from headquarters. Rose walked up to his window and he rolled it down.

"Stop telling Randy things," she said, referring to the Chair of Trumbull County.

"What are you talking about?" Thomas asked.

"You are telling Randy Law things about our party and if you're such a good friend of Randy's you won't find many friends here," she said coldly.

Earlier that morning, Randy had bragged to a member of the Canfield Republican Women's Club that he had a source inside the Mahoning party. The woman he spoke to was a friend of Rose's, and she told Rose that Thomas was spilling secrets to Randy Law, the chair of Trumbull County. Most people who mattered in Mahoning County, particularly the wealthy women, did not like Randy.

"Since you are such good friends with Randy, ask him to give us his life-size Trump cutout for the fair," she said. "We can make a lot of money with people taking pictures next to it. If you get his cutout, I'll help you with the RNC."

You have no power with the RNC, Thomas thought. *Otherwise I would have Jason Lovett's job by now.*

"I'm not a good friend of Randy. What did he say, anyway?"

Rose stretched out her finger through the driver's side window. "Stop talking to him," she said.

Thomas rolled up his window and drove away. Rose slammed his trunk twice with her hand.

Inside the headquarters' main room Joe was painting another Trump sign. He had heard that Thomas was leaving for a field organizer position in Wood County, on the other side of the state. He felt a lot of stress.

Canfield Fair

Thomas arrived to the parking area with boxes of supplies in his trunk. He walked to the tent and asked one of the young guys to bring a dolly to help him bring the T-shirts and boxes of buttons from his car to the tent. The two men returned a short time later with the supplies.

"They don't mind you drinking?" Thomas asked Dan Kavanagh, who, like most male members working on or around the tent, had a beer in hand.

Dan gave Thomas a crooked smile. "One time seven years ago we had a guy get really drunk. The cops came and confiscated all the alcohol out of our tent. I knew the sheriff's deputy and later that evening he gave most of it back. Then we all drank it together." He tipped the can to his mouth and took a long draught as emphasis.

"Jason Lovett fakes his door numbers," Dan said, changing the subject. He grinned. Thomas looked at him and asked for details.

Nicole and Don Manning arranged the white tables in a horseshoe shape around the inside of the larger white tent, and put two white tables in the back green tent. Thomas helped hook the canvas walls to the metal frame.

A young Republican spoke to Nicole, Don, and Thomas. "Rose Piper's cooking is really good. You have to try some. It's to die for." Don Manning nodded his head.

Davis Motel

Unofficial Update Ohio and Michigan August 28-30
To: Senior Staff Trump and Senior Staff Victory Campaign

Below are observations from the past few days.

Northwest Ohio

*A contact from Wood County said there has been exceptionally high demand for Trump signs and their supply is exhausted.

Northeastern Ohio - Mahoning County

*New county-purchased Trump signs arrived today and more will arrive tomorrow. Over 500 people are on a waiting list for Trump signs.

*In the last month up to 600 people per day are registering to vote in Mahoning County. There is a very high likelihood that these are Donald Trump supporters.

There were ~14,000 new registered voters for the primary and an additional

~6,000 previous democratic voters who crossed over to Republican side in the primary. The daily registrations of new voters are *in addition to* the primary voter registrations.

*A second mailing was sent out, this time to select Republican members of the county.

*The annual picnic for the Mahoning County Republican Party was Saturday, and a reporter from the UK Guardian newspaper attended and interviewed guests. I was not interviewed but I talked to the reporter. He told me that he "had not previously known that there was a crossover vote in Eastern Ohio."

*Up to 30 people are volunteering or working at a time in Mahoning County Republican Party HQ in the last several days.

Canfield Fair

*The Canfield Fair, the third largest county fair in the US and that takes place in Mahoning County, will start tomorrow and go through Labor Day.

*During the tent set-up Tuesday evening / night, we sold four Trump signs within fifteen minutes of bringing them to the tent still under construction.

Northeastern Ohio - Trumbull and Columbiana Counties

*Trump is receiving similar support in Trumbull and Columbiana Counties as he is in Mahoning County. This is based on conversations with those involved in the respective counties.

Michigan

*I chatted with a couple of Republican contacts in Michigan. They were surprised at the amount of support Trump is receiving in Michigan. However, they did not provide internal polling data.

Thomas Ryan

Wednesday, 31 August 2016, 69 Days
Canfield Fair

After your training tomorrow with the Victory Campaign I will be holding a training day in Wood County. Call the below conference line at 2pm today for our team's conference call – Tyler.

Thomas looked at the email from his new boss. There were no details: Tyler had failed to disclose his personal cell phone number on the email. Thomas sighed and looked outside the front of the tent.

Brenda Johnson was giving an interview to a Canadian Broadcasting journalist. Thomas walked out of the tent and up to another reporter standing next to the Trump wall. The reporter was from Al Jazeera. Thomas introduced himself to the man and his camerawoman.

"Wait, what percentage of Democrats crossed over for the primary election?" the Al Jazeera reporter asked. He looked Mormon, Thomas thought. *It must be the blue eyes, fair skin, and safe haircut.*

"Well, 6,000 out of roughly 35,000 Democratic voters did. What's that, seventeen or eighteen percent?" Thomas said.

The camerawoman for Al Jazeera moved around slowly, focusing on several red bricks in turn. Thomas' brick was safely in the trunk of his car, parked a half-mile away.

The sun bore down on those standing outside of cover, and Thomas walked to the white tent main entrance and through the back exit to the green tent that had the coolers full of water, Gatorade, beer, and soft drinks. He lifted the lid of a cooler and took a yellow sport drink. Dan Kavanagh was standing there. Thomas stood up and unscrewed the lid. He tipped the bottle up and took a long drink. "Are your daughters married?" Thomas asked.

"No." Dan smiled. "You know, my wedding was attended by a thousand people," he said. Thomas remembered this anecdote from the other day at the farm. "It's a great area to raise a family," Kavanagh said. "We'll miss you."

Rose walked up to Dan and Thomas and focused her attention on the taller one. "Give me the rest of your tickets," she said.

"I don't have them on me," Thomas said.

"You are leaving, so give them to me!" she shouted.

Thomas reached in his pocket and gave her one. "This is all that I have," he said. He walked to the front of the tent to escape Rose. Vendors who were setting up their own tents were stopping by to purchase Trump signs and MAGA hats. Many bought red bricks too, and wrote messages on them before a volunteer glued them to the wall. One volunteer put duct tape over the most colorful writings on the bricks.

Rose followed Thomas and planned to forcibly extract the remaining fair tickets from him but got distracted when she saw Nicole put two twenty-dollar bills into an already full money box. Rose grabbed a fistful of money out of the moneybox and brought it to her red car that was parked behind the green tent. She turned on the engine to run the air conditioner and counted the money, and stuffed the bills into a large brown envelope for the party to deposit at the bank.

Thomas' alarm went off. It was five minutes to 2:00 pm and he dialed into the Northwest Ohio field organizer conference call. Tyler was on time and introduced himself. He introduced the three new members of his team, including Thomas, and then talked about the upcoming training day. "Our training session will be fun. I use an air horn when someone says something stupid," he said.

Aren't we having the training in a library since you were not able to make a deal with the Wood County Republican Party to use their facilities? Didn't you just say these exact words? Thomas thought. He felt hot and exhausted.

CHAPTER 25

Thursday, 1 September 2016, 68 Days
Victory Campaign, Columbus, Ohio

Jonathan Schmidt handed paperwork to the fifteen new field organizers. He skipped Thomas and another person. "The RNC is hiring you, not the Ohio Republican Party," he said to Thomas. He walked to the young woman at the other end of the row and whispered the same thing to her.

Jonathan walked to the front of the room and started the training session. "Talking to the press will get you fired," he said. Thomas thought that he looked young. Politics was a young man's game, so it was not that unusual to have a twenty-four-year-old as Deputy Director for a statewide campaign.

"This afternoon we will give each of you a report of your social media presence," Jonathan said. This was a new practice – one implemented in the last week to address the issue of Victory Campaign field organizers posting anti-Trump tweets and other embarrassing things. Jonathan clicked to the next slide. "Your primary responsibility is to do whatever is necessary to help the local party chair," Jonathan continued.

That is exactly right, thought Thomas. *That's not what is happening in Mahoning.* Most of the field organizers were in their early twenties and had zero work experience. Many were immature and did not understand their own interests never mind the interests of other people, and they did not understand the power that county chairs wielded. *Jonathan and Tony are talented and hardworking. These guys are professionals,* Thomas thought. The two deputy directors took turns instructing the class for the orientation.

An hour later the class ended. "Hey Thomas, could you come to my office?" Tony Russo asked. Thomas followed Tony into an office filled with maps.

"I love the maps," Thomas said. Tony nodded but did not speak.

There was an old woman sitting in a chair against the wall. "I want to make sure that my daughter has the full responsibility of the college age demographic in Wood County," she said.

"Absolutely, she has all Bowling Green State University and the technical college." Tony said.

"Don't I have all of Wood County?" Thomas said. He was surprised by Tony's response to the request from the old woman.

"Yes, you have Wood County," Tony said.

The woman spoke again, this time with aggression. "My daughter was promised Wood County and all of the college students. She doesn't need someone else to take her territory." Bowling Green State University made up a significant part of the Wood County population, and would make up almost all of the volunteer force for the campaign. A key part of the field organizer job was recruiting volunteers. Furthermore, the party used the number of volunteers that a field organizer recruited as a core metric in performance appraisals.

Thomas realized that he was in the middle of an ambush, and he realized that he would not win by arguing. He remained quiet.

"Colleen has full authority over Bowling Green, and she does not need to report to Thomas," Tony said. The woman had a triumphant look on her face.

Thomas felt his face flush with agitation. The room was dark and he did not think that Tony or Colleen's mother noticed. He walked out of headquarters and drove northwest to Bowling Green State University. There was a BGSU College Republicans meeting that was starting in a few hours. If he hurried, he would be only fifteen minutes late.

Bowling Green State University

"We have a few special guests with us today," said the President of the College Republicans at BGSU. Rob Portman's representative spoke first, and then a representative from the NRA gave his pitch. Thomas stood up in the back of the room. The chair motioned for him to speak. Within ten seconds every eye focused on Thomas, his face, his hands. The students followed him as he took small steps and then paused, making points. Colleen gave the interloper a death glare. He ignored her. His stump speech was short and he started taking questions. He had the smoothness of a marketing executive. Thomas had not respected Colleen's mother's demand or Tony Russo's order to stay away from the key part of his county.

"I would like to ask each of you who wants to work with our team to sign this paper," Thomas held up a blank pad. He stopped speaking, the forty college Republicans clapped loudly, and young men crowded around him.

An hour later Thomas' boss called him and informed him that he would not be allowed to use the Wood County Republican Party headquarters because there was no agreement in place.

Another hour went by and Thomas received a message on Facebook. *You bastard!* Colleen's boyfriend attacked Thomas in a direct message after the young woman told her boyfriend that Thomas had wronged her by stepping on her turf.

Hotel in Bowling Green, Ohio

At 9:00 pm Thomas had his first Victory Campaign conference call. Justin Clarke started the call with a ten-minute combined pep talk and threatening soliloquy that entered the bizarre, particularly when he began to speak about his favorite Kentucky basketball team.

Next, each field organizer was required to tell how many doors they had knocked that day. The goal for everyone was one hundred fifty doors at a minimum. Thomas recognized the number that Jason Lovett had told him. Northeast Ohio went first.

"Trumbull County, one hundred fifty two-doors," Valentina said.

"Mahoning County, one hundred fifty two-doors," Chelsea said.

A few other field organizers in Jason Lovett's district answered, all claiming at least one hundred fifty-two doors. *I guess one hundred fifty is too suspicious?* Thomas thought. One guy said he did nine hundred and thirty doors. Thomas knew that in Mahoning County he was often the only person walking, especially on a weekday, and he would reach twenty to eighty doors.

Jason Lovett spoke. "We have walked 16,000 doors this week. I want to specifically congratulate my team."

What the hell? Thomas thought.

In Southern Ohio the district manager was honest but did not understand the game. One field organizer said he walked twenty doors. It was a completely rural district, Thomas knew, but he could not help feeling embarrassed for the guy. Thomas realized Tony Russo had taken away the urban and suburban parts of his district, and he had no office to meet with volunteers or a place to put up maps. Soon it would be Thomas humiliated in front of the Victory Campaign organization during the nightly conference calls.

Tyler got on the phone. Thomas' boss asked the first field organizer to announce his doors.

"Lucas County, fifty doors," the man said.

Tyler dressed down his worker in front of the eighty people on the phone call, telling him that there was no excuse and that he must do better.

No way! Thomas thought.

Justin Clarke ended the call and announced that his team in Ohio had walked 80,000 doors this week.

Thomas opened his laptop and sent an email to Director of the Victory Campaign, Justin Clarke, asking if Jason Lovett's doors in Northeast Ohio were phone calls or actual doors. Tyler responded to Thomas chastising him for going outside the chain of command. He said that the numbers represented doors, not phone calls. Thomas wrote back to Tyler, *I guarantee you that Jason Lovett or his staff did not walk anything close to the number of doors he claimed. I was the only person walking doors in Mahoning County most days.*

Ring

"Hey Thomas, this is Tony. You had a question on walking versus calling for doors?" Tony Russo asked. The Deputy Director of the Victory Campaign realized that Thomas could cause a problem and he needed to handle him right away. He was respectful.

"Tony, Jason Lovett is not walking those doors. I was there. I was the only person walking," Thomas said.

Tony listened and asked a few clarifying questions, but it was clear Thomas was getting nowhere.

"Can I fake the door numbers in Wood County?" Thomas asked. "I understand if you need to report some minimum number of doors to the national campaign, and there is no possible way I can make that goal with you taking the University away from me. Also, I will not be humiliated each night by Tyler for not meeting a goal that is arbitrary."

"It's hard work, Thomas. What did you expect?" Tony said.

"So to be clear, you are telling me that I cannot fake the door count to match Jason Lovett's fake numbers?" Thomas asked.

"No."

This is why Jason Lovett was laughing so hard! Thomas had an epiphany. *Jason Lovett knew my boss Tyler was either an idiot or sadistic.*

For two hours Thomas thought about possible actions that he could take. He could stay in Wood County and fake his numbers like two-thirds of the field organizers across the state were doing. It would be unlikely for anyone to make trouble for him for playing the game, Tony's answer notwithstanding. Thomas would be vulnerable to be labeled dishonest and fired for cause if someone kept close track of him; however, this too would be unlikely.

There were factors that could increase the risk of getting a bad reputation. He had been put in a position to make an enemy with the woman from whom he took the county. She would be looking to undermine him at every turn. However, if he managed to avoid open conflict and not get fired for either low performance or dishonesty he would have a spot working for the RNC. This is what he had wanted, because if Trump won the presidency Thomas would be toward the beginning of the line for a West Wing position, or better, a diplomatic policy posting in Europe.

That is, he would be first in line if Trump won the election. Northwest Ohio was going to vote for Trump in high numbers no matter what. Although the Republicans in this area tended to be religious conservatives, and even though local Republican politicos claimed that conservatives here would not support Trump, Thomas knew that they would pull the lever for Trump after Rob Portman, the US senator that Republicans in this part of the state venerated, got them into the voting booth. There was no possible way that a social conservative Republican was going to let Hillary win.

Northeast Ohio, Pennsylvania, Michigan, and Wisconsin were linked together and an entirely different story. Trump was going to win the White House by convincing the people in these areas to vote for him. He was doing exactly this; he spoke the message that blue-collar people needed to hear and demonstrated high energy and charisma. However, the RNC and the Trump campaign organizations were disorganized and weak in these same areas. Specifically, the campaign did not have the professionals that were usually on hand and necessary to handle a crisis that was bound to happen. Trump was winning, but he could lose without the people on the ground ready to act decisively. The media would continue to up their attacks against Trump. Someone would make a mistake, and no one would be present to fight the fire.

Thomas knew that his path to a position working at the White House was to stay in Wood County and to not make waves. However, Trump had to win the election. *Do I matter so much? Does it matter if I do nothing more for the campaign as long as I position myself for a job? Haven't I accomplished exactly what I came here to do?* Staying in Wood County would mean that he would be set up for a White House job should Trump win the election. It would also effectively remove him from the presidential campaign.

Thomas wrote a resignation letter. At 1:00 am he called and left a message on Tony Russo's voicemail.

- WINNING OHIO -

Friday, 2 September 2016, 67 Days
Thomas' Car

Do you miss Youngstown yet :), Dan Kavanagh texted.

I didn't take the RNC job, Thomas texted.

I heard. I can call them about Jason Lovett, Kavanagh replied.

There is no need. I'm from Indiana so I don't care about Ohio politics. I'm looking to retire anyway and go into private industry. Thomas texted.

There is a chance Jason Lovett will be fired, Kavanagh texted.

Thomas pulled into a rest area and bought another one-dollar coffee. He was running on four hours of sleep.

An hour later he pulled into the Davis Motel parking lot. The younger brother and Trump supporter gave him his key. "Back already?"

"It looks like I might be here for the duration," Thomas said.

He walked to his room and took a two-hour nap.

Thomas turned slightly to the side and pointed. "Yes general, you are correct. Increased gas flows from NordStream 2 will further weaken Eastern Europe's foreign policy position vis-à-vis Russia." The general nodded in grim agreement. Thomas heard a terrible noise. The room began vibrating. *What was happening? Why is this noise interrupting me? I am such a good presenter!* The noise and vibrations turned to darkness. The generals disappeared from their seats at the large oak table. He felt weightless.

He jerked awake, still sleep-deprived.

South Range Football Game

Thomas checked Facebook. Chelsea and Valentina had each blocked him. He put his phone in his back jeans' pocket and walked around the field to the visitor side. He saw an open gate that led to a path into the pine forest. There were several figures in the shadows.

"Hi Thomas," Kavanagh said. He laughed. "This is Umberto."

Thomas shook the hand of the Greek man who had an Italian given name. Kavanagh poured vodka for Umberto and Ben, another big fellow who stood at the edge of the woods.

"They don't like us to drink in the stadium." Dan said.

"This is just like Poland," Thomas said. He turned down a double shot of vodka. "They also drink in the forests."

"Umberto is a director at a company in the oil industry," Dan said. He turned to Umberto and Ben. "Thomas is looking to move to Youngstown."

Dan Kavanagh told the guys about the political drama. "Jason Lovett is faking his doors, I already called five party chairs in the area to tell them about him." In fact, Kavanagh had not made these calls.

"Jason tried to get rid of Thomas a few weeks ago, he told everyone that Thomas was a spy. I said to Mark that if Thomas is a spy please send ten of him. He is the hardest working guy here." Dan said. "He was motivating everyone," Kavanagh continued. "We found out that you were from Michigan."

I should invite the Kavanagh family to the Lake house. I don't think they get many vacations, and they have four kids in college, Thomas thought. At the Republican picnic at the Shriners club a week earlier, Thomas had asked Dan and Melanie's ten-year-old son Christian his summer plans. In front of his mother the boy had told Thomas that he wasn't going anywhere.

The four men walked inside the gates and to the steel cylinder grill. They ate hamburgers while several of their sons laid down a beating on the visiting team.

CHAPTER 26

Saturday, 3 September 2016, 66 Days
Canfield Fairgrounds, MCRP Tent

"Hi Thomas!," Nicole said. She was surprised to see him in the MCRP tent at the Canfield fair this morning. Nicole and Don were working hard selling Trump signs and T-shirts, and Don was talking to a large percentage of people walking by the tent on the fairground road.

"Hi Nicole, nice to see you again so soon," Thomas said. "I am helping O-rock with the Wood County third house race." O-rock meant the Ohio State House Republican Election Committee. "I realized that what they needed me to do I could easily do on my computer – it's database work. Maybe I can trade your campaign some non-walking volunteers for my walking doors for you guys?" Thomas said.

Nicole responded positively. "Really? What are you doing with the 3rd house race?" She asked. She knew that it was targeted by O-rock, and she wanted Don Manning's race to be targeted as well.

Thomas explained in detail. "You really should focus on your campaign first and send me only unused resources, that is, high school kids who can't work doors," he said. Thomas realized that his cover story was brilliant. It was mostly true, as his company did have a contract from the Wood County Republican Party. Even if O-rock was not the official client, his work would be key to reaching Bowling Green students for the state representative candidate.

Rose walked into the tent and bumped into Thomas. "They called me up and said you quit because you wanted more money," she said. She was noticeably cool to Thomas.

"I do have a job, but it is working for Wood County on database stuff. This is my area of expertise anyway." Thomas said. Rose didn't know what to think about this news. She walked away.

Thomas sent a text to Mark Munroe denying the rumor that he quit the campaign work because they were not paying him enough money. He mentioned his database work with Wood County.

Rose walked into the tent and headed to the back where the blue moneybox sat. She avoided looking at Thomas. Another woman saw an opening. Maggie Kavanagh was Dan Kavanagh's ethnic German mother. She was in her late 70s, like Rose Piper. "Thomas, could you help me fold these T-shirts?" she touched his arm lightly. He turned around and noticed a gentler woman than his previous taskmaster.

"Of course," he said. He walked with Maggie to the boxes behind the table and grabbed the first one.

Rose opened the drivers' side door of her red car and got out. She thought she heard laughing. *What is that?* Rose poked her head through the vinyl tent to see Thomas helping Maggie with folding T-shirts. She furrowed her brow.

"Thomas, would you mind bringing a box of buttons from the green tent up to the white tent?" Maggie asked. She used her sweetest voice. Thomas passed Rose walking back to the green tent and the chairwoman grimaced. She disappeared out the back of the green wall.

A news story popped on Thomas' twitter feed about the Trump Wall that was sitting in front of the MCRP tent at the Canfield Fair. Visitors poured money into the cashbox, buying red and gold bricks to place on the Trump Wall. Rose reappeared through the green tent wall to grab the cash out of the blue box and take it to her red car parked behind the green tent.

"Complaints Over Trump Wall at Canfield Fair," WMFJ wrote a controversial headline on their Twitter feed. It was true, a local Democratic Party activist had called the Canfield Fair Administration, the Sheriff's Department, and the media with his complaint.

Perfect!

Thomas thumbed a series of texts to every national and international media contact that he had made. He had close to fifty. He felt tugging on his sleeve.

"You need to come and help me with my Internet," Rose said. She grabbed his arm.

"What? I am folding shirts." Thomas said, half looking back towards Maggie. She sat in a plastic folding chair, staring at Rose.

"I need help with my Internet, let's go," she said.

Thomas walked to the Volkswagen, but as soon as he reached the car Rose left to go somewhere else. He walked into the tent and over to the table with the T-shirts next to Maggie Kavanagh. Don Manning saw him and walked up to him, shaking his hand in a friendly way. Nicole had told Don that Thomas had gotten a job with O-rock, the organization from which Don needed support.

"Trump might be here Monday at 2:00 pm," Don told Thomas after the younger man explained to the candidate his new database job in vague terms.

Whoa!

Thomas texted Lindsay McCoy, the weekend anchor of WMFJ 21 news. He heard Brenda Johnson's phone ring thirty seconds later. *Yep, she is talking to Lindsay*. Brenda confirmed that Trump was coming, but she said the details were not yet being released. It had taken Thomas two days to return to the middle of the campaign.

He texted fifty national and international reporters, and Brenda Johnson's phone lit up.

Thomas looked to his left and saw another handgun on the picnic table. One of the candidates was doing a gun raffle. He walked outside the tent, hoping the gun issue would resolve itself. He walked over to a young Asian man carrying an expensive camera and wearing a press credential. The man was taking pictures of the wall and the commotion at the Republican tent.

"Hi, my name is Thomas, are you press?" he asked.

"Yes, I'm a photojournalist from Bloomberg. My name is Rob, nice to meet you," he said. "Are you running for office?" he asked.

"I am just a volunteer," Thomas said. He and Rob talked about the response in the area for Trump.

"Why is Trump getting so much support in the area?" Rob asked.

Thomas explained his theory that voters were not motivated so much by anti-Muslim bias as they were motivated by anger at the lack of jobs in the area. They blamed trade policy for the closed steel mills and crumbling infrastructure. Thomas went on to explain that voters did not like the free-trade aspect of immigration, just as they rejected free trade itself. "These two concepts, immigration and trade, are identical."

"You are the most articulate person on these issues whom I have met," Rob said, a few minutes later. He shook Thomas' hand and gave him a business card.

"Let me know if you need anything. I am trying to help reporters as much as I can...you know, for favors later," Thomas said. He grinned at the last part. Rob laughed.

Thomas walked back into the tent and resumed helping Maggie Kavanagh. Her son arrived.

"Let's make a plan to get rid of Jason Lovett," Dan told Thomas.

"I'd love to, but I promised Tony Russo of the RNC Victory Campaign that I would hold off any action against Jason until November 9th," Thomas said.

"AHHHHH!"

Thomas and Dan walked out of the tent to see a man yelling and dancing around an old man in a wheelchair.

"That's Flynn the Felon," Dan said. "I'd stay away from him if I were you."

Flynn shouted obscenities in front of the gathering crowd. The wheelchair-bound man was a Hillary supporter and had rebuked volunteers standing around the tent for supporting Trump. The uncomfortable moment passed when the press came running to film the commotion.

Thomas noticed that the first wall was completely full of bricks. There was a second wall with two more rows of red bricks and three golden bricks.

Thomas saw Tracey. "Would you say a good word about me to Chris Horvath the next time you see him?" Thomas asked. Tracey was attending a State Party meeting in Columbus, Ohio on Monday where the head of the Ohio Trump campaign might be attending.

"Sure thing," she said. "Did you know that the first wall brought in $6,000?" Tracey was excited.

Davis Motel

Unofficial Report from Northeast Ohio – Tremendous Trump Support
To: Chris Horvath, Director Trump Campaign Ohio

There is tremendous support for Trump here. Since I talked to you last I have been knocking doors and generally helping everywhere in Eastern Ohio. The county party has sold 1000 signs in the first few days of Canfield fair. The response at doors overwhelmingly favors Trump.

My company now has a contract to help targeted local races to maximize turnout using data analytics. It's a data analysis job and online only, so I am back in Mahoning County, my favorite area.

Thomas Ryan

Sunday, 4 September 2016, 65 Days
St. Charles Catholic Church, Boardman

The faithful lined up for communion while Thomas stayed in his seat. He walked out of the pew, exiting near the wall, and hugged the brown bricks until he reached the double doors at the rear of the St. Charles auditorium.

A skinny dark-haired girl nearly ran into him. She had taken the similar but opposite path to the doors from the other side of the church. Thomas and Kayla Kavanagh looked up and at each other at the same time.

"Sneaking out early?" Thomas asked.
"Yeah," she said. She smiled with the smile of her father.

- THOMAS RYAN -

Canfield Fairgrounds, MCRP Tent

Melanie laughed, "Hi, Tom," she said, "Kayla saw you at mass today."

"She caught me leaving early," Thomas said, betraying Kayla's secret without realizing it. He smiled at Christian. Thomas walked into the tent and Rose Piper grabbed him. Doing tasks for Maggie yesterday had reminded Rose that Thomas was valuable. She was not going to have her man stolen today. She needed to clear up the situation with Thomas, the Republican Party, and the Victory Campaign first. Chelsea had told her some strange stories.

"Is there a court order against you, that you can't step foot inside the headquarters?" Rose asked.

Thomas laughed. "Oh no, of course I can go to headquarters." Thomas wasn't completely sure. "I have been a lifelong Republican but several years ago I ran as a Democrat during the Obama wave. The hardest person to tell about my plan to run for local office wasn't my conservative grandfather – I knew he would understand – the hardest person to tell was my barber," Thomas said. "The bottom line is, I got a job working for O-Rock helping with data analysis." He took a breath. "This area," Thomas pointed to the ground, "is the single most important area in the nation. This is ground zero, so I will be doing my data analysis on my computer but walking doors here."

"The RNC knows everything, and I have promised them that I would wait until November 9th to deal with Jason Lovett. He has spread lies about me since the beginning, for whatever reason. All along I had permission from Chris Horvath and the Trump Campaign to be in the state," Thomas said. Rose walked away. She was satisfied with his story.

Thomas noticed Maggie bickering with Jim, her husband. Melanie Kavanagh walked over to Jim, her father-in-law, and gave him a water bottle. It was hot and humid. Somehow the conversation between Maggie the mother-in-law and Melanie the daughter-in-law got to cats. "I hate cats," Maggie said, knowing that her daughter-in-law loved them. Melanie ignored the baiting and checked on Jim one more time to make sure he was hydrated enough to survive the Ohio summer heat and humidity.

Christian walked up to Thomas. The tall man asked the boy questions like he had done for his countless tutoring students over the years. "What grade are you?" "How are your grades?" "Do you think you can get As?" "Well, you should try to get As then," Thomas said while Christian gave one-word answers. The teaching personality burned brightly.

Dan Kavanagh arrived with Katherine and Kayla. The three of them were standing in front of the MCRP tent. Thomas walked up to Kayla first. "Can I have your number?" he asked. "Listen, I want to invite you and your family to my family lake house one weekend coming up."

Kayla gave him her number.

Thomas next walked up to Katherine and made the same offer. Dan watched.

"You all really should come," Thomas said. "We have kayaks and a pontoon boat. I'll be swimming."

Dan told his daughters that they could go if they wanted. "You all can come," Thomas said. "I may or may not be able to come."

Thomas walked into the green tent where an older woman was complaining about Jason Lovett. Thomas smiled. Rose grabbed Thomas. "Cynthia also has a problem with Jason too," Rose said. She introduced Thomas to Cynthia.

"Here, let me give you the contact information for the top Trump and RNC officials."

A sunbeam broke through a gap in the tent and lit up Cynthia's face. The sun had set enough for the beam to be nearly horizontal. "I will contact these people," the woman said.

Thomas checked his watch; it was getting close to the golden hour of television. Sure enough, he looked out the front of the white tent and saw media interviewing several people who stood near the wall. One reporter was making a live report for cable news. There was Mark Munroe, the party chair, live on Fox News.

Thomas remembered something and grabbed his phone. *Trump will be at the Canfield Fair tomorrow, estimated at 2 pm.* He sent the text to Kevin Schimp and Frank Hoagland.

I will be there! Frank responded.

When darkness fell, Chelsea and Valentina approached him. "We didn't know about you, Jason Lovett said that you were a spy, a Democrat! We didn't mean to treat you badly!" they both said, talking over each other.

"I understand the situation, don't worry about it," Thomas said. He walked inside the tent to help Maggie unpack new t-shirts for tomorrow.

CHAPTER 27

Monday, 5 September 2016, 64 Days
Davis Motel

Thomas got up out of the firm bed without thinking. After receiving the text last night from Dan Kavanagh to join him and a few others to build a new Trump Wall, Thomas had practiced lying down and getting up at 11:00 pm. A long time ago in engineering school Thomas and his roommate learned to do a similar thing during the grind of night after night of studying and of early-morning classes. *Lie down, get up, lie down, get up. Make it a rote action.* And so he had made it a rote action this morning.

His first conscious thought came when he was in the shower. *Trump is coming!*

Working through his sleepiness, Thomas thought hard to not forget anything, and he opened the door to the outside. A class eight truck idled in the gas station parking lot sixty feet away. Thomas stepped into the grey car and plugged the Home Depot address into his iPhone.

Home Depot

"Not used to mornings, eh?" Billy said, laughing. He was extra cheerful to highlight the juxtaposition of a professional carpenter and the silver-spoon kid from Indiana.

Thomas laughed. Dan stared. The corner of one mouth went up slightly.

"We need twenty pieces of two-by-sixes and..." Billy directed Thomas and Caleb to throw the wood onto the trolley.

MCRP HQ Backroom

Painting everything took the longest. Billy and Dan built the second wall in ten minutes while Thomas and Caleb cut bricks. They painted the frame red and the bricks red and gold. Thomas brought in fans from the main room, and found another two fans in the back room under piles of junk. He propped opened all the doors to get maximum airflow.

At 7:30 am they loaded the sign into the back of Billy's truck and used rope to tie it down. It made an enormous sail and was obviously unsafe. Thomas followed Billy's truck and the convoy drove slowly to the fairgrounds.

Canfield Fairgrounds MCRP Tent

10:30 am

"Hi, Thomas," Brian Wollet said. "How are things at the tent?"

"We are selling bricks like crazy," Thomas said. Brian Wollet was the Trump Regional Director for Northeast Ohio. It was an excellent sign that Brian was talking to him. Since Thomas took a job and resigned in one day on September first he was jumpy at Trump and RNC people.

"Thomaassss!" Rose yelled. She walked over to him and shooed away Brian. "Thomas, I need you to get change for this one hundred-dollar bill. I also need you to buy ice." Her hesitancy at associating with him had vanished because of the combination of jealousy and utility. She was jealous of Maggie Kavanagh and the relationship that seemed to be growing between her and Thomas, and she missed the utility that he offered her. He was good at almost everything, she thought, and so efficient, especially with her guiding him.

"Go, now," she ordered.

Thomas held his tongue and clenched his teeth. He walked out the back of the tent to make his way to the bank located on the fairgrounds.

"Hey, Thomas." Dan Kavanagh stood with Kayla and Matt Harris. "I have an idea." Dan smiled. "You seem to know how to find things. What if we made a giant brick for Trump to sign? Could you find a large piece of wood around here?" Dan said.

Thomas' eyes lit up. *Kavanagh has a great imagination*. "Like maybe a giant golden brick…do they have a maintenance facility here? They must have one." Thomas said.

"Yeah, there is one by the stadium," Dan said. He referred to the grandstands next to the racetrack.

"I'm on it," Thomas said. He walked away quickly, to the bank first.

Twenty minutes later he found the maintenance department and walked into the open garage. "I'm looking for a large piece of wood," he said. The first guy gave him a strange look, and the next guy said they couldn't help him.

"Listen, keep this to yourselves, but Trump is scheduled to arrive here around 1:00 pm." Thomas said. The time had been moved up from rumored arrival time of 2:00 pm, although he was not sure if these men knew that Trump was coming to the fairgrounds in the first place. "We want a large piece of wood to make an extra large brick for Trump to sign." Thomas said. He took a risk, and guessed that these men were Trump supporters.

The first maintenance guy smiled and walked to the back. He brought out a scrap piece of wood about eighteen inches long by eight inches tall. Thomas nodded and walked off quickly holding what might soon be an icon of the campaign.

The bags of ice were two dollars, not one dollar like Rose had said. He bought one bag.

Thomas saw Kayla and walked over to Dan. He handed the brick to Dan and Matt Harris chuckled. "You're amazing," Dan said, "and fast."

Back in the tent, Rose called, "Where is my ice?" Thomas gave her the bag and ninety-eight dollars in small bills. "Ice is two dollars now," he said. He walked away before she could assign him another task.

He sat in a chair in the rear tent and looked at his shoes. They were worn out from the door-knocking this campaign season. He looked up through a hole in the tent and saw snipers setting up on top of the grandstand. It was a few minutes past noon. The president would be arriving within the hour.

He overheard talking from behind the tent wall, "Have your people put on one of the name tags, the white ones with the blue lining. This will be a sign for our people to know who is authorized to be in the tent." Thomas walked out the back of the tent and saw a man in a suit talking to Tracey. He walked into the main tent and saw a pile of name tags next to the cashbox. Don Manning was wearing one. Thomas took a black marker and wrote his name and stuck the name tag on his shirt. He left the tent.

Whether the maintenance men had spread the word, or the other people had spotted the snipers, or the volunteers in the Republican tent had been bragging to those wanting to buy Trump signs, Trump hats, and Trump t-shirts that Trump was on his way, somehow the secret was out and a huge throng of people began to congregate outside of the tent. "Everybody out of the tent!" Mark Munroe shouted. He kept kicking people out, but it was not working.

Thomas was mingling with a crowd surrounding the Fox News reporter who was live across the globe at that minute. He overheard a girl say, "This is so exciting, I am from Indianapolis..." she said.

He tapped the girl on her shoulder. "You are from Indiana? I am from Columbus, Indiana and here volunteering on the campaign."

"Oh, that's so great," she said. "I'm here with my friend working the fair."

"Do you want to see if we can have an Indiana section and meet the President?" Thomas asked. His tone was completely serious. He would like having an ally in the tent.

"Really? I don't understand," the girl said.

"Follow me," Thomas said. He grabbed the girl's hand and pulled her through the crowd. He turned left and they walked around the tent to the back entrance. He led her through the green tent to the white tent and to the table with the cashbox. There were a few name tags left, and he snagged one. "What's your name?" he asked.

"Tiffany," she answered. She was in a daze.

He handed her the name tag. "This is your ticket. The Secret Service will watch for it, so you must keep it on at all times," Thomas said.

Bzzzz

Could you let people know that Trump will be meeting them at the Ferris wheel down Poland road? Mark Munroe texted Thomas and several other people. Yelling wasn't working, so he thought misdirection might. The press pen was also set up near the Rocket Ship ride six hundred feet south of the Republican tent.

Thomas grinned. He knew it was more important to stay in the tent than ever, and he saw Rose and Tracey break into a fight as they were positioning themselves.

"Stick close to me," he told Tiffany. She was frozen. He grabbed her shoulder and directed her until they were standing in front of one of the white plastic tables. No one said anything to Thomas about this new girl.

Throngs of people pressed against the tent and radiated outwards for one hundred fifty feet. The sea parted amidst loud chirping and yelling. *Whoop whoop.* The convoy was here and Secret Service members physically pushed people out of the way of the SUVs.

Two large green clad SWAT members walked into the tent.

"Everyone back!" the first man yelled. "Everyone behind the tables!" Thomas and Tiffany remained standing in front of the table, blocking the view of Rose Piper. She was furious.

The commotion got louder, and this time several suited men in their thirties who scowled and kept their hands up in a ready position barged into the tent, pushing people against the tables. "Get back, get back!" they yelled.

Dan Kavanagh stood at the tent entrance. He held up the giant golden brick to get the attention of the candidate. He waved the large piece of wood above his head and shouted. Agent Harper saw a threat out of the corner of his right eye and reacted. He grabbed Dan in between the upper arm and shoulder and pivoted his body. Dan went flying to the ground. The agent looked like a judo champion in a suit. It had been pure instinct from training.

"Ooouuufff," Kavanagh gasped as he landed in the grass

Mark Munroe intervened. "That's our Director of the Board of Elections!"

The agent let go of Dan. "Sir, please keep all objects on the ground," he said. The agent did not wait for a reply and walked forward into the tent. He joined his comrades shouting. "Stay back!"

On the left side of the tent, an African-American agent shouted a similar message. He walked up to Tiffany and Thomas and made a human barrier with several other agents. Someone reached their hand around Thomas and held out a pen. The agent grabbed it, replaced the cap over the writing end and placed it forcefully in the same extended hand. "Stay back!"

Thomas squeezed Tiffany's shoulder. "Use your phone," Thomas said. Her mouth was open and she was motionless. "Take pictures," he said.

Behind Thomas, Rose tried to push her way around the table. A man in a suit blocked her way. She tugged at the man's shirt. He swatted away the arm that he felt. She tugged again and spoke, but it was too noisy for the man to hear. Rose pulled at the man's suit coat with all her might.

"Ma'am, stop doing that," the Secret Service agent said. He turned and saw the short old woman.

"Get off the table!" said the African American agent. Caleb had climbed on top of the white plastic table to get a better view. "Get down right now!"

"Hi folks, what lovely people you all are." Trump was in the tent. Everyone including the agents stopped talking and yelling. "I want to thank you for such a warm welcome. I know everyone here is working hard on the campaign and I wanted to thank everyone of you." Trump said.

Someone shouted, "We are going to win Ohio!"

"There is so much support here, so much," Trump said. He walked over to Don Manning and allowed Nicole to take a picture with him and the state house candidate. The local candidates were positioned toward the front of the tent so that Trump could meet them.

Thomas saw silver hair. "This is the Indiana corner!" he yelled.

Governor Pence looked to the back of the tent and walked up behind the secret service agent. He shook Tiffany's hand. "This is where the election will be won. We are at ground zero!" Thomas said. Later that day, several producers used this phrase to frame their respective news reports on the Trump visit to Northeast Ohio.

Randy passed up a picture and Trump signed it before passing it back over the agent's head. They were not relaxing at all, yet the mood in the tent went from anxious to calm.

London, UK

Manuel Garcia walked through the glass hallway high in the skyscraper that towered over London. He had worked his way up the corporate ladder in investment banking after studying at Oxford and IESE Business School. Now at the director level, he was working late once again.

He turned right and walked through the door of the break room to get a cup of coffee. "This is live coverage of US Presidential Candidate Donald Trump's visit to the key state of Ohio at a local fair," said a talking head. The BBC anchor had a smooth voice, and she was in a small box on the right side of the screen while the live coverage of Trump at the Canfield fair was in the larger left box. There was chaos inside the tent, and someone shouted, "This is ground zero!

No, it can't be...

"Was... was that Thomas?!"

Canfield Fair MCRP Tent

Trump exited the tent followed by Pence. Secret Service and SWAT members left after them. The tide retreated and left a momentary emptiness in the tent. Then chaos erupted again.

Lindsay McCoy stomped into the tent and found Dan Kavanagh. "I was promised an interview with Trump! Why did you tell me to go down the street? You knew he wasn't going there!" she said. She made no attempt to lower her voice.

On the other side of the tent Rose was yelling. "I won't ever forget this. You were against Trump the entire campaign and I was his earliest supporter. I won't forget," she repeated. At the last second, Tracey had invited a few friends that slipped through the sidewall. They had met Trump and Rose had not.

Thomas thought it best not to mention he had done the same thing with Team Indiana. He looked down at his phone and thumbed a text to Chris Horvath. *Trump is going to win Mahoning County. Nearly 20% of Democrats crossed over in the primary and registered Republicans came out at a 60% higher rate than normal. The energy at the Canfield Fair is incredible. I just saw Trump.*

Chris texted back, *Well....*

"None of these guys want Trump to win!" Thomas said, to himself. He joined Lindsay and Rose with a fury of his own.

Secret Service Convoy

Thomas walked into the heat of the day and among the Presidential Candidate convoy that was parked amidst the massive crowds.

"Hey, Tommy!"

Thomas looked and saw Joe the retired cop behind the wheel of one of the black SUVs, one car behind the SUV that carried the counter-assault team.

"What are you doing?" Thomas asked.

"They're using me as bait," Joe said. He explained that the Secret Service told him to take the corners wide, "so that if a terrorist attacks they shoot my car!" He grinned. "I have the golden brick," he added. "I'll bring it back to the plane and see if we can have it signed there," Joe said.

"Hey Thomas, come back here," another voice said.

Thomas looked and Brenda Johnson was driving the next black SUV behind Joe.

How did I miss out on this gig? he thought.

CHAPTER 28

Tuesday, 6 September 2016, 63 Days
Davis Motel

Thomas woke up and looked at his phone. Tracey Winbush had friended him on Facebook last night. He stood out of bed and looked at his phone again. He decided to make the call. Maybe he could buy a farm in the area after the election.

St Charles

Deacon Dan sat in his office. A few more copies to make, and he would be completely prepared for the next RCIA class.

Ring

"Hello," he said.

"Hi, this is Thomas. I am brand new to the area and I want to join the RCIA class. I heard you two weeks ago saying that anyone interested should call you."

"Well, I did ask people to call the office by last Sunday," Dan said. The Deacon didn't want to have to make another booklet with all the inserts.

"I was travelling last week, but that should be it for the year," Thomas said.

The Deacon put him on the register. "Our first class is September 18th in the Luke room at 10:00 am."

- THOMAS RYAN -

Wednesday, 7 September 2016, 62 Days
Board of Elections

Thomas turned up a steep hill and pulled into the parking lot of the old Oak Hill Hospital. He walked through the large automatic doors and down a hallway, following the signs to the Mahoning County Board of Elections.

At one of the counters, he recognized Maggie Kavanagh and another young kid, although he couldn't remember his name.

I know half the people in here, thought Thomas. Dan Kavanagh had hired half the workers, which was made up of an equal number of Republicans and Democrats, selected by the Director and Deputy Director of the Board of Elections. "I would like to buy a large precinct map," Thomas told a woman whom he did not know.

"You need to talk to Mike, our IT guy. He does all the maps," she said. The woman pointed down the hall. "Walk down the hall and to the right and you'll see his office."

Thomas did as she instructed and walked to the office. The door was closed and the blinds were shut. He knocked.

"Come in," said Mike. After listening to Thomas' request he told him to come back after the map was printed. "I'll send you an email."

"Sounds great, thank you," Thomas said. He left the office and turned to leave when a lanky African-American man saw him.

"Thomas! What are you doing here?" Randy Taylor asked. Thomas told him about his map idea. "Let me give you the tour," Randy said. Randy took Thomas to every office but the Deputy Director's, and introduced him to the entire staff.

"Thank you for the tour, I really appreciate it. I'd better let you get back to work," Thomas said.

Randy laughed loudly. Thomas left the building.

Five hours later, Mike sent him an email notifying him that the map was ready. He walked directly to Mike's office.

"This thing is huge!" Thomas said. He grinned. Mike explained the precinct system and went into detail on the number of voters in each precinct, and how Mahoning County typically voted. "Mitt Romney received zero votes in 2012 in these three precincts," Mike said. He pointed to the middle of the map.

Mike took the map and rolled it up tightly, and put two rubber bands on the map, one on each end.

Knock knock

Maggie Kavanagh knocked on the closed door to Mike's office and opened the door to see the two men discussing the map. "That will be two dollars," she said.

"Oh, of course," Thomas reached into his pocket and pulled out his wallet. He gave Grandmother Kavanagh two one-dollar bills. "Thank you both for your help."

MCRP HQ

"How much did you pay for that thing?" Mark asked Thomas. The chair saw Thomas walk in with a rolled up map and head straight to the conference room where the outsider flattened it on the table and prepared to mount it on the wall.

"Two dollars."

"I think you overpaid," Mark said. He walked away.

What was that about? Thomas thought.

Caleb walked into the conference room and helped Thomas mount it to the wall. Thomas drew with thick black and green markers the boundaries of the US congressional district and the 59th state house race.

A few minutes later, Chelsea walked into the conference room. "I heard that Yale bid on the gun at the auction," she said.

Thomas and Caleb laughed.

Thursday, 8 September 2016, 61 Days
MCRP HQ

Thomas needed a way to bring in income since the RNC job didn't work out the way he had hoped. He typed in *youngstown.craigslist.com* and clicked through the tutoring jobs.

- THOMAS RYAN -

Football tutor: $60 / hour
Math tutor: $10 / hour

He closed and opened his eyes slowly and breathed deeply. He walked to the back room and saw Chelsea sitting in a chair. She held a cigarette in one hand and read her phone in the other. The pile of junk gave her some amount of privacy.

Thomas got an idea. He waded through the enormous heaps of political materials and other supplies and found what he was looking for. There were several floodlights with stands and extension cords, and large white boards that Joe was using for his oversize **Ground Zero** signs. All he needed was duct tape.

Target

Thomas walked into Target and headed for the home improvement aisle. He grabbed five rolls of duct tape and brought them to the check out.

"Would you like to save 5% on your purchase today by opening a Target credit card?" the cashier asked the woman in front of Thomas. The woman answered negatively, and grabbed her bags after the cashier printed the receipt.

The cashier looked up and saw a man intently staring past her. She pulled her head back slightly and then lowered it, scanning the duct tape rolls. Thomas put money on the counter, grabbed the plastic bags and walked out. *I am way too intense right now,* he thought. He noticed the cashier did not give the corporate mandated spiel to him. He felt enormous amounts of energy.

MCRP HQ

Wonder Boy brought in a map, Chelsea texted Dan Kavanagh

I know, Kavanagh responded. Mike had mentioned something to him.

Thirty minutes later, Dan Kavanagh stopped by headquarters. Chelsea and Dan walked in the conference room to see the large map taped to the wall with black and green markings drawn to show different political office boundary lines. "That son of a bitch," Kavanagh said. Chelsea laughed.

CHAPTER 29

Friday, 9 September 2016, 60 Days
Board of Elections, Mahoning County

Dan Kavanagh walked into Mike's office. "Can you print me some primary maps with voter data?"

Mike got excited. The deputy director mostly left him alone in his dark cave. He explained in detail what he could do.

"Yeah, give me four of them," Dan said.

An hour later he took the maps out to his old black SUV.

MCRP HQ

Dan Kavanagh put the four maps in a grid pattern to the left of the giant Mahoning County precinct map.

Mark walked in at 11:00 am and saw four new maps in the conference room, in addition to the large one that Thomas had mounted yesterday. The chair turned on his heel and walked out through the main room and out the front door. He got in his car and left the parking lot.

At 12:30 pm he returned with two official Mahoning County maps that he had purchased at Barnes & Noble. Thomas was sitting at one of the white tables working on his computer.

"Here are some much better maps." Mark said. He tossed the official county maps near Thomas and Caleb. "Billy and Joe will be arriving in an hour with several thousand Trump signs from Stark County. We will need a lot of help assembling them."

Mark walked into the chair's office and called several volunteers.

Over the next hour twenty people arrived at headquarters to help unload and prepare the Trump signs that were en route.

A half hour later a white pickup truck pulled into the parking lot, and the volunteers did exactly what they were supposed to do. Mark walked around the room and laughed and joked with people. "Hey Thomas," he said, "No fake work today!"

Conference Room MCRP HQ

At around 5:00 pm, Matt Harris arrived at headquarters carrying a black poster that had embarrassing Trump quotes written in white text. The quotes were out of context utterings that Trump had said throughout his career. Matt Harris leaned around a chair to put the poster on the wall next to the maps.

Jason Lovett walked into headquarters at that moment to prepare for a meeting later that evening, and he saw the back conference light turned on. "What are you doing?" Jason asked. Matt ignored the RNC Victory Campaign field director and pressed the poster flat against the wall. Jason walked up to the poster. "You can't post that here," he said.

Matt Harris blocked him with his body. "Back off Jason, this isn't your building."

"You can't put up a poster at headquarters that mocks the Presidential Candidate," Jason said.

"Get out of my way," Matt said. He walked past Jason and pushed him.

"Don't touch me," said Jason.

Matt and Jason began yelling.

Matt texted Dan Kavanagh.

A fight is about to go down at headquarters between Jason Lovett and me.

Dan Kavanagh looked at his phone and thought for a second.

He called Mark first. "Matt Harris and Jason Lovett have gotten in a fist fight. Something is going on at headquarters," Dan said. Mark was the senior board member sitting on the Board of Elections in addition to being the MCRP chair.

Kavanagh hung up the phone and called Tracey, the other Republican board member on the Board of Elections, and told her the same thing. This made Matt Harris, the financial director at the Board of Elections, look immature and less of a threat to Dan Kavanagh's Deputy Director position.

South Range Football Away Game – Akron

Thomas walked to the brand-new stadium in Akron and walked up and down the visiting side of the field. He didn't see anyone he knew.

The stadium cost at least $10 million dollars, with full grandstands, a press box, large concession facilities, and locker rooms under the stadium. The high school was new too.

This is all from the 2009 stimulus package, he guessed. The local school boards had used part of Ohio's share of the $900 billion Obama and Pelosi stimulus package as collateral to issue bonds that funded world-class athletic facilities first, and new high schools second. At least this is how it appeared to Thomas.

At the end of the third quarter South Range was winning, and Thomas noticed the team had improved their teamwork. He sent an email to Michael Glassner and Chris Horvath about the possibility of adding an additional 20,000 votes in Northeast Ohio and Northwest Pennsylvania by adding a union bug to the walking lit targeted at crossover voters. Union members often refused to vote for a candidate whose lit did not have a small printer's union insignia, colloquially called a bug, on the card.

Saturday, 10 September 2016, 59 Days
Davis Motel

Thomas stared at the ceiling first. He felt unable to move for a moment, and then he rolled over on his side and faced the wood paneling about eighteen inches away from his face. He was sore. He was tired.

For over fifty days, he had worked without a single day off. His short naps in the middle of some days were helping somewhat, but he felt the wear and tear on his body.

MCRP HQ

A copy of the *Vindicator* lay on the front desk. "Brenda Johnson chosen as Presidential Delegate," declared the title below the fold.

"Do you mean like one of the voters of the President in the Electoral College?" Joe asked, "Like what we learned about in fourth grade? Brenda is one of those?"

Brenda Johnson walked in at that exact moment. She held her head high and looked much taller than her five-foot frame. Thomas walked over to her and showed her a comparison of the Trump lit versus one of the local judges. The judge's business card had a union bug on the card, while the Trump lit did not. "I think Trump could pick up another 20,000 votes in the region from crossover Democrats if he reprints this lit with the union bug."

"That's a great idea," Brenda said.

Karen interrupted the conversation and pointed at Brenda. "She is going to put Trump in the White House and Hillary in prison," she said.

Not quite, Thomas thought. No one was walking today. Chelsea wasn't in her office.

Apartments in South Youngstown

"Put these addresses in your RNC database and give random answers on the doors." Jason answered. The Victory campaign field director and field organizer stood outside a set of apartments on the south side of Youngstown. "Remember, you need one hundred fifty-two," he said. Jason winked. One hundred fifty-two doors seemed to be the magic number that did not raise any suspicion.

Chelsea started thumb typing the addresses on her RNC Advantage app. *Supporting Trump and Portman, Not home, Supporting Trump, Supporting Hillary.* Jason Lovett got in his car and drove away.

MCRP HQ

Thomas gathered the trash bag from the kitchen, the women's restroom, the men's restroom, the back room, the conference room, the chair's office, and from the front desk. He lugged the bags out to the dumpster. No one else had been willing to take out the trash, and headquarters had been a disgusting mess until he took control.

Mark Munroe saw Thomas at the dumpster when he pulled up in his Ford. He followed Thomas into headquarters. "OK, folks, everybody out today. Folks, you have all worked too hard and it is time to take a break."

Thomas looked at his watch. *2:08 pm.* He left without questioning Mark and drove south toward Columbiana, where there was a street fair in this northernmost Appalachian city.

Columbiana Street Fair

A woman's hands danced over the strings of a harp. Notes reached the microphone that was connected to a PA system. Harp music flowed over the plaza. Thomas looked to his right and saw two women sitting at harps, one woman playing the violin, one woman playing some sort of flute-like instrument that wasn't a flute, and another woman playing some octagonal type accordion. The harps went silent for a moment while the violin, accordion, and flute picked up the tempo, approaching a foot-stomping beat. The music slowed again and spread a calm, feminine ambience to the pedestrians walking about the fair.

Thomas walked into a large tent where most of the vendors were packing their things, and doing so quickly. "What is going on?" he asked a heavyset woman at a soap table. "There are big storms coming," she said. As she spoke a flap of the tent lifted with a gust of wind.

Thomas walked outside of the tent and looked skyward. The sky was purple and gray, churning in anger. He pulled up a weather map on his phone.

RUN!

He ran. He looked back and saw the sheets of rain advancing down the street like the unstoppable Prussian Army of the eighteenth century.

The storm moved toward him at forty miles per hour. He didn't make it to shelter, and rain poured on him as he reached his car.

MCRP HQ

Brenda Johnson stayed in headquarters even after Mark suggested everyone leave. She was making calls for volunteers and VIPs for the upcoming Trump Canton event that would take place Wednesday.

Ding-a-ling

Jason Lovett burst through the main door and walked to the conference room where he and Matt Harris had nearly come to blows the previous night. "Get out, this is my conference room," he told Brenda.

"Who are you?" Brenda said. She knew exactly who Jason Lovett was, but she was sending a signal that he did not know who she was.

"I am the regional director and I need to use the conference room," Jason responded.

"I am using the room now, I'll be done in a while." Brenda said.

"You need to leave right now," Jason said as he stepped into Brenda's personal space.

Brenda walked out of the room with her phone up to her ear. She called Justin Clarke, the Director of the Victory Campaign to complain about Jason Lovett. Within minutes Tony Russo called Jason Lovett to tell him to lay low. Jason walked out of headquarters with his head slumped low, and Brenda walked back into headquarters to resume her calls.

Sunday, 11 September 2016, 58 Days
MCRP HQ

Ding-a-ling

Thomas walked into headquarters following another megachurch Catholic experience at St. Charles. The news ripping across Twitter said that Hillary was suffering an unknown ailment. He didn't wish anyone ill, but the optics were terrible for the Democrats. People think of their President as a protector before anything else, and a protector does not faint on the street.

"Did you hear about last Friday night at headquarters?" Dan Kavanagh walked out from the kitchen holding a can. He answered his own question. "Matt Harris and Jason Lovett got into a fight."

"What?" Thomas asked. "What about?"

"Some poster thing. Matt texted me and I called Mark and Tracey. Jason is lucky that Mark arrived first or I would have joined Matt and beat Jason to a pulp," Kavanagh said.

Thomas wondered why Dan had called both Mark and Tracey. He should have wondered why Dan was telling him, too.

"Anyway, I'm just leaving. We are driving down to Marietta today to see my son at college," Dan said.

"Can you let me know how many Trump signs you see?" Thomas asked.

CHAPTER 30

Monday, 12 September 2016, 57 Days
Davis Motel

Thomas' old roommate from Boston knocked on his motel room door at 7:00 am. Thomas pulled on his pants, trying to make the early morning deadline that Court had set last night.

"What are you doing in there?" Court called through the door. Thomas opened the door and they walked around to the other side of the motel where Court had parked his white SUV when he and the two girls arrived late last night.

"Let's get a coffee first, we can go to Dunkin' Donuts," Thomas said.

They drove to Dunkin' Donuts, missed Rose by minutes, and headed north on Market Street to the Board of Elections. Thomas wanted to introduce Court to Dan Kavanagh.

Board of Elections, Mahoning County

Dan Kavanagh and Matt Harris were in the back of the Board of Elections offices, standing in Matt's office where he did his work as Financial Director.

"I wanted to introduce you to Court. He is a friend from the old days and he wanted to see ground zero for himself," Thomas said.

Matt and Dan looked Court up and down. Court wore fashionable business casual clothes and had enormous forearms. He had the charm of a salesman. Court and Matt talked about one RNC race they had both been involved in two years earlier.

Dan invited Court to see his office and the crew walked to the larger executive suite. "Is that where you get your votes here in Youngstown?" Thomas asked. He pointed out the large windows and to the cemetery on the hill. Everyone laughed.

Thomas and Court left to see the Trump Wall at headquarters.

Dan Kavanagh and Matt Harris looked at each other after the two men had left. Their eyes were wide.

MCRP HQ

At 10:00 am Thomas, Court, Chanel, and Channing walked through the front door of headquarters. Thomas wore his normal jeans and button-up shirt. Court was one step dressier, and the women wore navy blue sheath dresses. Marq stared at Thomas first, then the girls, and then at Thomas again. The other volunteers were quiet.

"This is our wall," Thomas said. He gave each of the three guests a red brick to sign. The crew walked to the back room. "Here is where we make the signs, and everything else," Thomas said.

Brenda Johnson had been in the back room talking to Joe. Thomas walked up to her and introduced her to Court and the sisters. "How do you girls wear those shoes?" she asked. "You two are gorgeous," Brenda said.

Tracey Winbush showed up at headquarters, and looked at Thomas quizzically. *What was he up to now?* She talked with Chanel.

"You know, Thomas is an expert at policy papers," Chanel said. Tracey had explained her idea on making a policy paper for the inner city.

"Thomas!" Tracey called out. "You are an expert at writing policy papers?"

"Yes he is, he has written a lot of them," Chanel said. "He can send you an example," she added.

"I want to see one," Tracey said.

"Ok, I'll send you one then," Thomas said.

"You are always hiding things!" Tracey said. She felt like her idea might now become a reality.

Conference Room

Chelsea hid in the conference room to avoid interacting with Thomas and the guests that looked as though they had stepped out of a fashion magazine.

Ring

"Hi Chelsea, this is Tony. Listen, you have done such a good job there in Mahoning County that Jonathan and I are giving you three additional counties," Tony Russo said. He said a few other words and hung up abruptly.

Chelsea opened her résumé and added the three counties to her area of responsibility.

Tuesday 13, September 2016, 56 Days
MCRP HQ

Ring

"Hi, Thomas? This is Susan from Bloomberg News. I am a producer and we are doing a story on the people around the Trump Wall in Youngstown. Do you have the number for Billy?" She said. Thomas gave the New York producer the contact information she requested.

He hung up the phone and felt a tapping on his arm. "Thomas, what do you want to do? I can help you get a job around here," Rose Piper said. She continued, "Tomorrow is my birthday. I have to go prepare for my party."

"Are you turning fifty-nine?" Thomas asked. He kept his face straight but his eyes sparkled.

"Haha, you trickster!" Rose said.

Rose walked away and talked with the volunteers standing around the front desk. "Thomas thought I was turning fifty-seven years old tomorrow!" she said. She laughed.

Brenda Johnson's House

Thomas arrived at Brenda Johnson's house in Boardman for a Trump volunteer party. A crew from the British channel ITV was interviewing Trump volunteers in the backyard, though they avoided talking with Thomas.

An older man took his guitar out of his case and strummed the chords to a folk song he had written himself, the ballad of a steel mill closing and how Trump would reverse the economic decline of the area.

A local candidate walked up to the picnic table and sat down by Thomas. "Take a look at my lit," he said.

Thomas took the postcard size paper in his hand. "Not bad," he said.

"The volunteers aren't carrying my lit," Larry said. He had an angry tone.

You need to be knocking on your own doors, Thomas thought. He said nothing.

"Say, do you think you could help me with my campaign strategy?" Larry said.

"Sure, I'd be happy to. One thing, I've heard that you own several rental properties and that you rent rooms, is that true?" Thomas asked.

"Yeah, I have over thirty units," Larry said. He was annoyed that Thomas changed the subject.

"I am looking for a place to stay because I'm in a hotel room right now."

"All my rooms are full," Larry said. "So when can we meet to work on my campaign?"

"I'm really busy," Thomas said. He turned away from the local candidate.

CHAPTER 31

Wednesday, 14 September 2016, 55 Days
MCRP HQ

Ring

"Hello, is this Thomas? This is Kamilah. You are on the VIP list for this evening. Be at the facility by 5:30 pm at the latest. There will be a VIP check-in table and someone will escort you to the seating area." Kamilah said.

Thomas responded with a few words and hung up the phone.

"Hey Thomas," Tracey said. She walked over to the white table where he was sitting. "Can I have an example of a policy paper? Chanel spilled the beans on you."

Thomas laughed. "Sure," he said. He opened up Word and pulled up a paper on the Eastern Mediterranean Sea Natural Gas Conflict. "This one was done for the State Department a few years ago," he said. Thomas copied the policy paper to an email and sent it to her.

Tracey opened the document. "Wow."

In the conference room Caleb received a call from Victoria, the deputy director for Millenials on the Ohio Trump Campaign.

"Hi, this is Caleb," he answered.

"Hi Caleb, this is Victoria. Would you like to meet the Presidential Candidate tonight?" she asked.

"Yes," Caleb said. His throat tightened.

"Now, don't tell anyone about this until after the fact, OK? Get to the Canton rally by 5:30 pm and find me. I will be on the floor so you will see me." Victoria said. "And make sure not to tell anyone." She said again.

"Ok, thank you so much," Caleb said. Victoria was off the line.

Caleb walked to the main room where Tracey and Thomas were talking. "Thomas, are you going to the rally tonight?" Caleb said. Thomas nodded. "Can you give me a ride?"

"Sure, that's not a problem. Let's leave here around 4:15 pm sharp," Thomas said. "I have VIP seats so I have to be early."

Caleb didn't respond. He nodded his head and walked away.

Davis Motel

Thomas arrived at his tiny room at around 3:00 pm. He opened the door and hit the air conditioner switch.

Nothing.

The lights did not turn on either. "OK," he said out loud. He propped the door open, and changed into his suit and dark blue tie and climbed back into his car.

Canton Trump Event

"Caleb, would you come with me please?" Victoria said. She had approached the two men and singled out the younger one.

"I have to go, Thomas," Caleb said.

"Go where? Aren't you coming to the VIP area?" Thomas asked.

"I'll find you later," Caleb said.

Thomas watched Victoria and Caleb walk into a hallway.

Caleb turned the corner and saw two Secret Service men standing at the ready. They nodded to Victoria. She and the high school senior walked past the first checkpoint. Victoria motioned Caleb to turn left down another hall and past another Secret Service agent, this one a woman. Victoria pushed a door open and Caleb followed her into a medium size room with five other high school students.

"Hey guys, thanks for all your work," Trump said. "It's really great the work you have done on the campaign." He motioned for Caleb to come up and stand next to him in front of the Trump campaign backdrop.

"What's your name?" the Candidate asked.

"I'm Caleb. We're going to win Mahoning County for you," he said.

Trump laughed and gave two thumbs up for the camera. "I know you guys are working really hard. It's so great."

Victoria motioned for a young woman from Canton to step forward.

Caleb texted Thomas

I just met Trump!

Thomas texted back.

That's amazing! Good for you!

Caleb was good at keeping secrets. Thomas realized that he had been the chauffeur for the evening, not the star. He grinned.

He turned and introduced himself to the short matron standing next to him. "Hi, my name is Thomas Ryan. I'm from Indiana helping out on the Trump campaign in Youngstown." They were both standing on the stage behind the podium where Trump would give his speech.

"Hi, I am Mrs. Timken," the woman said. She was the heir to the Timken fortune and a major financial backer of the Republican Party. She was also the reason why there was a civil war brewing within the Ohio Republican Party – she was only supporting candidates who themselves supported Trump. *Why don't I recognize this man?*

Thirty minutes later the rally started as the earlier ones had: loud music, an opening prayer, an introductory speaker, and then the Candidate. Trump was improving his speech, Thomas noted.

Those in the packed hall shouted "Trump, Trump, Trump!" Thomas instinctively reached into his front pocket and grabbed earplugs he always carried with him. The press was already publishing first reports of a half-empty and lackluster showing.

Thursday, 15 September 2016, 54 Days
MCRP HQ Back Room

"Did you stay in Canton and get anything to eat while you were there?" Marq asked.

"I figured the half-life of parking my car in Canton was about two hours before it was up on blocks," Thomas said.

"What do you mean?" Marq asked. He spoke in a slow Southern Ohio drawl.

"When Caleb and I drove to the rally last night I was nervous about finding a place to park…" Thomas said. He stopped his joke. Marq was staring at him. Thomas got a black look on his face as he realized something was wrong.

"Why?" Marq asked. "That was my hometown for nineteen years."

The food probably was excellent in Canton, but the city was not, in fact, a nice place though it had been at one time, Thomas thought. He turned away and walked out of the room, down the hall, and to the main room of headquarters.

MCRP HQ

Thomas loaded up Tracey's policy paper on Microsoft Word and began typing. He had been working on it for an hour when someone tapped him on his shoulder.

"Thomas, could you take a look at my lit piece?" Larry said.

"Sure," Thomas said. He took the piece and gave it a once over. "It looks great," he said and handed it back.

Larry was a bit annoyed. He walked away.

Bzzzzz

Thomas looked down and saw that Tracey was texting him about the memo. He responded.

I will send you a draft tomorrow night.

Friday, 16 September 2016, 53 Days
MCRP HQ

Marq and Karen were running the front desk again today, and Karen could not contain her excitement. "I heard that Trump might be back in Youngstown on October 3rd," she said. Two days earlier Marq and Karen had been volunteers for the Canton event. Karen returned to her normal small talk. "Hillary is such a criminal, when are they going to lock her up?" she asked.

Another volunteer rejoined the conversation, "Obama and the Muslim Brotherhood are protecting her," she said.

Obama doesn't like Hillary, Thomas thought. *Isn't this obvious to anyone else?*

Victory Campaign, Columbus, Ohio

Chris Horvath answered his phone.

"We are thinking of having Trump come two more times to Youngstown, once on October 3rd, and then again on October 20th," a feminine voice said. She was calling from New York.

"I'll have Kamilah get started on the arrangements," Chris said. He hung up the phone and sat at the plastic table that he used as a desk. He began playing solitaire on the computer.

MCRP HQ

"Thomas, how many signs do we have?" Brenda Johnson asked. She had walked up to him while he was concentrating on Tracey's memo.

Thomas stood up at attention to face her. "There are 280 completed signs left, and an additional 1000 signs without wires," Thomas reported. "We were shorted 1000 wires by Stark County the other day," he said.

"Oh, we can't run out of signs, that will look terrible," Brenda said. "What are you doing on your computer?" she asked.

"This is a policy memo that I am working on with Tracey. It addresses inner city issues and the minority vote," Thomas said. He turned his laptop around and showed her.

Brenda was not happy. "Tracey needs to be walking and holding signs instead of taking credit for everything," Brenda said.

Thomas closed the laptop and asked Brenda to follow him to the small storage room across the hall from the women's bathroom. Once there he pointed at the boxes of signs. "We do have enough signs for two weeks or so, if we can get the wires. I tried stealing the Rob Portman wires out of his signs, but they are a non-standard size," Thomas said. Rob Portman was a clever politician, even if the voters in the area disliked him. He had ordered signs slightly wider than every other candidate to make it impossible to remove the wires and to put them in signs that were in demand.

Thomas and Brenda walked to the main room. Brenda left and Thomas returned to his memo.

Ding-a-ling

A well-dress woman in her fifties walked into headquarters. Thomas hopped out of his seat to meet her.

"My name is Thomas, how can I help you?" he said.

"My name is Wendy, I am on the Ohio Supreme Court," she said.

"Oh, I am actually from Indiana and helping out on the Trump campaign, I apologize for not recognizing you," Thomas said.

Wendy was pleasant and she and Thomas began talking about the presidential race. "Trump is going to win, because he will win Ohio and Michigan," Thomas said. "Some people know that he will win Ohio, but nobody realizes that he will win Michigan. It makes sense, since in Southeast Michigan retired union auto workers make up the population – like my cousins and uncles," Thomas said.

"Interesting," said the judge.

Mark Munroe appeared. He had received Thomas' text ten minutes earlier that a justice was in the building. Thomas returned to his computer.

Ding-a-ling

Chelsea walked into the headquarters carrying a Stone Fruit Frappuccino. "Jason is here," she said to Thomas. Thomas looked up for a second and then down at his policy paper.

Ding-a-ling

Jason Lovett burst through the headquarters door and made a beeline to the conference room. He slammed the glass door shut. Thomas did not look up from his work.

After twenty minutes Thomas thought he would be more productive at Kinkos and packed up his things to leave. He grabbed two

Vetrans for Trump buttons from the display case, smiling at the misspelling. *Maybe these will be worth something one day.*

South Range Football Game

Thomas saw Jim Kavanagh watching the game next to the field and he walked down the hill to be with Jim. They talked football plays and Bible stories.

Halftime came and went, and Thomas walked to the visiting side of the field. Dan Kavanagh saw him. He waved Thomas to come into the forest where three men were drinking outside of the official stadium grounds.

"You have to stay here, Thomas," Umberto said. "This is a great place to live. It's a great place to raise a family."

Ben nodded. "It's not as fast-paced as the big city, but it's not bad."

Dan mentioned how much better the offensive line looked this game.

Thomas walked to the home side of the field and found Joe. "Alexis is around here somewhere," he said. She came running past as if someone called her name. She was fast.

The game was nearly over and Thomas pulled out his phone. He emailed Tracey a draft of the policy memo as the clock reached zero on the giant scoreboard.

Tracey texted him.

Whoa.

A few minutes after this she texted him again.

Do you want to join me at the pastor's meeting next week up in Cleveland? Trump is meeting local religious leaders and you can come with me.

CHAPTER 32

Saturday, 17 September 2016, 52 Days
Davis Motel

Thomas pressed Send and the latest version of the urban renewal policy memo arrived in Tracey's email one second later. He looked at his watch. It was 7:30 am and he was going to be late to the Katrina Pierson meeting downtown.

Church Downtown Youngstown

As it turned out, Thomas and Tracey arrived at the church at the same time, and the two of them beat everyone else. The state representative candidate for the 58th district hoping to represent Youngstown had not arrived. There was light rain.

"She's almost here! Corrine better get here soon," Tracey said. She was referring to Katrina Pearson, Trump's national spokesman and Corrine Sanderson, the state representative candidate. The entire point of the exercise this morning was to have Katrina Pearson give the kick-off speech for a group of Party volunteers to knock doors in the inner city for Corrine. Yet Corrine was not here.

Tracey and Thomas walked to the curb in front of the church. A large black SUV pulled up, and a short, slender Black woman exited the front passenger seat. Thomas thought that this was the state representative candidate and walked up to her holding an umbrella. The woman looked up at him and smiled while she ducked gratefully under his umbrella.

Thomas heard Tracey's voice the same instant he saw a large African-American man walking quickly around the back of the SUV. *SIG Sauer P226,* Thomas thought.

"Hi Ms. Pearson," Tracey started, "I am Tracey Winbush, the Vice Chair of the Mahoning Republican Party."

The Black man was Katrina's bodyguard. He had his own umbrella and Thomas backed away.

The minor celebrity and crew made their way inside the church where the Youngstown *Vindicator* Newspaper had set up a makeshift studio to interview Katrina.

"Go buy food for the volunteers," Jason Lovett ordered Thomas. The volunteer ignored the regional director.

Five minutes later Katrina Pearson took a picture with Thomas, and he told her the local response that he was finding at the doors for Trump.

YSU Football Game

Caleb and Thomas climbed the home grandstands at the YSU Penguins football stadium.

"Jim!" Thomas said. He saw Grandpa Kavanagh sitting in a box seat. "Is anyone sitting by you?"

"Take a seat," he said. Thomas introduced Jim and Caleb to each other. Jim explained to the two younger men the weaknesses of the YSU defense.

Thomas and Caleb walked in the concourse to buy chicken tenders. They saw Melanie and Christian. "Kayla's around here somewhere," Melanie said.

Thomas walked from the two Kavanaghs and straight into another one. Kayla talked to him for several minutes until he turned away to speak to another person he recognized. The Kavanagh daughter stayed by his side until Thomas and Caleb left.

Back at their seats Caleb and Thomas ate chicken tenders and nachos with cheese sauce.

"You know, Kayla lost her phone this morning. She was really upset about it. It was one of those new iPhones," Jim said.

Thomas texted Dan Kavanagh on what steps he might be able to take to locate the phone. *Where did she lose it?* he texted.

Western Reserve Road around NorthPoint Gas Station

Thomas was on the phone to a friend. "The campaign is crazy here in Ohio. You would not believe some of the things that have happened," he said. They started to talk strategy for after the election.

Honk honk

Thomas looked up and saw Melanie Kavanagh waving at him while driving her crossover vehicle. "Do you need a ride?" she shouted.

He waved her off and continued talking on the phone. She turned south.

Thomas turned around and moved a few feet more off the road and took methodical small steps in the grass.

Sunday, 18 September 2018, 51 Days
St Charles RCIA class

Thomas couldn't find the Luke Room at St. Charles. It was the first day of RCIA and he was wandering around the foyer and halls of the eight-thousand-member-Catholic church in Boardman. He saw a couple of people walking past him and tailed them.

Inside the Luke Room a man in his sixties stood at a podium, explaining the RCIA process to about twenty-five people sitting around tables arranged in a U shape. He wore a red and gray Ohio State football journey. Thomas and one other young man wore suits, while everyone else was dressed casually. Two leaders of the class, a husband and wife, wore flip-flops.

"Let's go around the room and introduce ourselves," Deacon Dan said. He started, and then asked the RCIA candidate sitting next to the podium to do the same. Ten minutes later Thomas pushed back his chair and stood.

"I have returned to the United States from living in Poland, and I knew I was at the right place when I recognized the Polish steeple," he said. Several people, including Deacon Bob, laughed. Deacon Dan directed his focus on Thomas. Thomas finished, "My name is Thomas Ryan, and I'm looking to come home." Several women clapped at the turn of the phrase, for they also viewed Catholicism as their spiritual home.

The last five people introduced themselves, and explained why they wanted to join the church. Deacon Dan welcomed everyone a second time.

"During this class, we will not discuss two things. We will not discuss the Real Presence of Christ in the Eucharist, and we will not discuss women priests," Deacon Dan said. "Everything else is open for discussion."

"Wait…." Thomas interrupted. "Isn't the Real Presence of the Eucharist the central theme of Catholicism?" Thomas asked. The class looked at him.

Deacon Dan walked over to Thomas and put his hands on Thomas' shoulders. Thomas understood this as a corporate training move to control an unruly student. "By the way, the dress code is casual here, so no need to worry about what you wear," the Deacon said.

Thomas vowed to himself to always wear a tie and coat.

The Deacon walked back to the podium and droned on about the topics the class would cover over the next school year.

Poland Library

Headquarters was closed, so Thomas drove to the Poland library. Caleb had told him a few weeks prior that it was a nice place to visit. He pulled into the parking lot and saw the flowing stream amongst the limestone rocks next to the library and parking lot.

The library itself was situated in the city center of Poland, Ohio, yet it had a feel like it was in the countryside. Someone had spent a lot of time planning and landscaping the building and grounds.

Thomas walked into the lower entrance accessed from the rear, and saw a modern coffee shop decorated with tile floors and wooden highlights on the walkout basement floor. Upstairs he saw wooden ships positioned throughout the library, and stone busts of philosophers lining the walls. He sat at a table and plugged in the power cord of his MacBook.

Reince Priebus Takes a Swipe at Republicans Not Supporting Trump

Thomas saw the headline of the RNC chair and realized that he was angling for a top job in the Trump administration should Trump win. *Trump is going to win.*

It was the oddest thing, Thomas felt someone staring at him. He looked up, and Tracey Winbush was staring directly at him from an oversize poster taped to the end of a bookshelf.

"Read more," said the quotation on the poster.

Monday, 19 September 2018, 50 Days
MCRP HQ

Thomas first met Ed while both were standing outside the headquarters' front door. Ed was smoking and Thomas had walked away from some annoying volunteers to get a breath of fresh air. Thomas saw a man who looked like the previous Canadian Prime Minister. Ed had an executive look about him, and was calm in demeanor. Thomas introduced himself.

"Are you an attorney?" Thomas asked. He figured this man was part of the Rob Portman campaign.

"Oh no, I'm just a volunteer. Sharon and I come on Mondays."

"Well, nice to meet you," Thomas said. He walked inside.

"Oh, I am going to be a widow!" said Sharon Kaufman. She was lamenting and walking around headquarters with her hands in the air.

"What's wrong with Ed?" Thomas asked. He put together that Ed and Sharon were married.

Brenda walked up to Thomas. "I am cancelling my vacation to Florida and going to the pastors' event in Cleveland on Wednesday," she said. "I can't believe that Tracey is going! Do you know what she did during the primaries?" Brenda asked. "She was the most obnoxious person – she was bullying the Trump supporters and she should lose her vice chair position." Brenda continued.

"I'll work for you, Brenda," Joe said. He was making Trump signs in the corner of the room.

"At least *someone* will work for me," Brenda said.

"What can I do to help?" Thomas asked, getting the hint.

"I need a database of Mahoning County Trump volunteers and their emails and phone numbers," she said.

"Let me see what I can do," Thomas said. He could easily make such a database and it would build him one more ally.

Ding-a-ling

Tracey walked into headquarters and saw Thomas talking to Brenda. Thomas walked over to the Vice Chair. "Do you have a ticket for me to the Cleveland event on Wednesday?" he asked.

"Well, there are no tickets to the 9:00 am roundtable event since it is so small. You would have to be at headquarters at 6:00 am for the drive to Cleveland." Tracey said.

Thomas recognized what the Dilbert creator Scott Adams called a "fake because" when he saw it. He realized that Tracey was backing down on the offer to take him to Cleveland. He did not show his disappointment. He walked back to Brenda.

"My husband might die!" Sharon moaned as she wandered over to Brenda and Thomas.

"What is wrong with Ed?" Thomas asked.

"He has food poisoning, but he won't let me bring him to the doctor. He's so stubborn. I don't want to be a widow!" she wailed.

"I just talked to him, I'm sure he'll be fine," Thomas said. This calmed Sharon and she returned to the front desk.

Ding-a-ling

A rough-looking man and his wife walked into headquarters to buy a couple of signs and a MAGA hat. Sharon convinced him to purchase a red brick as well. The man walked to the white plastic table where Thomas gave him a thick dark pen to sign the brick. The man brought up the topic of guns.

"My wife keeps my gun in her purse," he said.

"Isn't it dangerous around these parts to have your wife carry a gun?" Thomas asked. His voice was too loud.

Marq and Billy started laughing. "You know, Joe was really agitating Rose Piper the day before she shot Yale," Marq said. "It could have been him!" Thomas put the glue on the brick and the visitor stuck it on the wall. The visitor walked out of headquarters wondering what these guys were laughing about.

Tuesday, 20 September 2018, 49 Days

Vindicator Article

Corrine Sanderson, the Republican Candidate for the 58th State House Seat stated that she might not vote for Trump. In an interview with the Vindicator during Katrina Pierson's Visit to Youngstown Corrine Sanderson said she had questions about certain Trump policies....

"What the hell is this?" Brenda Johnson nearly shouted. She put down the local paper on the table and fumed. A representative from the national Trump campaign had come to Youngstown and specifically headed up a volunteer day for college kids and other volunteers to knock doors for Corrine, and Corrine had returned the favor by blasting Trump in the media.

Tracey walked into headquarters and past Thomas and Brenda. She headed to the chair's office in the back and shut the glass doors.

Brenda saw an opportunity. "Thomas, do you want to ride with me to Cleveland?" she asked.

"Yes," Thomas said.

"We are leaving very early, around 5:30 am or 6:00 am. I will text you the specifics," Brenda said.

Thomas worked on job applications for several hours, ignoring the chaos at headquarters.

Ding-a-ling

Dan Kavanagh and his two older daughters, Kayla and Katherine, walked into headquarters. Thomas walked up to Dan and began chatting. Katherine stayed close but Thomas avoided eye contact with her and focused his attention on Dan.

Dan walked to the kitchen to grab a beer and Thomas turned around and saw Kayla watching him from several feet away. He walked towards Kayla and she backed away as he approached her. *That's strange,* he thought.

"Stay right where you are," Thomas said. "Why are you backing away?" He could see Kayla physically shrinking from his presence.

"How is college going for you?" he asked. "How are your classes?"

"They're fine," she said. She stared at him.

"What are you studying again?" Thomas asked. He had asked her before but he couldn't remember.

"Biology," she said.

Dan Kavanagh walked into the main room and Thomas turned to talk to him.

CHAPTER 33

Wednesday, 21 September 2016, 48 Days
Church Parking Lot at 0530

There it is. Thomas saw the white bus in the parking lot next to a few cars. It looked like an airport shuttle bus. He wheeled his car into a parking space, turned off the engine, grabbed his phone and MacBook, and walked across the dark asphalt.

"Hi Tracey," he said. The vice chair stood next to the bus.

"It's way too early," she said. They both laughed.

Brenda Johnson stepped off the bus. "Up here Thomas," she said. She had saved a seat in the back of the bus. He followed her up the short stairway and to the back left side. The seats faced each other, and there were little tables that would come in useful if he wanted to use his computer.

One by one, a dozen pastors, male and female, Black and White, made their way up the stairs and took seats around the bus. Everyone could see everyone else.

"Good morning folks, this is your driver. Let me know if anyone needs to stop, but hopefully we will make the trip in under two hours," the driver said. He started up the engine. It sounded rough.

The driver turned right onto Meridian Street and Thomas realized that the shocks were shot. The rear of the bus jolted violently at each pothole.

"I would like to say a word of prayer," said a pastor. He was sitting in the front of the bus. Thomas had his eyes closed for sleep, not for prayer. The pastor spoke briefly.

"I have a word of prophecy from the Lord," another pastor said when the first pastor ended his prayer. He quoted from the book of Hezekiah from the Old Testament, something about God's wrath and burning fire.

Make it stop, Thomas thought. His own prayers were not answered.

"...and thus says the Lo-rd," said the pastor. He was finished.

There was a brief silence.

"The Lord has put a word on my heart," said another pastor. Thomas groaned and he heard a few others do the same.

Thomas turned to Brenda Johnson and said, "If they break out the snakes I am getting off the bus," he said. Brenda laughed.

Brenda changed the subject. "Can you help me with this list? I am trying to get a database of Trump supporters so that we can reach out to them for upcoming events," she said. Thomas opened his computer and connected it to the data signal from his phone. The Realtor and the analyst began to work, and the noise and jolting from the bus discouraged the pastors from praying anymore.

Cleveland

A man of about sixty leaned over to Thomas. "What church do you pastor?" he asked. The two men were sitting in the pastor's section at the front of the church. Brenda sat one seat to the right of Thomas, who sat one seat to the right of a Baptist minister from a small town in Northwest Ohio. Brenda had the idea to pretend that Thomas and she were ministers so that they could sit in the front. Thomas had readily agreed.

"Oh, I don't have a church right now," Thomas said. He introduced himself and then started in with the theology. "Have you ever thought about the story of Solomon and Bathsheba and motherhood?" he asked.

"Do you mean David and Bathsheba?" John asked.

"Well, most people know the story of David and Bathsheba, but not many have considered the implications of Bathsheba and Solomon," Thomas said. He went on to explain his hypothesis.

"Where did you study?" John asked. Thomas was making a convincing show that he was a pastor.

An African-American pastor of the Cleveland church walked up to the podium. "Good morning and welcome," he said. He started the morning's program.

An hour later, several of the pastors left their seats to approach Trump and lay hands on him. Thomas didn't dare push the charade that far. He was afraid he would be asked to pray.

"Let's go get a coffee," Brenda said. The two of them walked out of the church and relaxed at a coffee shop for an hour before returning to the building. Next up was a taping of Sean Hannity, Trump, and his supporters.

Another two hours went by, and Thomas and Brenda boarded the bus home. Thomas sent the policy memo that he had prepared for Tracey to several members of the senior Trump campaign staff.

Country Club, Youngstown

"Hey Caleb, look at that car," Thomas said. He pointed at a cherry-red Ferrari. "Here, take my picture," Thomas handed Caleb his phone and crouched by the car. Caleb took several shots.

Caleb and Thomas walked into the Youngstown Country Club, and to the ballroom with the large glass windows where the Treasurer candidate was having her fundraising dinner. Sonia saw the two and waved, and walked over to them.

"Caleb, you are sitting over there with Chelsea, and Thomas, your seat is right here," Sonia had her hands on a chair at a place that had "Thomas Ryan" written on a card in front of the water glass. "We are just about ready to get started, so I better take my seat," Sonia said. She walked away and sat by her husband.

"Please, would everyone stand for the singing of our national anthem," Mark Munroe addressed the donors.

A woman stood up at the podium and sang the national anthem. The crowd was much too small and it was awkward.

What is the minimum size where we must sing the national anthem before beginning any activities? Thomas texted Caleb.

Caleb looked back at Thomas, smirking and holding back a laugh.

Mark introduced Mrs. Ohio to the forty people following the song. She was a friend of the candidate, apparently.

CHAPTER 34

Thursday, 22 September 2016, 47 Days
Yankee Grill

Brenda Johnson sat with several of her friends for breakfast at a favorite diner on Market Street. "Hey Thomas, over here," she called when she saw him walk past the cash register. Thomas sat next to Brenda.

Thomas felt tired and he blinked purposely. He felt that he was having trouble following the conversations. He needed sleep.

The food helped. He noticed Brenda's phone start to buzz.

"Oh, I have to get to headquarters," she said. She seemed disoriented.

Thomas wolfed down the rest of his food and left money on the table, trying to catch up to Brenda in the parking lot.

The Guardian Newspaper Main Office, London, UK

Paul grinned and watched the hits on the Web come to his exposé on Brenda Johnson and the Mahoning County Republicans supporting Trump. He had timed the release of the piece perfectly. Just as Trump was gaining momentum from the Hillary health scare on September 11th, the *Guardian* story was going to bury him.

Twitter lit up.

His editor walked over to his desk. "Congratulations, Paul, you've gone viral."

MCRP HQ Conference Room

What is going on? Thomas watched Brenda Johnson frantically switch between thoughts. Her phone rang nonstop.

"What is the problem?" Thomas said. He turned to the Internet and saw several quotes from Brenda trending on Twitter.

> "If you're black and you haven't been successful in the last 50 years, it's your own fault. You've had every opportunity, it was given to you. You've had the same schools everybody else went to. You had benefits to go to college that white kids didn't have. You had all advantages and didn't take advantage of it. It's not our fault, certainly."

> "Growing up as a kid, there was no racism, believe me. We were just all kids going to school."

> "I don't think there was any racism until Obama got elected. We never had problems like this...Now, with the people with the guns, and shooting up neighborhoods, and not being responsible citizens, that's a big change, and I think that's the philosophy that Obama has perpetuated on America."

You have ruined us all! Brenda received an angry text from a Trump campaign member. Thomas saw it pop up on her phone.

"I have to explain myself to the press," Brenda said.

Thomas felt a nervous energy as he realized the enormity of the problem.

MCRP HQ

Peter Milano of WKBN arrived to headquarters first. He and his cameraman had jogged out of their own studio and then risked angering the Youngstown and Boardman police to drive down Market Street from the broadcast center to the MCRP in ten minutes.

Thomas met them at the door. "Hi, my name is Thomas," he said.

"What is your last name?" Peter asked. He was aggressive.

"Thomas will be fine," Thomas said.
"Who are you?" Peter asked next.
"I am a volunteer," Thomas said.
"Yeah, right," the cameraman said.
Thomas felt aggressiveness and hostility from the two men.
"Where is Brenda Johnson?"
"Why don't you wait for her outside?" Thomas asked. Brenda was in the conference room on the phone.
"We have a right to be here," Peter said. He started to walk to the back of the room and Thomas stood in his way.
"You need to leave," Thomas said. Peter was surprised at the authoritative way Thomas spoke, and felt intimidated by the change in the volunteer's expression. This guy was dangerous.
The cameraman felt the change too, and he hoisted his camera on his shoulder and pressed record.
Thomas did not move and looked down at his phone.
"Where is Brenda Johnson?" Peter asked, but not politely. He raised his voice. If he could start an argument at the MCRP it would make for great newsreel footage.
Thomas continued to stand and look down. He typed on his phone.
Brenda Johnson opened the conference room and greeted Peter. "Do you mind if we do the interview outside?" She asked.

MCRP Parking Lot

Brenda, the reporter, and the cameraman walked into the middle of the parking lot outside headquarters. Thomas stayed next to Brenda and fielded dirty looks from the reporter.
"Do you mind if I watch the interview?" he asked the reporter.
"No, I don't care," Peter said.
"Listen, let me give you my contact information in case I can give you further information as the day progresses."
This guy changes his demeanor on a dime, Peter thought.
The interview started, and was streamed live to the local news station for their morning show. Brenda spoke about the *Guardian* article

while Thomas stood next to her, on camera, with his head down while he typed on his phone.

Flash – Youngstown Racism Meltdown –
To: Senior Trump Campaign Staff

Brenda Johnson needs to be pulled off the air immediately.

The interview was not going well at all, Thomas could tell. Reporters often were experts at their jobs, and like police officers, could trap a subject into saying what they wanted them to say. This was happening now.

Thomas sent a series of texts to the Ohio Trump campaign.

WMFJ was next to arrive in the headquarters parking lot.

Marq and Karen watched Thomas return from the parking lot into the main room, momentarily free of the press. He paced in front of the four Trump walls, talking aggressively to someone on the phone. They had never heard Thomas utter one angry word until now, and it scared them.

Trump Tower

Michael Glassner was already working to solve the problem. Thomas' email from Youngstown arrived first, followed by a notification from Twitter of a trending news story.

He picked up the phone.

Chris Horvath's Office

"Hi Michael, we have the chair of the Mahoning County Party on the line. Can we make it a conference call?" Chris said.

Chris Horvath would have been taken completely off guard by the call from the national campaign office, except that Mark Munroe called him and gave him five minutes of lead-time. Mark had received Thomas' texts and immediately called Chris Horvath.

Stone Fruit Coffee Shop

When the third set of reporters arrived at headquarters Thomas told Chelsea that they needed to leave the building. Chelsea suggested going to Stone Fruit. They managed to exit the parking lot while chaos continued to build.

At the coffee shop they set up their computers at a high circular table. "It doesn't matter what Brenda did or said, the *Guardian* article paints her as a racist," Thomas said. "Brenda is not a racist, and it's tragic what has happened to her. However, she needs to be replaced... who can replace her that would cancel the narrative the media is building?" He asked. He stood up and resumed pacing.

"Tracey," he said.

"Chelsea, can you call Tracey and ask if she would be willing to be the Trump County Chair to replace Brenda?" Thomas asked as if he was the one who had authority.

Chelsea dialed. "Tracey, I'm sitting here with Thomas and we want to know if you would be willing to take over the chair position?" Chelsea asked. She nodded to Thomas.

He sent off several more texts to the leadership of the Ohio and National campaign.

"It is crazy, we left headquarters...what's that...OK, goodbye," Chelsea said. Tracey said she was getting another call.

"Tracey said that she would be willing to replace Brenda, and that she was getting a call from the campaign so she had to hang up on me," Chelsea said.

Thomas felt a surge of energy; adrenaline was countering his sleep deprivation. He paced again while texting the fifty local, national, and international reporters he had met over the past months.

Flash Message

Brenda Johnson is no longer with the Trump Campaign. Tracey Winbush will replace her as Mahoning County Chair for the Trump Campaign. You can confirm with the Ohio Trump Campaign Manager Chris Horvath. Please do not use my name as your source.

Chris Horvath's Office

Chris's phone rang. "What? There is no decision yet," he told the first reporter to phone him. He thought again and changed his answer, "Well, obviously, we will be replacing Brenda, but there is no decision yet on who is replacing her."

Several reporters claimed that they had an inside source and that they knew it was Tracey. "Who is your source?!" Chris asked. The thirtieth reporter to call his personal cell phone told him. Chris was furious. Thomas Ryan had forced the campaign's hand and would make him look weak and indecisive unless he put Tracey as the county chair. There was no going back.

Chris called Thomas. "Stop talking to reporters!" Chris said.

"I don't talk to reporters," Thomas said.

"I just had a reporter tell me that you told him that Brenda Johnson is fired and Tracey Winbush is the new Trump County chair!" Chris said. He was yelling.

Thomas was silent.

"Listen Chris, I am a volunteer. I walk doors, and if a reporter walks into headquarters I give them your contact information so they can reach out to the campaign."

"I told you not to talk to reporters!" Chris screamed.

"I don't talk to reporters," Thomas said.

Chris ended the call and threw his phone on the floor.

Standing in a Stone Fruit coffee shop on the other side of the state, Thomas controlled his breathing. *Chris doesn't realize that I made him look like a genius.*

CNN Headquarters, Atlanta, GA

"Yeah, cancel the trip," the VP of political reporting said. He was speaking to his best producer. Mary was in the process of arranging a flight to Pittsburgh for her political reporter. The VP of political reporting continued, "The Trump campaign already replaced Brenda Johnson with an African-American woman. They were fast, you gotta hand it to them."

MCRP Parking Lot

By noon the national and international press stopped calling headquarters. Why cover a story that made the Trump campaign team look competent?

In contrast, local press stayed at headquarters until they completed their live 5:00 pm and 6:00 pm broadcasts. The Youngstown *Vindicator* was there at headquarters too, interviewing as many volunteers as would speak into a microphone, hoping for outright racist comments. *The Warren Tribune Chronicle* took the national press' lead and left the property.

Thomas watched the circus and walked away from any reporter who approached him. His phone shut down from overheating.

MCRP HQ

At 6:20 pm the last reporter left the headquarters parking lot. Mark Munroe walked inside and over to Thomas, who sat at his computer. Mark put his hands on Thomas' shoulders. "Thomas," he said. He sounded like a father. "You were really on top of things today."

The damage from the Brenda Johnson story was contained to Mahoning County. They would suffer a vote count loss, as the *Vindicator* was sure to pound the racist narrative for the next six weeks. However, national media calculated that to cover this story would be to announce to the public that the Trump team could handle a crisis.

Thomas had prevented a catastrophic political contagion from spreading outside of Mahoning County. He had also won Mark Munroe's approval. He knew which one of these things was the more important, but his feelings betrayed his thoughts.

The Georgetown Italian Restaurant and Bar

Mark cut into a steak and brought the fork to his mouth. "What a day!" he said. Dan Kavanagh sat to his right and Tracey on his left. Matt Harris sat across the table.

"Trump is finished, isn't he?" Matt Harris asked.

"Oh no, I'm not sure if you saw what happened. Around noon the press stopped calling the headquarters. It looks like the Trump campaign handled a crisis extremely well," Mark said. "Don't you think so, our new Trump chair?" he asked Tracey.

"You said it Mark, what a day!" Tracey said.

Unusually, Dan Kavanagh had not touched his food. No one noticed, as they were busy eating their own dinners. The Georgetown had an excellent cook.

Kavanagh leaned back slightly while the other three were talking. He was staring past Matt, somewhere distant. Living in a house that his father-in-law owned was tough enough on his self-image. Eating in a restaurant that his brother-in-law managed wasn't always a pleasant experience. Now, he had to listen to a party chair who he couldn't control praise an outsider for saving the day. The party that he had served for thirty years was slipping away.

Dan appeared to have a full and rich life from the perspective of an outsider looking at him. In reality none of it was his. He should have been happy, but he felt something sinister. Today he should have joined in the celebration, but instead he felt like mourning. Thomas Ryan had quit the RNC job located somewhere else in one day and returned to Youngstown. Dan had been glad to see him go, though Dan had acted friendly toward the outsider during August. With Thomas Ryan in the area to act as a conduit with the national campaign, Trump might actually win the presidency.

The demons of envy and wrath wrapped their spindly arms through the voids in the soul of the Deputy Director of the Board of Election. He would come up with another plan to destroy Trump. He had a few helpers.

CHAPTER 35

Friday, 23 September 2016, 46 Days
Texas

Ted Cruz clicked a button on his mouse and switched windows from his Reddit account to the national news. "Where are the stories about racist Trump?" he asked.

Standing in a door, a young woman answered him, "I haven't seen any."

"That son of a bitch has good crisis management. This amateur hour stuff is all an act. They know what they are doing," Cruz said.

The news this morning did not cover much on Ohio and Mahoning County, with the exception of a couple of articles that mentioned Tracey Winbush as the new Trump County Coordinator. Since Brenda had been removed within hours and someone within the campaign had notified all the press, there were no stories about the seemingly racist interview, as this would only help Trump since his team had handled it so well. Ted Cruz recognized the situation.

"Dammit, this guy is good. He might win," Cruz said. He frowned and turned in his chair to stare out the window. He thought for a moment. "We have to endorse him today."

The slender woman walked away to her own desk and began preparing a press release.

Ted Cruz grabbed his Android phone. He sighed, resigned to

fate, and tweeted his endorsement of the Republican Presidential Candidate.

Italian Barber

A large, jolly Italian man put his hands through his customer's thick brown hair and massaged his scalp. Thomas closed his eyes and leaned back while the barber washed his hair. He was glad to be out of the headquarters building, and he was ecstatic Ted Cruz had just endorsed Trump. *Mark was not joking, I did save the day yesterday,* he thought. Sharon had done an excellent job of answering the angry phone calls and preventing a forced error. She remained very calm on the phone. Tracey had done her part by stepping into the Trump County Chair position to let the world see a Black woman at the helm. It was such a tragedy for Brenda Johnson. She was by far the smartest and hardest campaign worker Thomas had met, and she had been solidly for Trump since the beginning.

He thought back to the Republican picnic at the Shriners Club. Thomas remembered how he had tried to break up the interview, but the *Guardian* reporter had sensed this and kept walking away. Flattery and six hours worth of tape had been her undoing. They managed to splice together some quotes that did appear bad when taken out of context. In reality, most people in Mahoning County felt like Brenda did, and most people in the area were not bad people.

"You have great hair," the barber said. Thomas looked at himself in the mirror.

"I have a great barber," Thomas said. They laughed.

MCRP HQ

"This is unacceptable," the caller said.

"I know, I know, I agree with you," Dan Kavanagh said. "It's that new guy's fault, Thomas Ryan. He pushed for Tracey to replace Brenda." Kavanagh was fielding calls from Republican Party members who hated Tracey and were furious that she was the new Trump

Chair of Mahoning County. Kavanagh attempted to direct this fury at Thomas.

Chelsea walked into headquarters as Dan got off the phone. The two of them walked out the back of the building where they smoked together, as was their habit. "That bastard, Thomas," Kavanagh said. "Is he even a part of the campaign?" Dan asked.

"No," Chelsea answered. Chelsea wondered what Dan Kavanagh had in mind because she and Thomas had worked together yesterday morning to remove Brenda quickly and replace her with Tracey. It had been Thomas' idea, but Chelsea had made the phone call.

Kavanagh sensed Chelsea's hesitancy with his line of attack, so he tacked left. "I just don't trust him. We don't know anything about him," Dan said.

Spread Eagle Tavern, Columbiana

A few hours later, Dan met up with Ben and Umberto at a bar in Columbiana. There was a football game in Lisbon, farther to the south, and the three men had a tradition of drinking before they arrived to their son's football games, usually in the second quarter.

"That Thomas is a piece of shit," Kavanagh said.

Umberto's expression froze. Ben agreed with Dan. "Why do you say that?" Umberto said. He had talked with Thomas a few times at the previous games and found him charming.

"He is hitting on my daughter," Dan said. "He even friended Katherine on Facebook." Dan paused. He thought that this was the perfect setup: Katherine was beautiful and Thomas was older than her by some number of years. There was nothing creepier in modern America than a man appearing to be attracted to a younger woman. Bizarrely, an older woman sleeping with a young man was praised by society, while an older man who showed interest in a younger woman was considered mentally ill. It was like America in the last decade had moved to some sort of reverse patriarchy. Juvenal had written parallel stories in his *Satires* on Rome.

"I just realized...he was moving in on me to get access to my daughter. I saw it the other day when I was at headquarters," Dan said.

"What a bastard," Ben said. He liked Dan Kavanagh. Umberto said nothing.

Lisbon, Ohio

Thomas turned the wheel sharply right and then sharply left. He climbed out of the car and walked quickly up the hill. After a minute he realized he was walking the wrong way and turned down a side street. He caught a glimpse of football fans heading the other way and turned again, this time joining the latecomers for the South Range – Lisbon football game. He passed family after family, and groups of young people walking to their Friday night entertainment.

Once inside the stadium, he ran straight into Melanie Kavanagh standing next to the home grandstand with Christian.

"Thomas! Thanks so much for looking for Kayla's phone. I drove by you the other day and wondered if something had happened, if you needed a ride somewhere. It hit me as I was driving away that you were looking for her phone," she said.

"Well, I didn't find it," Thomas said. "I thought that she might be able to use the location services…I worked on these phones before while making a learning app." He pulled up an app on his phone. "A few other guys and I made this," he said.

"Oh wow, how many did you sell?"

"Only a handful, it wasn't successful commercially," Thomas said. "Is Dan around?"

"He's around somewhere," Melanie said. Thomas left.

Thomas ran into Ben and Umberto standing at the fence. Umberto ignored him and Ben gave him a dirty look. *That was strange*, Thomas thought.

He found Dan.

"Everyone knows about the crisis you solved," Dan said. He was acting a bit strange, but not overly unfriendly. "The big problem is that now Tracey is in charge," Dan said in reference to his boss at the Board of Elections. Mark and Tracey were the two Republican board members, and together with the two Democratic board members they chose the Director and Deputy Director of the Board of Election.

South Range crushed Lisbon. Thomas left the stadium with the throng of people and walked down the hill to his car. Except his car wasn't there. *Where is my car?* he thought. He couldn't remember. He was too tired.

Two hours later after walking up and down the hilly streets of Lisbon, Thomas was physically exhausted. He walked into the police station. The officer on duty offered to drive him around. They walked out to the parking lot. "In back," officer Smith said, pointing at the cruiser. Thomas continuously clicked his unlock button on the FOB while the police officer raced through the streets. A gray sedan flashed its hazard lights at the push of his clicker.

"I need a day off," Thomas told the officer. He got in the car and drove back to the Davis Motel.

Saturday, 24 September 2016, 45 Days
MCRP HQ

"Hey Thomas," Tracey said. She called for Thomas to come to the chair's office. "I am looking for a technical coordinator for my coalitions. I need someone who can keep track of everything."

"Yes, I can help you," Thomas said. He brought his computer and set it on his lap. Within a few minutes he had created shared folders on Google Drive.

"Oh, Pence is coming to Columbiana County on Wednesday!" Thomas said. He fired off an email to Kamilah asking for VIP tickets.

Annette walked into headquarters and saw Thomas in the chair's office with Tracey. She walked through the open glass doors.

"Thomas, is anyone walking the doors today?" the German reporter asked. She wanted to find out what the voters thought about the campaign days before the first debate. Annette also wanted to know what it was like to knock on random peoples' doors and ask personal political preferences. She found the whole American experience interesting and odd. She wasn't quite right, though. The doors were not random.

"Umm." Thomas looked up from his computer. He saw Jenna, a high school junior from South Range sitting at the front desk. "Let's the three of us go out and knock some doors," he said. He stood up and walked to the front of the main room in headquarters. "Jenna, do you want to join Annette and I?" he asked.

"To knock doors, OK!" Jenna answered. She was almost jumping up and down out of excitement.

Thomas thumbed through his phone to the RNC Door knocking app, and found a list of voters whose doors were partially completed. "We can take my car," he said. The Indiana man, the German reporter, and the South Range Dance Majorette piled into the gray car. Thomas put the air conditioner on full blast. It was a beautiful morning, but hot.

Doors, Poland, Ohio

"Absentee voting has just started," Thomas said. "Typically in America, people can vote up to six weeks before the actual Election Day, and roughly half of all voters vote absentee." Thomas turned the wheel and merged onto Canfield-Poland Road. "Almost all candidates get this wrong and wait way, way too late to walk doors. Also, by now every voter will have received multiple negative mailings, turning them off from the political process this election cycle. From now until Election Day it will get increasingly hostile at the doors. Really, the purpose of going to the doors this late in the campaign is to send information up the chain of command. That is what I'm doing," Thomas said.

Jenna stared at him from the front passenger seat. Annette asked, "What type of reception is Trump getting at the doors?"

"He is getting a positive reception, but a lot of that depends on which doors we are knocking. For example, many traditional conservative Republican voters in Ohio voted for Kasich, Rubio, or Cruz in the primary election, but they will vote for Trump at a high percentage even if they claim to not like him. This is because they dislike Hillary much more than they fear Trump."

Thomas launched into a twelfth-grade civics lesson that Jenna recognized. "The president actually has very little domestic power compared to the executives of most countries. The president of the United States has almost dictatorial power in foreign policy issues since World War II, and this power has only grown in the last several decades. However, Congress is the body that controls domestic policy. Many Republican voters, especially those that support more traditional candidates, know this nuance of American politics. They know that a president is limited in what he can do domestically," Thomas explained.

He noticed Jenna looking at him. "Jenna, what do you want to study?"

"Well," she said. She paused. "I would like to be a doctor."

"How are your grades?" Thomas asked.

"Pretty good," she said.

"How good is pretty good?" Thomas asked.

"3.8."

"That is good. You should try to finish this year and next year with as many As as possible, and then in college you need to have at least a 3.8, then you have a decent chance at medical school." Thomas said, now in full teacher mode.

Jenna nodded.

Thomas turned the wheel again and pulled over to the side of the road in the Boardman neighborhood. Jenna took some lit and the German reporter grabbed some for Thomas. The two teams walked on each side of the road.

The first two houses had nobody home, and then the next two were big Trump supporters. Thomas and Annette walked to the center of the street. Jenna looked a bit sad. "How are your houses?" Thomas asked.

"They were not Trump supporters," she said.

"Why don't you join us for one or two more and then we can head back to headquarters?" Thomas said. Jenna smiled, and the hop returned to her step.

The three walked up to a middle-class ranch house and Thomas rang the bell. "Hi, we are walking for Don Manning who is running for local office," Thomas started his canned introduction. It was awkward with two people at the door, and now there were three. Still, the two girls and one man made it more of an interesting combination than a threatening one. The woman looked at each of their faces.

"Is he Democrat or Republican?" the woman asked.

"Republican," Thomas answered.

"We are all Republicans here," the woman said.

Annette lunged forward and nearly pushed Thomas off the porch. "Hello," she said in formal and accented English. "Do you mind if I ask you a few questions? I am from the German public-service television ZDF."

"Annette is a reporter who is following us around today," Thomas added, softening the interjection.

"Oh, how interesting. My cousin went on vacation to Bavaria this summer!"

"Yes, what do you think of Trump?" Annette said in a staccato fashion. She didn't see the friendly social cue.

"Oh," the woman said. "Well, we aren't too sure about Trump, but we support the other Republicans: Rob Portman, Bill Johnson." She referred to the US Senator and US Congressman.

Annette asked another question about Trump and his view of women. The woman gave a less than enthusiastic answer.

Jenna hopped off the porch, and Thomas and Annette followed in slower fashion. "That woman is definitely voting for Trump," Thomas said.

"What? But she said…" Annette responded.

"Voters like that will pull the lever for Trump. She was a conservative Catholic voter, and there is no possible way that she will vote for Hillary." Jenna looked at Thomas, surprised at his tone. Thomas fell into his German mannerism. During his time living in Germany he learned that Germans take equivocation as weakness rather than politeness. So he told Annette exactly what he thought and he told her as if it were complete fact.

She responded well to his tone. "Interesting," she said. The three of them reached the car and Thomas drove them back to headquarters.

MCRP HQ

Brian Wollet, the Trump Campaign Regional Director Northeast Ohio, saw the trio walk into headquarters. Thomas was acting chummy with the tall blonde reporter. "You have to see a local football game," Thomas told Annette. "It really is part of the culture here."

Joe interrupted before Annette could respond, "Tommy boy, I want to invite you to the Grasshopper tonight."

"The Grasshopper?" Thomas said.

"Yes, it's my daughters birthday – you know, Alexis's mother. There are a bunch of people coming," Joe said.

Thomas agreed to come, though he was unsure of the whole thing.

Grasshopper Bar

The music was too loud. Thomas strained to hear Joe. "What is your relationship with Dan?" Joe asked.

"Dan?"

"Yes, Dan Kavanagh. What is your deal with him?" Joe asked.

"I mean, I just met him when I arrived. He invited me over to the farm, his family seems nice," Thomas said.

"Dan Kavanagh is a bad guy," Joe said. "He fired my wife from the Board of Elections," Joe continued.

Thomas then thought about Joe making the signs to earn money. Thomas didn't think of what Joe was really telling him. Joe was a former cop and could understand people's motivation well, yet at this moment Thomas could not understand Joe's motivation.

"Alexis really likes you," Joe said. Thomas thought Joe was trying to set him up with his single daughter, but this was a wrong analysis. Joe was trying to warn Thomas because he had helped with his granddaughter.

"Do you have two dollars? There is the Queen of Hearts game. You could win eleven thousand dollars." Joe was shouting over the loud music.

"What is the Queen of Hearts game?" Thomas asked. He pulled two dollars out of his wallet.

Joe took the money and a few minutes later came back. "You lost."

CHAPTER 36

Sunday, 25 September 2016, 44 Days
St. Charles RCIA Class

Deacon Dan looked relaxed in his football jersey. "We have a special guest today, and she is going to teach us the most important part of being a Catholic. Debbie, would you come up here?" he said.

A tall woman rose out of her seat and stepped to the podium at the front of the room.

"Our Catholic faith can be summed up in the following statement. As Jesus said, we must love others with all of our heart," she said. "When we are selfish we distance ourselves from the community and can find ourselves isolated. When we don't love others we can find ourselves outside of the church. The most important commandment is to love others unconditionally."

Isn't she forgetting the first part of that saying? Doesn't the New Testament instruct us to love God with all our heart and strength, and then to love our neighbor as ourselves? Thomas thought.

MCRP HQ

Tracey and Brian sat in the chair's office while Brian Wollet hosted the daily Northeast Ohio Trump Campaign roundup conference call.

"We have six Saturdays left," Brian said. "The number-one priority is to recruit volunteers to hit doors and phones."

Phones don't matter, thought Thomas. *Although a phone-in town hall would be nice.*

"Trump has run an amazing campaign," Tracey said when Brian paused. "I don't know how I didn't see it in the primary campaign."

Brian resumed talking. "Don't talk to the press, anybody. On a positive note, Mahoning County has been very high-functioning and the entire Northeast region has been high-functioning as well." Brian paused. "Brandon Moffett is involved."

So the Deputy Director Trump Campaign is now claiming credit for the doors the German Reporter and I are doing! Thomas looked impassive.

"Thomas is helping me organize here in Mahoning," Tracey said.

"That's great," Brian said. "In region 4, that's us in Mahoning and the surrounding counties, we knocked 17,000 doors."

Thomas slumped dramatically in his seat. The cheerleader, German reporter, and he had been the only people knocking doors in Mahoning County yesterday. They hit about twenty-five.

"The press will be at headquarters on Monday for the debate," Brian said. He referred to the first of three debates. Brian started listing email addresses of additional Trump campaign officials, and Thomas scrambled to record them in a draft email on his phone.

The call ended.

San Francisco 49s HQ, Two Miles North of MCRP HQ

A group of thirty or so Republicans marched up Market Street to the headquarters of the San Francisco Forty-Niners, owned by the DeBartolo family. They were protesting the quarterback who was kneeling during the national anthem. Brenda Johnson led the group, and she carried an enormous American flag. Matt Harris, the former chair of the Mahoning County Young Republicans and current Mahoning County Board of Elections Finance Director, was near the back and avoiding the WFMJ TV cameras. He was worried that there would be an incident.

MCRP HQ

"Hey Thomas, do you want to volunteer at the Pence event? You can bring a couple more people if you want to," Brian said. He walked out of the chair's office and walked to the white table where Thomas had been eavesdropping on the conference call.

"I'd love to," Thomas said. Brian walked away and Thomas called Sharon and Ed, two Trump campaign volunteers, to invite them to the Pence event as VIPs.

Chelsea walked into the chair's office where Tracey remained seated in the leather office chair. "What does Brandon think? She asked.

"He's in great spirits," Tracey said.

Mark walked by Thomas carrying a large box. He went into the back conference room and installed a second TV to complement the large TV hanging in the main room at headquarters. There was going to be a VIP room during the debates.

Monday, 26 September 2016, 43 Days
Dunkin' Donuts

A red car inched up in the drive-through line at Dunkin' Donuts. "What is taking so long?!" Rose cried. She hit her horn at the stopped car in front of her. She heard unintelligible shouting from the same car in reply.

Rose found Thomas' number on her phone and hit his name. Normally she texted him, but this time she called. Thomas answered on the first ring. "Thomas, I am going to invite Brenda Johnson to the debate tonight," she said.

"OK," Thomas said.

"Brenda worked harder than anyone for the Trump campaign," she continued. "She deserves to be there way more than Tracey."

Thomas listened. The phone line went dead.

Rose screamed at the car in front of her to pull up to the empty window.

MCRP HQ

Phyllis, the vulgar front desk volunteer, noticed that Sharon was not at headquarters yet, and she went on a rant speculating various indecent activities she imagined Sharon doing.

Thomas looked up from his table and recognized narcissistic/antisocial personality disorder projection. *Why is this woman allowed to be here?* He noticed that this was a pattern of negative gossip. The other day Phyllis had badmouthed Nicole when she was not at headquarters, and now she had targeted Sharon. Phyllis was in her late seventies, and at various times had claimed to be a cheerleader in high school, a professor at YSU, and a connected person to the powerful people of Youngstown. She was never any of those things, but found a listening ear from the volunteers at headquarters.

Thomas left to eat lunch, and returned to work on his computer, filling out job applications. Chelsea was not at headquarters this afternoon, so he took up residence in the back conference room.

Ding-a-ling

Thomas turned around and looked through the glass door of the conference room to see Dan Kavanagh and Kayla walk through the door.

Dan scanned the main room at headquarters and did not see Thomas. *Where is he? He is always here.* He noticed a head bobbing behind the glass door at the back of the room. *Even better,* he grinned in his crooked way. His eyes were emotionless.

Kayla felt her father's hand on the small of her back as he guided her to the back conference room. Dan opened the door. "Hey Thomas, what are you working on?"

Thomas responded with some non-answer, but Dan wasn't listening. "Well, I have to get ready for a meeting with Mark," he said. Kayla stood at the door while Dan walked away.

Kayla walked into the conference room.

"Kayla, do you want to join me at the Pence event Wednesday?" Thomas asked. "I have an extra VIP ticket."

"No, I have a physics lab," she said.

"How are your grades so far?" Thomas asked.

"Not good, although I like physics," she said. She explained that she had trouble with biology.

"Interesting. You might be better at logic rather than memorization," Thomas said. They both remembered Kayla losing her phone. "Biology is not a good subject to study if you are bad at memorization. Physics or computer science, or subjects that require logic or imagination rather than memorization, might be better for you to study."

Who is this guy who thinks he can tell me what to do? Kayla thought. "Uh-huh," she mumbled.

Thomas saw the reaction and sat down at his computer. Kayla stayed in the room until her dad came to get her fifteen minutes later.

What was the point of that? Thomas thought.

Thomas walked out of the conference room where Joe and Billy were working on signs.

"Ahh, here comes our pretty boy," Joe said. "He is spoiled."

Thomas thought that Joe was upset that Thomas did not go to the second bar after the Grasshopper the other night. This was only partially correct. Joe was frustrated that Thomas did not listen to him at the bar, that he was not seeing Dan Kavanagh for who he was.

Tuesday, 27 September 2016, 42 Days
MCRP HQ

The debate was not until the evening, but the crowd began to arrive in the late afternoon to the headquarters building. Several reporters planted themselves around the room, and Thomas counted at least three professional cameras. Mark Munroe did several interviews with members of the press while sitting in his office behind the double glass door.

Thomas Ryan reserved a seat in the conference room with Chelsea, Caleb, and several other Young Republicans. He started teaching Chelsea and Caleb about human motivation using psychological models on the whiteboard. Chelsea half ignored him at first, but then something switched in her head. It all made sense. Thomas really understood people. Chelsea took another drink from her beer can and began to tell the young men and women sitting in the room.

"Guys, guys, listen. Guys, guys, be quiet," she said. "Thomas is a genius!" She threw an empty beer can at a young man from Trumbull County who did not heed her order to be silent. "Listen!" she shouted.

Kayla stared at Chelsea, and looked at the whiteboard. Everyone else stopped talking and looked at Chelsea. *What is going on?*

Trump struggled as the debate progressed. Thomas stood up and left the conference room to get some food from the layout in the main room. Kayla followed him out of the conference room, and walked over to her father who had four young people surrounding him. These were a few of the Republican workers at the Board of Elections, and acted as Dan's flying monkeys to do whatever task he needed to be done. They thought of Dan as the cool uncle in addition to their boss.

Dan saw Thomas holding a piece of chocolate cake and talking with a Japanese reporter. Dan felt tightness in his chest that turned to anger. Thomas walked away from the reporter and towards the conference room when Dan walked up to him, flanked by four young men, including Matt Harris, Kyle Morrow, and two others.

Thomas saw Dan Kavanagh's face flash a millisecond of anger. It was the strangest thing. At that instance Kavanagh brought his hand down sharply on the small plate with the chocolate cake.

Smack! The cake tumbled to the carpet.

Thomas shoved the image of the face out of his mind. "What in the world?" he said. Kavanagh was staring at him, as were the other four people. Thomas saw Kayla standing to his side with a curious look, but not a hostile one.

"Dan, I can't help it that your daughter friended me on social media!" Thomas said. His voice was charming and light-hearted. "I can't help how sexy I am!" he continued. He bent his knees and picked up the cake without bowing to Dan.

Dan's look went from that of a shark to one of confusion. Kyle Morrow started laughing. Kayla looked puzzled. The first attack had failed.

Thomas texted a friend later that night.
Something is wrong with Dan Kavanagh.
The reply was instant.
Be careful.

CHAPTER 37

Wednesday, 28 September 2016, 41 Days
MCRP HQ

Sharon put her hands in front of her in a prayer-like fashion and bowed for the sixth time that morning to one of the four Japanese reporters. He bowed back out of politeness, and Thomas walked up and bowed as well. One of the Japanese reporters was a woman and she covered her mouth and giggled at the scene. Finally, the lead reporter made it past Sharon and walked back to the men's room.

"Thomas," said the woman reporter, "we are looking for streets with Trump signs. Where could we find these?"

"Do you mean like in neighborhoods, so you can get a camera shot up a street filled with Trump signs?" Thomas asked.

"Yes, exactly," she said.

Thomas unfolded Mark Munroe's Mahoning County map and smoothed it out on the white plastic table. He pointed in a sweeping motion from Austintown, around through Boardman and over to Poland in a five mile radius circle around Youngstown. "This area here is where you are most likely to find a street like that," he said. "Downtown Youngstown will be mostly African-American voters, but to the west and to the south you will find working class neighborhoods of white voters who are big Trump supporters." He continued, "Too far west or too far south you will either get rural areas with only farms or more traditional Republicans who might not be as vocal in their support of the nominee. They might not have as many signs."

The three other members of the Japanese table crowded around the table as Thomas explained neighborhood characteristics. They began to speak Japanese amongst themselves, and it was clear they were planning to take the maroon minivan out driving to find some of these neighborhoods.

"If you want, I can come with you and we can knock on a few doors. You can see what it is like," Thomas offered.

"Oooohhhh," the woman said.

"Thank you so much, but we only need to take a picture of the street," the head reporter said.

Thomas realized that it was well outside their comfort zone to interrupt strangers in their home. Thomas walked away and the four reporters continued to strategize their afternoon. Sharon walked by and bowed again, and in unison all four of the reporters returned her bow.

Two Norwegian journalists were wandering around headquarters and Thomas approached them. "Hi, I'm Thomas. Is there something you want to see?" He was thinking of the signs that the Japanese reporters wanted to film.

"We actually just got back from one neighborhood," said the lead, a woman. Her assistant was a young man.

"Would you like to see our brick factory?" Thomas asked. He smiled. "You know, where we make the bricks for the wall?"

"That sounds interesting," the reporter said.

Thomas led the Norwegians to the back room and showed them the saw station and painting station for the red and golden bricks, and he showed them the enormous signs in the back room. The reporter raised her camera in the way an infantryman raises his M4, and immediately started to shoot. Thomas kept out of the frame.

"By the way, would you mind talking to the Japanese reporters and giving them the address of the neighborhood that you visited? They are looking for photos too, and I don't think your media market crosses," Thomas asked. The Norwegians nodded and kept taking pictures.

Thomas walked outside and to his car. He needed to change clothes and then drive to the Pence event in Leetonia.

Leetonia High School, Leetonia, Ohio

Thomas got out of his car at 2:20 pm at the joint middle school and high school in the small town of Leetonia, Ohio. He wore a dark gray suit and dark blue tie. A cold front had pushed through in the morning, and it was less than eighty degrees with a clear blue sky and low humidity. He walked through the large parking lot and around a yellow school bus parked at the curb. Two teachers who were talking at the back of the bus nearly jumped back when they saw him walk past. *They think I am Secret Service*, Thomas thought. He tried to smile reassuringly at the teachers, but at that moment a bell rang and kids streamed out of the building.

Several boys walked up to him and jumped back. Thomas looked to his left and saw the real Secret Service advance team arriving. Twenty men in identical suits, haircuts, and body builds to Thomas split into two teams, with half walking in the double front doors and the other half walking around the building. Thomas thought about following them in the building, but then thought again, and stayed outside. The kids were pointing and yelling at all the men without smiles.

Thomas knew that the Secret Service would clear the building and set up the metal detectors and control points to get access to the building; it would take a while, so he decided to walk around the building. At the back of the building there were several state police cars and Columbiana sheriff's deputies patrolling.

"Are you Service?" a sheriff deputy in a tactical vest asked, "Do you need to go inside?" he asked Thomas.

This guy thinks that I am Secret Service too, Thomas thought. He shook his head and kept walking around the building.

He played the role and stared down the elementary kids when he walked to the front of the building. They loved it. Several third-grade boys raced up close to him before turning and running away, while the girls covered their mouths and laughed with each other.

Thomas saw Chris Horvath, the head of the Trump campaign, walking in from the parking lot with Frank Hoagland the 30th State Senate candidate and former Navy Seal. He walked up to the two men assertively.

"Hi Frank, nice to see you here!" Thomas said. Frank smiled wide and recognized Thomas right away.

"Thomas, great to see you! Thanks for all your help in Carrollton and other places." He said.

"You are going to win, and win by a lot," Thomas said.

Chris Horvath had a sour look on his face. *How does this guy know Frank Hoagland?!* he wondered.

An hour later, Thomas was escorting VIPs to the reserved area behind the stage. He found himself next to the congressman's wife and they talked about the campaign.

The drum corps signaled the start of the festivities. Frank Hoagland strode onto the stage. "Everyone stand and face the flag," he ordered. Everyone did, with haste. He led the crowd in the Pledge of Allegiance.

A few speakers later Governor Pence spoke while his wife and daughter walked near Sharon and Ed. The Youngstown volunteers met the Columbus, Indiana natives.

Once the Pence family left the building, Thomas walked outside to find a large bus where he helped load 30,000 pieces of lit into his trunk to take back to the MCRP headquarters.

Moretti Farm

Katherine was chatting with Brooke on her iPhone while scrolling through Facebook. She saw several pictures of Thomas pop up on her feed. She clicked "like" on all of them.

The Georgetown

It was almost 9:00 pm by the time Thomas drove north and arrived at the Georgetown on the south side of Youngstown. There had been a $250 – $1000 a plate fundraiser for the Party and one of the candidates at the Moretti's private club and catering business headquarters tonight. Thomas figured that by wearing his suit and his Trump volunteer badge, and by walking in late no one would give him trouble. He was right.

Thomas walked to the back where there was a bar and ordered coffee. He began sending Dan Kavanagh a series of tweets of all the people who were attending.

Is Tracey there? Dan responded. He asked several other questions.

The dinner ended and Thomas walked up to several people, including Mark.

Kayla was working as a busboy for her uncle, and when she walked by Thomas he gave her his empty cup and then ignored her. She tweeted about the interaction later that night.

Moretti Farm

Dan arrived home just after Kayla. "What was Thomas doing at the Georgetown?" he asked his daughter.

"I have no idea," she said.

"That guy has some nerve," Dan said.

Kayla was confused. *Do we like Thomas or not?* she thought.

MCRP HQ

Thomas made one last stop at headquarters because he had forgotten his power cord earlier in the day, and he needed it to do any work on his computer. He pulled up to headquarters and walked inside and found his cord. As he was walking back out to his car a minivan pulled up to the front door. Tracey and Randy, an associate at the Board of Elections, were inside.

Randy saw Thomas. "It's awfully late," he said.

Thomas realized that he was not supposed to have seen Tracey and Randy together. *This must be why Dan was asking about Tracey, he is afraid that he is going to be replaced by Randy,* Thomas thought. He sent a text on what he had seen to Kavanagh.

Thomas felt badly for Dan and the other Kavanaghs. At least ten people and several young people in college were depending on Dan Kavanagh's job to provide for their needs, and many people were trying to take his position away from him.

Thursday, 29 September 2016, 40 Days
MCRP HQ

Brian Wollet picked up the *Vindicator* paper from the front desk. A picture of Brenda Johnson at the Pence rally in Leetonia was above the fold. Brian didn't say anything and walked back to the chair's office.

Thomas walked over to the front desk to see the paper that Brian had laid down. *It's only local coverage, not national.* The *Vindicator* and other local press might be hammering the story until Election Day, but the regional, national, and international press had moved on to other stories. A smile broadened across his face.

"You can go to hell!" said Phyllis.

The momentary happiness that Thomas felt faded as the woman who seemed to be at the front desk cursed out another person. Thomas looked over his shoulder to see whom she was cursing at this time.

The President of the Ohio Senate.

"Senator, my name is Thomas," he said, positioning himself between Phyllis and the man in the suit. "Welcome to Mahoning County!"

Back Room MCRP

Thomas climbed a stepladder and used duct tape to attach a rear light to hang the large pieces of white poster board that he had positioned to be his backdrop. "That should do it," he said. He had completed his TV studio with minutes to spare. Now he hoped that anyone who walked into the back room would obey the signs that he had printed and taped to a row of chairs. *QUIET PLEASE, FILMING IN PROGRESS.*

He wasn't actually filming, but he had built a studio so that he could Skype with tutoring clients. Thomas had found a potential client on Craigslist and he was going to interview her shortly. The student was in China, where it was 7:00 am. He dialed her number and began a transpacific communication with a foreign national of a hostile country, who happened to be sixteen years old and taking AP History at an international school in Beijing.

South Range Legacy Football Stadium

The lights were off. *Why are the lights off?* Thomas thought. A few weeks ago Dan Kavanagh told him that on Thursday evenings the dads gathered at the football stadium to repaint the lines and the numbers. Thomas had wanted to join the effort to meet more people locally.

He looked up the football schedule on his phone. *Of course,* he thought. *Tomorrow is an away game.*

CHAPTER 38

Friday, 30 September 2016, 39 Days
MCRP HQ

"I was interviewed by the BBC this morning," Munroe said. He had walked up to the table in the center of the main room where Thomas was working on his computer.

Thomas closed a job application and looked up. "Oh, really? What was it about?"

"The usual," Munroe said. He meant the usual questions concerning the level of support that Trump had in the area and what people thought of Trump's campaign platform.

Thomas thought Mark looked happy. *He is the center of attention on the world stage right now.* Thomas shut down his computer and put on the South Range windbreaker that he had bought the other day. Sharon walked into headquarters.

"Oh, the South Range fan!" she said. "By the way, how old are you? I asked my husband the other day and he said, 'Thomas is at least 30.'"

"That's right, I am at least 30," Thomas said. He laughed and Sharon joined him.

Bar in North Lima

"What?" Umberto asked Dan.

"That bastard is 40 years old and he is harassing both my daughters and hitting on one of them." Dan said. "Just the other day I saw him corner Kayla in the conference room at headquarters." Kavanagh raised his voice in anger. It was feigned, and Umberto could tell, but he was playing along with the story.

Why does this guy hate Thomas so much? Umberto thought.

Ben tried to change the subject.

"I think this guy thinks he can take my job," Dan said. Dan did actually think so, but it was not his primary motivation.

"Nah, he doesn't have a chance," Umberto said.

South Range Away Football Game

Don Manning saw Thomas. "Hey there, the boys are looking great!" he said.

"South Range has an excellent team," Thomas said. He smiled. "What are you eating?"

"They are selling these pulled pork sandwiches at the concession stand," Don said.

"I'm going to go get one right now," Thomas said. He walked away from Don.

Thomas mingled through the crowd and made it to the concession stand. Ten minutes later he had ordered, received, and eaten the pulled pork sandwich. *It is good,* he thought.

Thomas walked around to the visitor side of the field where Dan, Umberto, and Ben usually hung out from the second quarter on. He saw Umberto and waved. Umberto didn't respond. Thomas walked up to Umberto. Umberto walked away and Thomas stopped pursuing him. Thomas was not sure what was up with Umberto. Last week Ben treated him badly in Lisbon, and today Umberto did. *Are these hillbillies so full of envy? What is going on? Is he just drunk?* Umberto had been drinking, that was obvious, and Thomas rationalized away his behavior.

Kavanagh and another guy were grilling hamburgers and hotdogs on the steel grill up the slope on the visitor's side, just like at the South

Range home stadium. "I'd like a hamburger," Thomas asked the man who held the spatula.

"Of course, it will be ready in a minute," the guy said.

Thomas walked to the concession stand and paid the three dollars fifty cents for the cheeseburger. He decided to get cheese at the last minute. Kavanagh seemed neutral to friendly.

"Is Randy trying to take your job?" Thomas asked Dan.

"He sure is. He has been scheming for years to get it," Dan answered.

"I noticed that he is about to finish his associate's degree at YSU," Thomas said. "It makes sense if he wants your job."

Kavanagh stared at Thomas. *Did he know?* Dan Kavanagh had dropped out of YSU and Dan could not tell if Thomas was hinting at this.

"I want Catholics to take over the Republican Party here in Mahoning," Thomas said. He had irony in his voice. Kavanagh's father was a Lutheran like Thomas' own parents, and Thomas thought that Kavanagh had converted to Catholicism for marriage.

Dan Kavanagh's stare became hostile for a moment. He grunted.

"Randy thinks that because he is close with some of these factory owners he can become the chair," Thomas continued. "The Republicans need to have someone like you in charge."

What is this guy's game? Kavanagh wondered. *Why is he saying I should be chair? Is he trying to throw me off something?*

"I plan to be chair from 2018," Kavanagh said. "I know the votes that I need. Mark has been chair long enough."

Kavanagh crossed his arms and took a few steps down the hill. Thomas decided to leave. He walked away and for the first time left a South Range game early.

Poland Football Game

Caleb put on a giant bulldog head to complete the outfit, and ran out to the field with the cheerleaders at the end of the halftime marching band performance. He danced for a few minutes and ran back to the track adjacent to the stands. He saw a man standing in the handicap section and waving at him.

"Thomas!" he said. "Did you see the band?" Caleb had played in marching band for several years and was proud of their ability.

Thomas walked down from the stands and took up a post on the chain link fence by the twenty-yard line. He looked back at the brick and steel grandstands with a glass-covered press box. *This must have cost $20 million.*

An hour later Poland lost a well-fought contest.

South Range Away Football Game

"That Thomas is a great guy, isn't he?" Don Manning said. He had a freshman son on the team just like Dan Kavanagh.

"You think so? I caught him lying the other day. He seems to be sneaky," Kavanagh replied. This response took Don Manning by surprise.

"Come on guys! One more score!" Number 14 yelled to his teammates. South Range was in double overtime and had possession. The quarterback started the play and ran to his left before cutting up the field. A linebacker with especially good spatial reasoning skills guessed correctly the moment of the quarterback's cut and hit the ball squarely with his shoulder pads. The ball flew free from the quarterback's grasp and onto the field where a safety picked it up. The safety ran in the rain for a touchdown. The game was over. South Range had lost.

Dan fumed at the loss that ruined the perfect season for his boys. He raged internally at the games that Thomas was playing. *How dare he tell me I am unqualified to run the party. Some Pence religious nut thinks that he is smarter than everyone. Well, he's not smarter than me.*

Fireplace Lounge

Thomas followed Caleb to the Fireplace Lounge, where they met Don and Nicole. The place was packed, but Don had a table already and the two men walked to the back.

"How was the BBQ sandwich?" Don asked Thomas.

"What sandwich?" Thomas said. He noticed a slight change in expression on Don's face.

"The pulled pork sandwich that you said you were going to try," Don said.

"Oh yes, I remember. It was tasty," Thomas said. He realized that Don didn't believe that he had ordered one. *Was he offended that I walked away from him?*

Saturday, 1 October 2016, 38 Days
MCRP HQ

"Hey Caleb, do you know of a Trump supporter that we can visit right now?" Thomas asked. "The anchor of ARD, that's like the German PBS, asked if we could knock on a couple of 'random' houses in the area." He used air quotes.

Caleb made several calls. "I got someone."

Thomas walked back to the ARD team of the apparently famous anchor, a producer, a lighting guy, and a camerawoman. "Yes, we can take you to a neighborhood with us and you can film us," Thomas said.

"That would be super!" the anchor said.

Thomas and Caleb walked out to his car and the Germans piled into their rented van with a quantity of expensive gear.

Poland, Ohio

"So here's the plan, I'll tell the Germans that I will go on one side of the street to find someone home, and you start one house away from your friends house. Let's hope no one is home at that first house. Just don't knock," Thomas said. They were arriving in the neighborhood.

Thomas parked his car and the German van parked behind him. He got out and explained to the Germans that this time of day not many people were home, so they were going to walk to a few houses.

"OK, can you ask the person at the door if they would be willing to repeat the interaction with the cameras, like do everything twice?" the anchor said.

"That's no problem," Thomas said. He walked over to Caleb and relayed the message.

The plan worked perfectly, and in five minutes a mini outdoor studio popped up on the porch of Caleb's longtime friend. The Germans were amazed at randomly finding such a prepared Trump supporter.

YSU Football

Thomas and Caleb drove to the YSU Game and walked over to the tailgate parking lot. Senator Rob Portman was hosting a BBQ before the game. "Look at the senator!" Thomas said. Portman was taking his picture with the YSU cheerleaders. Thomas and Caleb walked up to the crowd, and the cheerleaders took a picture with both of them. Caleb did not smile.

Rob Portman was an establishment Republican and had many policy positions that differed from those of Candidate Trump. Most of the people in Northeast Ohio preferred Trump's policies to Portman's. Still, he was a sitting US Senator. Thomas was excited.

One thing that most Trump supporters did not realize was that Chris Horvath, Trump's Ohio Campaign manager, had run Rob Portman's US Senate race in 2010. This meant Chris knew Portman's general strategy and where his strengths lay, namely in the central and western parts of the state. Rob showed up to the tailgate party today, but it was his only stop in Northeast Ohio for the entire campaign other than in Cleveland. He had to show the flag, but he knew to leave well enough alone for the most part and trust that Trump voters would tick his name on the ballot at a high rate.

Likewise, the Trump campaign was emphasizing the Eastern part of Ohio while ignoring most of the Central and Western part, with an exception or two. Chris Horvath knew that Portman voters in the central and western parts of the state would probably vote for Trump at a high rate, for once an establishment Republican stepped into the voting booth it was unlikely that he would allow for Hillary to become President. This was the entire point of the "NeverTrump" movement, to specifically lower this Trump and establishment vote linkage. The data showed that Trump needed roughly 85% of Portman voters to vote for Trump in order to carry the state. Current polling data showed that 83% of Portman voters were admitting that they would also vote for Trump.

Thomas and Caleb watched the game and walked around to the locker room exit. A friend of Thomas had arranged for QB1 to meet them after the game. The quarterback of the Penguins had been home-schooled and was a huge Trump supporter.

Tracey saw a picture of Thomas pop up on her Facebook feed. He was face to face with QB1 and waving his arms, describing the two-pronged Ohio strategy, according to the description of the picture. "How did he do that?" she asked herself.

Sunday, 2 October 2016
St. Charles RCIA Class

"Folks, you need to tell us who your sponsor is in two weeks," Deacon Dan announced. Most of the students in the RCIA class who were converting had already chosen a sponsor. Deacon Dan avoided looking at Thomas, who had not found a sponsor yet. *He might have to leave the class, oh well!* Deacon Dan thought. "Remember, we are here for you, and there are several assistants who would be happy to sponsor you." Deacon Dan gave a grin that would fit nicely onto the face of any corporate training expert.

Thomas looked around at the assistants – those people who were Catholics and who attended the RCIA class to help new potential converts on their journey to join the Church. Most of the assistants and potential sponsors were divorced, women, or both. There was one broken-down man who had been divorced and his helplessness showed. A woman who had a habit of sitting by Thomas had gone through two husbands and was on her third.

The class was soon over. One of the friendly leaders of the class, a plump middle-aged woman, walked up to Thomas after class. "Perhaps you would be more comfortable at one of the more traditional parishes in the diocese," she said.

"I am fine where I'm at," Thomas said.

"It's just that the Catholic Church is a large body, and there are many different types of believers," she continued. She looked concerned.

Thomas' face fell. The woman walked away.

Boardman Park

Thomas drove from St. Charles to Boardman Park where the Republicans had set up a tent for the local candidates and Trump. People streamed into the tent to purchase Trump signs.

"You look nice," Mark said. Thomas was wearing a tie under his fleece.

"I just came from St. Charles," Thomas answered.

Mark grimaced slightly and walked to the parking lot to retrieve more signs.

CHAPTER 39

Monday, 3 October 2016, 36 Days
MCRP HQ

The BBC reporter and camera crew returned to headquarters, this time to interview Tracey. She sat in the chair's office for several hours, giving phone interviews to reporters once the BBC crew left headquarters.

Tuesday, 4 October 2016, 35 Days
MCRP HQ

"Thanks for calling, Tracey, but I won't be able to help. It's just that I am overwhelmed with work," the woman's voice answered through the phone. Tracey moved her thumb down the list to call another member of the party to be one of her co-chairs.

Thomas waved through the glass door and she motioned him into the chair's office. "Can you help me organize the list of Party members?" she asked. Tracey had not been successful in finding other co-chairs for her Trump effort, so she had to coordinate the mass emailings herself.

"The databases are all set up; I just need the names and email addresses," Thomas said.

Tracey sent him a file from the computer in the chair's office, and Thomas loaded it into the shared Google folder.

VP Debate

Thomas sat in the VIP room for the Vice Presidential Debate. "Pence is doing an excellent job!" he said. After the first ten minutes it was no longer a race. Pence, the former radio professional, made Tim Kaine sound like he had the talking points of a blue haired Antifa member.

"It's as if Pence is the father figure in a Southern Indiana farm house. He has such credibility and calmness." Thomas said.

An hour later the momentum of the campaign shifted in Trump's favor.

Dan Kavanagh hated everything about Mike Pence. He hated everything about Donald Trump.

Wednesday, 5 October 2016, 34 Days
Mahoning County Country Club, Girard, Ohio

Thomas gave a presentation at the Rotary Club lunch meeting. He noticed the liturgical nature of the meeting, from the opening hymn to the closing commitments each member made to attend future meetings. It struck him as odd.

After the presentation he met several other business owners, including the senior Mr. Cafaro, owner of a large percentage of the commercial real estate in Trumbull County.

Canfield Republican Women's Club

The Canfield Republican Women's Club was only slightly less strange than the pageantry at the Rotary club. At least no one was singing the "Star-Spangled Banner" to a small indoor audience.

"I would like to present to you our speaker tonight, Sergeant Vincent of the local veterans organization," a short woman said. The old soldier walked with a limp up to the podium. Everyone clapped.

Thomas squinted as the man spoke. His lecture was about the vulnerability of veterans and suicide awareness.

"When life gets so desperate these kids don't know how to cope. They reach for the gun and put it up to their face," he said.

Thomas leaned back in his chair and looked to his left. A seventy-year-old woman in pearls and expensive jewelry put on a Russian stone face.

The sergeant got more graphic. "Bang!" he shouted. He slammed his fist on the podium.

Oh baby Moses, Thomas thought. He saw the wealthy Republican donor clutch her purse tightly without making a sound or movement from the waist up.

The blonde woman stood up from the table at the pause and walked around the table. She started clapping and Thomas joined her. Soon the room filled with noise and the sergeant took his seat, relieved that he was no longer speaking in public.

"Just a reminder ladies…and gentleman," the blonde woman said, "Tonight's donations will go to the veterans organization of Youngstown."

Thomas didn't hear exactly which organization, but he was glad the episode was over. He looked at his watched and walked out of the dinner so that he could catch the end of the chili cook-off on the other side of town.

Chili Cook-off, The Avian, South Range

Most of the people were filtering out of the hall to the parking lot when Thomas arrived. He saw Dan Kavanagh at the door and walked past him to see who was still in the building. Inside, he saw Mark standing by a large metal pot full of chili. Mark held his head down. He had lost even with his specialty recipe.

It had not been a fair contest, as the judges were not about to award anyone anything unless that person was of Italian stock, and sure enough, a rotund and cheerful Italian man was glad-handing everyone. His chili really was good, and he beat the WASP Republican County Chair.

Dan Kavanagh made his way back to the main room. He wanted to know what Thomas was talking to Mark about. Kyle Morrow followed Kavanagh to the back corner. Dan carried a slice of cake and walked to the backside of the table to be next to Mark.

Kyle walked up to Dan and slapped the cake out of his hand, just as he had seen Dan do to Thomas a week earlier.

What an idiot, Thomas thought. Kavanagh was momentarily stunned.

Thursday, 6 October 2016, 33 Days
MCRP HQ

"Thomas, I need to ask you a question," Tracey said. She grabbed the doorframe of the conference room and peeked her head inside.

"Ok," Thomas said. He looked up from his computer.

"Why are you voting for Trump?" She asked. A Japanese cameraman popped around her and aimed the video camera at Thomas. He squinted from the LED spotlight mounted on top of the apparatus.

"Chris Horvath yelled at me pretty good the other day. I am not allowed to speak to the press," Thomas said. Tracey had ambushed him. The Japanese reporters had tried several times to get Thomas to talk to them on camera, and they almost succeeded getting Tracey to set Thomas up for a surprise interview.

Thomas, the Japanese cameraman, and Tracey walked out of the conference room and into the main room. Thomas walked up to the Japanese leader of the four reporters and asked if they were looking for anything else that he could help them with.

"Did you find your street signs?" he asked. He referred to the picture that they wanted to photograph – a long street filled with Trump yard signs in front of most of the houses.

"Oh yes, thank you very much," the man said. "The Norwegians told us a street to visit and it was in the area that you showed us on the map."

Thomas walked to his computer and looked over the Facebook message to Melanie Kavanagh one more time.

Hi Melanie, This is Thomas. I am going through the process to be confirmed at St. Charles, as I was never confirmed earlier. As part of this process I need to find a sponsor. There are a few people who are "leaders" in the St.

Charles RCIA class who offer to be sponsors, but I would prefer to have someone as a sponsor who is male and not divorced. So far, I have not met a person who fits either criterion. If you do know a potential sponsor please do let me know, even if he attends another church in the area. Thank you!

Thomas hit Send. The Morettis had about a thousand relatives in the area, and Thomas was hoping to meet one of the uncles. He was serious about not wanting to have an angry divorced woman as a sponsor as well. There was a big risk by sending this Facebook message, but he had not seen Dan be overtly hostile to Catholicism. Dan had managed to hide his rage.

A few hours later, Thomas went to the back room and set up his makeshift-tutoring studio. He turned on the bright lights on the homemade stands, and put his iPad on a box to use as the camera. He hit the button and taught the young woman sitting in a room in Beijing American history for ninety-three dollars per hour.

Chelsea walked to the backroom to sneak in a smoke and saw the bright studio lights behind the piles of junk. She approached the studio and stared at Thomas. She walked away, shaking her head.

Friday, 7 October 2016, 32 Days
Bliss Hall, Youngstown State University (YSU)

The syncopation of Chopin was difficult, and that is what made the Etude piece so pleasing to the ears. Thomas ran his fingers down the keyboard and back up, switching between his index finger and middle finger and back again quickly.

Knock Knock

The door flew open. "Oh, you aren't Melissa!" A young man stood at the doorway to the practice room.

Thomas turned first and then stood up from the bench. He introduced himself.

"I heard Chopin and I thought you were my TA," he said.

"I just play a bit here once in a while," Thomas said. He realized he was in no danger of getting kicked out, a thought that had crossed his mind. He talked with the man and learned that the student specialized in early twentieth-century classical music.

A few minutes later, Thomas resumed practicing, giving his mind the musical foundation to improve his creative and logical thinking.

MCRP HQ

Today his timing was perfect. Thomas thought he smelled something tasty when he was just outside of the main door of headquarters, and he confirmed his suspicions when he walked in and saw Chelsea filling a plate from several metal rectangle tubs sitting on the counter.

"Pamela had a fundraiser this morning. These are the leftovers," she said.

Thomas did not have to be told twice. Fresh-cut fruit, bacon, sausages, scrambled eggs, waffles, syrup – it was delicious. Thomas walked back and filled his plate again. And then he did it a third time. Chelsea stared. Thomas had run a three-mile circuit on Highway 7 and Sharrott Road at 6:00 am before piano practice, and he was hungry.

Thomas was singing in headquarters, from the food and the earlier music practice, by the time he polished off the third plate.

"Did you see the news?" Chelsea said. She stared at him in a peculiar manner.

"Not yet, what's going on?"

"Read the news," she said.

When you're rich they let you do it, you can grab 'em...

Thomas laughed, weakly at first and then loudly. "October Surprise!" he said.

Chelsea was not laughing, and there was an emergency call with the victory campaign in a few hours. Chelsea let slip that the rumor was that the RNC was going to withdraw all support for Trump and focus only on Rob Portman.

Thomas realized a couple of things right away. He knew that the Mike Pence performance at the Vice Presidential debate had changed the momentum for Trump. Pence had crushed Tim Kaine by any measure. Furthermore, two weeks worth of absentee votes were already in the books, at least fifteen percent of the total vote. The press and candidates underestimated how quickly a race was won or lost by absentee voters.

However, the press would have their talking points for the next week or more. This vulgar audio release would give non-Trump voters a "fake because" reason to not vote for him, although they were not going to vote for Trump anyway. The tape would also give other politicians an excuse to distance themselves from Trump.

Still, which Trump voter would change their mind because of this tape? Men who had already decided to vote for Trump? Absolutely not. Women? That is whom the media would be targeting. However, women know better than men how base people can be. Had these media people ever cleaned a public women's restroom? These were almost always much dirtier than a public men's restroom. Thomas didn't think that women in general would vote for Trump at a lower rate due to a naughty comment.

That left the evangelical vote. This was a legitimate worry, and made up fifteen percent or more of the Republican electorate. However, would an evangelical voter really stay home or outright vote for more abortions and Hillary over a man who had said a disrespectful word about a woman? Thomas doubted it. The evangelical voter might make a scene about holding their nose and voting for Trump, and that was the worst-case scenario.

The locker-room comments were a nothingburger in his opinion, although every establishment Republican talking head on Fox News and CNN strongly disagreed with this analysis.

Board of Elections Mahoning County

Matt leaned on the door in Dan Kavanagh's office. "Trump is finished," he said. "What an idiot," he added with a laugh.

Dan Kavanagh laughed too, but he wasn't so sure. "You really think this is the end for Trump?" he asked.

"I mean, can the holy rollers really vote for this guy now? Come on…" Matt said.

"What does that mean? Will they remove Trump?" Dan asked. He remained seated and turned his chair to look out at the Oak Hill cemetery outside his window.

"The RNC is deciding what to do right now. Probably they will just have Pence become the candidate by a vote of the executive committee."

Dammit! Kavanagh thought. *That bastard from Indiana will become more powerful!*

MCRP HQ

Rose Piper burst through the front door at around 5:00 pm. "Thommaaass!" she said. "You have to be a host for Sunday's dinner."

"Is this the dinner that I'm paying $45 dollars for?" he asked.

"Don't talk back. I will beat you," Rose said. "There will be many judges there, and I want you to dress in your nice suit and escort them to their seats.

Thomas understood. As a condition of her parole it was grey territory for her to approach a judge outside of an official setting.

South Range Football Game

Thomas stood on the visitor side of the field, watching the game with Dan Kavanagh. He seemed to be nicer this evening.

"Trump will stay in the race," Thomas told Kavanagh. "It is too late to change anything, and fifteen percent of the vote is already in."

Dan Kavanagh nodded at the absentee vote percentage. He knew Thomas was right.

"By the way, I asked Melanie if she would connect me with one of her cousins to be an RCIA sponsor," Thomas said.

Kavanagh stared at him.

There was a loud crack and both men turned their attention to the field. A young man was down on the field, his leg jerking unnaturally. The wide receiver screamed, and the athletic trainer bumped up his quick walk to a jog. Thomas felt nauseous. He remembered back to his biology class when the helpless chicks a day or two from hatching flopped around when the biology teacher made the students crack open the eggs.

Three coaches ran out to the field and the players each went to their respective sides of the fields and took a knee. Thomas saw across the field to the home side a coach was leading the boys in prayer.

"That's Seth," Dan Kavanagh said. "He breaks a bone every year."

Thomas tried to keep his facial expression neutral.

The ambulance sitting just outside the end zone flipped on its emergency lights and drove onto the field. Momentarily, the EMTs had loaded the adolescent on a gurney and shoved him into the back of the emergency vehicle. The ambulance turned on its siren and drove off the field, disappearing down an access road.

Thomas followed the ambulance with his eyes, and heard one loud unified clap. He turned his head back to the field. The kids had all taken formation at the line of scrimmage and South Range was ready to run what looked to be a running play.

What the hell?

Kavanagh walked back from talking with the other fathers. "He broke his leg. He's done for this season."

Thirty minutes later, the South Range Raiders resumed their winning streak. For Thomas had returned to his position standing at the sidelines, resting his arms on the fence.

CHAPTER 40

Saturday, 8 October 2016, 31 Days
MCRP HQ

"Trump has widespread support among the people in the area," Tracey said.

"Don't you think that his comments that recently came to light will hurt him at the polls, especially with women?" asked the reporter. He sat across from Tracey while bright LED lights shined on them both. Professional cameras were also arranged behind each person and pointed at the interviewer and interviewee.

Tracey stumbled over her words in a long answer.

"That's all we need," Jim said. "Hit the lights," he told the cameraman who then turned off the bright lights.

"How did I do, Tom?" Tracey asked Thomas, who was watching the interview from his station at the white plastic table.

Thomas paused, then answered with a slow, clear voice. "I am just a volunteer."

The reporter burst out laughing, followed by Tracey, the cameraman, and then Thomas himself.

Moretti Farm

"Did Thomas Ryan ask you to find a sponsor for him?" Dan asked.

"Yes," Melanie answered.

"Stay away from that creep," Dan said.

He walked out of the kitchen and then out the door to the gravel driveway. He got in the black SUV and drove down the dirt driveway.

NPR Regional Studios, Kent, Ohio

The recent Trump tape is likely to have no impact on the race. The constituency most likely to be offended – evangelicals – is registering no change in their willingness to openly support Trump at the doors. Non-Trump supporters are becoming more hostile to Trump, using the leaked tape as justification.

M.L. Schultze looked at the latest text message from Thomas. "Hmmm," she said. She got on the phone and called several of her colleagues.

MCRP HQ

Thomas noticed the volunteers treating him with more respect. The scuttlebutt among Republicans was that Pence would replace Trump as the Presidential candidate in the next day or two. They wondered what role the man from Indiana would play in the campaign and administration. Thomas knew that Trump would not quit the race.

Thomas heard talk at headquarters that the Victory Campaign had issued a directive specifying they would no longer support "walking doors" for Trump. Rob Portman would be the focus now.

Sunday, 9 October 2016, 30 Days
Highway 7 next to Tiffany's ½ mile north of Davis Motel

It was one of those ironic things that find unlikely timing. *What would happen if I broke down here?* Thomas thought. He looked to his left at Tiffany's, the strip club a half-mile north of the Davis Motel.

Clunk, scrapppee

Thomas stopped his car in the middle of the road, and then backed into the driveway of the strip club. He had planned to attend mass before going to the RCIA class. Instead, he got out of the car and crouched low. The exhaust pipe had broken off and was leaning on the ground, in the wrong way too, meaning he could not drive forward.

He got back into the car and put it in reverse. He waited until traffic cleared, and then drove backwards down highway 7 to the Davis Motel.

Once there, he texted Deacon Dan. No response. Next he texted Adam, a young man in his RCIA class who was converting so that he could marry a Catholic girl early next year.

Hey Thomas! I am just driving up from Columbiana. I can pick you up. Adam responded right away.

Adam was true to his word. Ten minutes after that the two young men walked in together to the RCIA class. Deacon Dan's face tightened when he saw Thomas.

St. Charles RCIA Class

Deacon Bob led the lesson for the morning, explaining how it was a "fact" that most of the Old Testament never happened.

Thomas did not hold his tongue. "Do you know about the burial mounds?"

"What burial mounds?" Deacon Bob responded. He dreaded Thomas.

"Since the Ottoman Empire controlled the Middle East for roughly four hundred years, very little archeology took place until the British conquered Egypt. Even then, the archeologists focused mainly on Egypt, and only about one hundred out of the almost one million burial mounds in the Middle East have been analyzed. This means that we have an absence of evidence of what happened. We do not know for a fact that Jews did not come out of Egypt. Yes, that is the current academic scholars' educated opinion, but lots of data is missing."

Deacon Bob moved on to the next topic, explaining that scholars knew the Old Testament was written quite late because it predicted events, and it wasn't possible to be this accurate unless the books were written after the Babylon captivity.

After thirty long minutes, the class ended. Just as the week prior, a woman walked up to Thomas. This one was skinny and petite. They were the only two left in the classroom. This was the woman who was on her third husband. "You will never find a woman," she said.

Thomas was surprised at the outright rudeness. It took a moment, and he realized what she was saying. *Unless I submit to a divorced woman as my Catholic sponsor, and then obey her in everything, and then get with the program to accept this non-Catholic RCIA teaching as Catholic dogma, I will be isolated. This woman is threatening me!*

Thomas walked up to the chalkboard and explained to this woman his theory of the Mountain of Truth.

"You have a lot to learn," she seethed.

Thomas thought he heard hissing.

Thomas walked to the main fellowship hall to find Deacon Bob. He realized one more thing about the morning's lecture, specifically when Deacon Bob referred to Moses in the Pentateuch and how the writers had used heroic language. Due to recent scholarship on the Jaspers' shift or axial age, there was a literary argument that the Torah was written early in history, not late.

Deacon Bob saw Thomas first when Thomas walked through the double doors. He turned, "Where do you live?" he asked.

"I live here," Thomas said.

"Where is your address?" Deacon Bob asked. He wanted Thomas gone.

Thomas saw the hatred in Deacon Bob's stare. He turned around without answering further and left the fellowship hall to attend the mandatory mass at 1:00 pm.

Moretti Farm

Dan woke up late and looked at his phone. He saw several texts from Thomas asking for help with his car. He clicked ignore and walked downstairs to eat some leftover sausages.

St. Charles Parking Lot

"Mary," Thomas called. He saw the woman whom he had met a few weeks earlier at the mailing effort at Republican headquarters. She seemed disoriented.

"Thomas," she said. "My husband is dying. The hospital isn't doing what they need to be doing!"

"Oh, I am sorry to hear that," Thomas remembered her talking about walking to St. Elizabeth from Republican headquarters. Mary was distraught.

"Here," Thomas said. He took a piece of paper and wrote his phone number on it. "If something happens, you can give me a call." He gave it to her.

She got in her car and left.

Caleb pulled up in the parking lot. He had received a text from Thomas.

"Thanks for helping me today," Thomas said. "My car is at the Davis Motel. Could you please not tell anyone that I'm staying there?" Thomas asked. Until that moment, no one knew the location of his home base of operations, located on the other side of the woods behind the Moretti compound.

Davis Motel

It took an hour for Caleb, Thomas, and the Davis Motel maintenance guy to jury-rig the exhaust pipe with hangers. Thomas slowly drove the car up Market Street. It was loud, but it worked.

Pep Boys

Bishop Tobin of Indianapolis is named Cardinal. He will be moved to New Jersey.

"Of course," Thomas said. Indianapolis was a notoriously loose diocese. Not many people realized that Mike Pence's priest in Columbus Indiana openly flirted with Buddhism, perhaps one reason why Pence had attended Protestant Evangelical churches for years. Bishop Tobin had protected this priest just as his predecessor had done for decades. Thomas was not qualified to know if the priest was a heretic, but in his opinion the priest did not follow orthodox Catholicism.

Thomas remembered that shortly after Pence was picked as the Vice Presidential nominee, the priest had given the New York Times a long interview where he implied Pence's mother wept for Pence as a "fallen child." The Buddhist priest didn't even follow Buddhism correctly.

"Thomas," said one of the Pep Boys associates. "Your car is fixed." Thomas walked up to collect his keys. In only three hours he had a brand new exhaust system. Money really did solve everything in America.

St Maron's Catholic Church

"Where is Thomas?!" Rose was anxious. "You, there, come here!" She assigned another young man instead of Thomas to escort the judges. The other man bowed his head and obeyed.

Thomas walked into the Maronite church and church hall complex at that moment.

"Thomas, I don't need you anymore. I found someone else." Rose said, clearly annoyed that he was late.

"Sounds good to me," he said. He walked into the banquet hall. A large banner said that the dinner was to honor Clarence Smith. Thomas had no idea who Clarence Smith was, but he aggressively introduced himself to people standing around the dessert table.

"I am Monsignor Siffrin," said the man in a collar. He and Thomas talked for moment.

Thomas mentioned how he had figured the artists at Bliss Hall at YSU would leave a door propped open just as the artists 'back in Boston' had done the same. "So I practice the piano now at YSU," Thomas said. He liked telling his secret of how he knew how to pirate piano playing time to a priest, or monsignor.

"Why don't you stop by my office one day?" the Monsignor suggested. Thomas had told him that he was converting to Catholicism. Thomas agreed and walked away.

"Hey Thomas, I complained to Matt Borges about Jason Lovett," someone said. Matt Borges was the Ohio Republican Party Chair. Thomas turned to his side and saw that Matt Harris, the Board of

Elections Finance Director and orbiter of Dan Kavanagh, was speaking to him. Thomas nodded his head and nabbed a small sausage.

Monday, 10 October 2016, 29 Days
YSU Bliss Music Hall

The music room was the first stop of four stops downtown today for Thomas. Three would be before lunch, and one would be in the evening. Music helped Thomas think. He felt tired. It had been over seventy days since he'd had a real day off.

Board of Elections Mahoning County

"Hey Mike," Thomas said, opening the door after a quick knock. "I'm looking for absentee voter data." Thomas said. "Do you release who has voted?" Thomas already knew the answer.

"Yes, every night for the past two weeks I have been uploading a list of who has voted. You can't see how they voted, but you can see all the information we have on each of these voters." Mike said.

"Where do I find this file?" Thomas asked. Mike showed him.

Thomas stepped out of the darkened IT center and Maggie caught him. She had watched him enter the hallway fifteen minutes earlier. "Thomas, take this." She shoved a cookie in his hand. "Thank you for looking for Kayla's phone," she said. Maggie looked up at his face. Thomas had lost weight over the past months.

"Oh, don't worry about it," he said. "Is Dan around?"

"He's in his office," Maggie said.

Thomas walked down the hall and to the left to the Director and Deputy Director's office. He had been in it once before, with Court. He walked in and Dan looked up while sitting at his desk.

"Hi Tom, what brings you to Oak Hill?" Dan Kavanagh asked. His voice sounded a touch flat, Thomas noticed.

"I am gathering absentee voter data from Mike."

"Mike does a great job," Dan said. He picked up a copy of the *Vindicator* and opened it. "The polls don't look good," Kavanagh said.

"That's why I want to see the raw data. I don't know that I believe the polls," Thomas said.

"Come on, this is ABC, these guys are professionals. Do you think they are making up numbers?" Dan asked.

Thomas seemed not to understand Dan wanted only agreement. "Well, sometimes their samples are incorrect: for example, they could be using Republicans in irrelevant states, and sometimes people don't tell their true feelings to pollsters," Thomas said. He noticed a cloud come over Dan's face. That was new.

"What do you think are Trump's chances of winning?" Kavanagh asked.

"Sixty percent," Thomas answered honestly. The cloud on Kavanagh's faced darkened. Thomas felt like he should leave.

St. Columba Cathedral

"Can I schedule a meeting with Monsignor Siffrin?" Thomas asked. A woman behind the bulletproof glass smiled. Thomas continued, "I met the monsignor at a fundraiser yesterday and he invited me to come and see him at his office. I know he's busy, so could you let me know when he might have time?"

The secretary opened a book. "How about a week from Wednesday, at 10:00 am?" she asked.

"Sounds great." Thomas smiled.

Candidate Forum Southside Baptist Church, Youngstown

It was already dark at 6:00 pm when Thomas wheeled into the church parking lot. He was running late.

Inside was packed, but he saw Caleb and Chelsea in the crowd with a free seat next to them. He walked over and sat in it. The three young people made up the majority of the white attendees in the fellowship hall.

Larry Pashin, a county commissioner candidate, walked up to the podium. His shoulders slumped forward and he hung his head. Thomas noticed that he gripped several three-by-five cards.

Pashin cleared his throat and forgot to introduce himself. "I am running to be the county commissioner," he started. Thomas felt empathy for the candidate; it was obvious he did not like to speak publicly. "I like the Blacks," Larry said.

Chelsea raised her head from her phone and Caleb turned to Thomas.

"I like the Blacks," Larry repeated. "I...I own an apartment complex do...downtown and have many colored tenants."

What is this guy saying?! Thomas looked at Chelsea and Caleb. They were all thinking the same thing.

It appeared that Larry was shrinking into his skin, and his face became even more like a mouse. He sighed loudly and looked down at one of his index cards. The blue ink had smeared from the sweat running down his arms and dripping off his hands. He could no longer read his prepared bullet points. The audience was not hostile, but Larry remembered his first oral book report in elementary school. He hung his head lower and looked again at the smudged index card.

He grunted in an exasperated way, and said for the third time, "Uh, I like Black people."

The pastor of the church and master of ceremonies walked up to him and put his arm around Larry's shoulders. "We all like Black people here," he said. The pastor gently guided the candidate off the stage. Larry hung his head lower and shuffled back to his seat.

Thomas, Chelsea, and Caleb tried to stop laughing by gripping their mouths tightly.

After the candidates had given their spiel, and one Democrat and Republican almost came to blows, Thomas approached the Judge whose signs he had assembled.

"Hey judge, several of us are going for drinks and to watch the game," Thomas said. He did not want to ever serve on jury duty if she won her election.

"I love baseball," she said.

MCRP HQ

Thomas arrived at the headquarters after midnight and after Chelsea and Caleb. The field organizer of three counties and the high school student had turned on the PA system. They took turns singing at the podium.

"I..I…like the Blacks," Caleb said.

Thomas burst out in laughter.

Chelsea walked on the mini stage and began singing. "Grab 'em, grab 'em, grab 'em," she started. Caleb pushed her slightly to the left and they both leaned into the microphone. "Grab 'em by the pussy," they sang.

Thomas fell to the floor, holding his stomach. Caleb and Chelsea tortured him further by singing the refrain of the County Commissioner candidate and the Access Hollywood tape over and over.

CHAPTER 41

Wednesday, 12 October 2016, 27 Days

Judge Christian walked into headquarters at 2:00 pm, earlier than her usual time of after 6:00 pm. She had a spring in her step.

"Congratulations on the endorsement!" Thomas said.

"Thank you, Thomas," she said brightly.

"Should I decide to attend law school, would you be willing to give me one of the three letters of recommendation?" Thomas asked. He struck immediately.

"Kiss-ass!" Joe shouted. Susan, another volunteer, nodded in agreement.

"I would be happy to write a recommendation letter for you," the judge said.

"What a brown-noser!" Joe shouted. He held a paintbrush in one hand.

Thomas wrote down in a draft email. *Judge Christian is willing to provide a future reference.*

Thursday, 13 October 2016, 26 Days
Davis Motel

I do not know anyone who might be your sponsor.

Thomas looked at the Facebook message from Melanie Kavanagh.

She waited until the last minute, but she wanted to let me know before the game tomorrow, Thomas thought. *This isn't good. I have misunderstood the situation with Dan.*

Thomas decided to not talk with Dan about anything religious from that moment forward.

MCRP HQ

Thomas pushed the chairs together with his "Do not Cross" signs as the final step in setting up his amateur TV studio in the back room. Soon, he was connected to Beijing.

His Chinese pupil had not done her essay and so the two of them worked together to write it for her English class.

Friday, 14 October 2016, 25 Days
MCRP HQ

Bzzzz

Thomas looked at his phone. The Monsignor needed to move back their appointment on Wednesday by an hour. Thomas had the idea of asking him to be his sponsor.

South Range Football Game

Joe was not sitting in his chair on the home side of the Raiders' field, and Jim was not standing at the sidelines. Thomas wandered a bit, but did not recognize anyone. He walked around the end zone to the visitor side and stood behind the players to watch the game.

The first quarter came and went, and the second quarter commenced. He felt lonely.

"Thomas!"

Thomas looked up, startled. He had been thinking while the minutes ticked down to halftime. Christian ran up to him and grabbed his arm.

"Thomas, my grandpa is on the other side!" he said. He jumped up and down. The ten-year-old pulled at Thomas. "He wants to talk to you. Come on!" he said.

Thomas turned and followed him, walking toward the ambulance beyond the end zone, and then to the concession stand, and finally down the hill to the edge of the field on the home side.

Katherine stood talking to her grandfather. This was the first time that Thomas had seen her at one of her brothers' football games. Her black hair was in a ponytail, and she wore a leather jacket with blue jeans.

Thomas stopped. Christian pulled on his arm again and he walked to the pair.

Katherine kept talking to Jim. She took a breath and Jim stuck out his hand. "Nice to see you Tom," he said.

"The team is looking good tonight," Thomas said. Jim agreed. Katherine stared at the field.

"Katherine," Thomas said. She turned to face him. He felt she did not like him interrupting her conversation with her grandfather, and that she did not want to talk to him. "The other day I ran into Kayla at mass, when we were sneaking out early, but I haven't seen you there."

Thomas' bluntness surprised Katherine. She looked down, "I am not much of a mass-type person," she said.

"Are you in the young Catholic's phase of pseudo-atheism?" Thomas asked. He had intended the comment to be light-hearted, but it was piercingly direct. Katherine looked away. "Well, don't let the phase be too long," said Thomas. Now he looked toward the football game and Katherine turned her head back to him.

"Listen, Katherine," Thomas began again. "Your dad has an extremely tough job. There are so many snakes in the Republican Party. Your dad pretends to be a bad guy, but really he is a good guy, deep down inside. He pretends to be bad, but he is good." Thomas repeated. He paused and smiled. "I, on the other hand, am a bad boy but I pretend to be good."

Katherine stared at Thomas. Jim interrupted. "Oh no, Dan really is a bad guy."

Thomas and Katherine each turned to the grandfather and stared at him. Thomas looked at Katherine and saw her blank face. In that one second Thomas realized that something was wrong, dreadfully wrong.

Katherine turned and walked away without a word. She walked over to a group of high school senior boys who crowded around her. Thomas stood by Jim a bit longer. He felt a pit in his stomach. "The girls like the bad boys," Jim said. "The boys like Katherine," he continued. Thomas walked away and up the hill. He looked back. More young men were surrounding the former homecoming queen, nudging each other to get closer.

Thomas left the stadium. He knew he would not be back.

In the Forest

2:00 am

Two men and a woman gathered the three Molotov cocktails and put them in an old backpack. The short man put the backpack on and tightened the straps.

"Listen, I'll run out by the big tree near the road and watch for cops," the tall man said. He held his black plastic whistle. "When the coast is clear of cars, I'll blow my whistle in two short blasts. That's when you should run around and light the bottles. I will run over to you and throw one into the building."

He looked at the young woman. In the darkness, her purple hair looked black. She grinned. "In thirty minutes," he said. He had read somewhere online that the best time to cause havoc was 2:30 am. Maybe it was true, or maybe he was risking more by waiting, but in any case he was riding on the adrenaline now.

Beaver Township

2:05 am

"There they are," the Mahoning County Sheriff Deputy said to his partner. It was unusual for two deputies to ride in the same car.

A black SUV raced past the sedan and up the long driveway, blue and white LEDs sending a cascade of light dancing on the side of the house. The cop yanked the steering wheel and blocked the driveway.

"Hit the lights," Rob told his partner. The full-sized Ford drove on the grass and up to the house. Sarah, the new deputy, had beaten them to the punch. Rob walked to the back of the house while Sarah joined John at the front door.

The front door was open and she walked in. "Attention everyone, party's over," she shouted. She held a long D-Cell Maglite.

A few kids scrambled to the back of the house, into the waiting arms of the supervisor in charge.

Minutes later, Katherine Kavanagh looked out the back passenger window of a cop car for the second time in five months, wondering where she had gone wrong in life.

MCRP HQ

2:15 am

Chelsea, Caleb, David, and Thomas remained at headquarters very late. Caleb arranged several mattresses in the back room that were inexplicably buried amongst the junk. Thomas had tried to leave headquarters fifteen minutes earlier, but Chelsea and Caleb had tackled him and wrestled him to the ground.

He pretended to fall asleep on the ground and the three young Republicans walked to the backroom. Thomas got up and ran out of the building.

Caleb heard the bell on the front door and ran out of the back room, through the Trump brick kiln that was really a circular saw and paint station, and through the main room of headquarters. He burst through the door to the parking lot only to see Thomas pulling away. "Thommaasss!" he screamed.

Thomas saw Caleb running after him as he pulled away.

Republican Headquarters, North Carolina

2:30 am

The fire burned brightly. The three Antifa members watched the broken window for a minute and saw the liquid spread across the floor, peeling Trump signs through the heat.

The iPhone police scanner beeped.

"Let's go!" the tall man said. The three of them ran to the back of the building and into the woods.

Flames consumed the entire Republican Party County Headquarters in North Carolina.

CHAPTER 42

Saturday, 15 October 2016, 24 Days

Poland, Ohio

Thomas walked off the porch and down the driveway to the cul-de-sac. He walked up the next driveway and rang the bell. There was noise behind the wooden front door, and then a woman opened it in a jerky motion.

"Hello?" she said.

"Hi, my name is Thomas, and I am out walking for my friend Don Manning, who is running for local office," Thomas said. He handed the woman the lit piece. "By the way, the presidential race is crazy, isn't it…" he said.

The woman laughed. "We support Trump here!" she said.

"Well, listen, it's such a beautiful day I'll leave you to enjoy it," Thomas said.

"Thank you," she said. She closed the door.

Thomas made a note on the RNC door-walking app on his iPhone. He made a mental note as well. *Voters don't care about the Access Hollywood Tape.*

Moretti Compound

For once Katherine received the attention from her father that she craved. It was negative attention, but at least he finally noticed her.

Dan yelled louder.

"I was so upset, I couldn't help it," Katherine said. "Thomas came up and harassed Grandpa and me. He called you a bad man!"

Katherine knew how to parry her father's accusations. Her father stopped talking. She saw his face getting red. He turned around and grabbed a coaster from the end table. He hurled it against the wall and walked out of the room.

Columbiana County Republican Party Headquarters (CCRP HQ)

Chelsea and Caleb were awake when Thomas returned from gathering intelligence at the doors in Poland, Ohio. Thomas walked to the back room that was now a makeshift campsite with the field organizer and high school student sleeping on mattresses that the two had found late last night.

"Let's go get breakfast in Lisbon," Thomas suggested. He picked up a pillow on the floor and threw it on the old mattress.

"Come on, let's go," he said again. The two others followed Thomas out to the gray sedan.

A few minutes south of headquarters, the car skirted hills and Mennonite farms. Twenty minutes later, they turned into a parking lot in the city center of Lisbon. There was a sleek, streamlined silver diner, and Thomas had eggs and steak.

A little while later, the three of them made it to the CCRP HQ. This headquarters looked right out of 1920s small town Americana. The inside was trimmed with rich walnut and political knick-knacks.

Thomas sat in a large, upholstered leather chair. "Why can't Mahoning headquarters be like this?" he asked.

MCRP HQ

The reporter from the *Vindicator* turned on the camera. "Phyllis, why are you supporting Trump, especially with his comments about women recently coming to light?" the reporter asked.

Phyllis gave an incoherent response. The reporter kept a straight face and looked at the Trump sign with a backward S sitting behind the receptionist. *This is going to make great copy,* he thought.

Sunday, 16 October 2016, 23 Days
Davis Motel

Phyllis has to go! Thomas thought. He watched the video interview of Phyllis while getting ready for church. He texted Dan.

Dan Kavanagh responded.

Let Mark know.

This morning his gray car started brilliantly. Thomas drove past Tiffany's one more time on his way to St. Charles.

Moretti Compound

"Who let this guy in the MCRP?" Dan said. He was raging against Thomas to his daughter Kayla.

"He's an asshole," Kayla said.

Dan stopped his rant and looked directly at his daughter. "Why, what did he do?"

RCIA Class

Thomas arrived early to the RCIA class and sat in the corner near the outside window. The twice-divorced leader who had threatened him with a life of loneliness walked up to him and sat down.

Acting as his corporate career had taught him, the Deacon walked into the class exactly on time. He wore the same Ohio State Football jersey. "Welcome, everybody," he said. He flashed a broad smile and turned his head to the left to look at each student. His smile faded when he looked at the back corner.

Thomas sketched a picture in his notebook.

"We know, for example, that the bread and wine is not really the blood or body of Christ," the Deacon said.

Thomas stopped drawing and looked up. He interrupted the Deacon. "Isn't that the heart of Catholicism, the doctrine of transubstantiation?"

"Yes, but not like you think. The bread and wine doesn't actually change," The Deacon said.

"I am sure that it does," Thomas insisted.

The woman who had recommended that Thomas attend a church closer to his conservative views reacted physically. *What's going on here?* she thought. Slow realization spread across her face.

The class ended. Thomas walked out of the class without talking to anyone, and purposefully ignored the woman sitting next to him, who stared at him and willed him to be gone.

Monday, 17 October 2016, 22 Days
MCRP HQ

As the judge and her friends had been doing for three days a week since July, the crew set up the phone bank and called a thousand voters in Mahoning County. Thomas worked on his computer in the main room. He had seen earlier campaigns on both parties use phone banking, and it never seemed to be effective at generating an increase of votes. Hopefully it would be different this time, for he liked the judge and her deeply knowledgeable husband.

"I'm pushing off early today," the judge said. She waved to Thomas and walked out the front door. Thomas googled the baseball game. *Yep, she's going to watch the playoffs.* He wished he could go too.

Tuesday, 18 October 2016, 21 Days
The Avian

Thomas finished his chore for Mark and set up the flagpole in the main dining room of the Avian. The Republicans were going to have another fundraising dinner for Pamela and her run for County Treasurer. He walked to the entrance where Sonia, the campaign manager, stood.

"Where is Pamela, anyway?" he asked.

Madam Rhonda's Psychic House, Canfield, Ohio

Madam Rhonda had once been interested in politics. Decades earlier she had managed her uncle's campaign for township trustee, and she fondly remembered setting up the maps in his office, and making lists of houses for him to visit. She had enjoyed designing a simple palm card that he could hand out to their neighbors and prospective voters.

She smiled genuinely at the current candidate for Treasurer in Mahoning County, as she was happy to see a woman run for office. Rhonda turned over a card.

"Is that good?" Pamela asked.

"Not yet, my dear, there are four other cards still to go," Rhonda said. She pursed her lips, thinking how great it was that the Republicans had a candidate with significant means running this year. She was tired of her taxes increasing, and Mahoning County itself had begun to layer on the regulations for small businesses. It was time for a *laissez faire* approach to government.

"Am I going to win?" Pamela asked.

It was the tone of her voice that tripped a switch in Rhonda's brain. There was a quality in her client's voice that was more than the typical nervousness, though certainly nervousness was there too. Rhonda blinked, and her cheek twitched twice before she regained her composure. She felt her eyes getting wide. Her throat dried up, and for a brief moment she left her character behind. The fortune teller stared at the candidate and spoke directly, knowing the answer before the words left her lips. "How many doors did you walk?"

The Avian

Several prominent members of the Republican parties spoke during the dinner, including Matt Borges, the Ohio Republican Chair, John Husted, the Secretary of State of Ohio, and Bill Johnson, the local congressman.

Thomas was sitting between Mark and Rose, the party Chair and Chairwoman, and he was sitting across the table from John Husted, the Secretary of State and ultimate authority over all the Boards of Elections in the state.

"Trump is going to win Ohio," he told the table. "Trump has

support all over the state, but especially here. What were those numbers from the primary election?" Thomas asked Mark.

"We had double the normal Republicans vote in the primary, with the extra votes going for Trump. This included 6,000 crossover voters," Mark said. He gave data and left the conclusions for someone else.

"Right, and I see the same things at the doors. Even establishment Republicans who don't particularly like Trump are going to vote for him. Hillary was the worst candidate the Democrats could have chosen. In the voting booth, even the Rob Portman voters in Cincinnati will pull the lever for Trump to keep Hillary and Bill out of the White House."

"Interesting," John Husted said. "What do you think about the local candidates in the area? Do they have a chance to ride on Trump's coattails?" he asked. He looked at Thomas.

Dan stood thirty feet away at the dessert table with a county commissioner candidate. He held a beer in his hand and watched his boss' boss question Thomas.

A few minutes later, Thomas thought he would like a piece of cake. He walked back to the dessert table where Dan and the commissioner candidate were standing.

"Great party, huh?" he said.

Dan took a sip from his bottle. "Pervert," he said.

Thomas kept walking to the dessert table without responding. He returned to the VIP table, and resumed the conversation.

Moretti Farm

Bing

Thomas Ryan texted Dan.

Don't call me a pervert again.

Dan looked at the text.

Dan was very drunk. Thomas Ryan could go to hell. Who did Thomas think he was, talking to Dan's boss and the Secretary of State?

He typed on his phone, *pervert*.

Bing

Thomas Ryan responded.

I guess I could be even nicer to you in front of Mark.

"What the hell does that mean!" Dan said. *You leave Mark to me. Pervert.*

Thomas Ryan responded a final time.

What is your problem! stay away from me.

Dan Kavanagh had an idea. He began to formulate a plan to stop Trump using Thomas. Finally, Thomas showed that he would react when provoked in the right way. People thought that he was cool like a robot, but he wasn't a robot. The third debate was tomorrow.

I am going to ruin this punk's life, and stop this embarrassment of a candidate, Trump, in his tracks, Kavanagh thought. He poured himself a shot of whisky and downed the rest of the bottle.

CHAPTER 43

Wednesday, 19 October 2016, 20 Days
Board of Elections, Mahoning County

"Matt, can you come to my office?" Dan said. Matt was in the hall. He noticed Dan looked hungover and upset. He followed Dan to the Deputy Director's office.

"I warned people about Thomas Ryan, yet I didn't see what he was doing to my own family," Dan said. "This bastard harassed both Katherine and Kayla, and now he has assaulted Kayla."

Matt Harris' desire had vacillated between Kayla and Katherine for a few years. He channeled this frustration in the most pathetic of traditions. "What?! When did this happen?"

"Just the other day, he pushed up on Kayla when she and I went to headquarters. Kayla told me that she was afraid of going to headquarters as long as Thomas was there. She wouldn't give me details until last night. I am going to kill the bastard," Dan said.

"You should," Matt said. "You know, the press will be at the debate tonight. Why not just humiliate him in front of the entire world? Maybe we can make national news and put an end to Trump while we are at it."

Matt fell into Dan Kavanagh's trap.

"Why go to jail? We can ruin his life anyway," Dan said.

Matt nodded and thumbed out a text to Chelsea, the object of his current begging. Next, Matt posted on Twitter that the secret was out. Chelsea and Kayla joined him in cryptic Twitter postings. *It's on tonight!!!* Matt Harris tweeted.

St Columba Cathedral

"I'm looking for a sponsor," Thomas said. "I want a male over 40 who is not divorced."

The Monsignor looked at him and did not react. Thomas thought that the Monsignor reminded him of his Canadian thesis director from graduate school. Both were thoughtful and polite, and intelligent.

"Well, I can be your sponsor, but we would have to use proxies for some of the ceremonies since I have responsibilities here," Monsignor Siffrin said.

"Listen, I would love to have you as my sponsor, and I understand how busy you are. I certainly am not looking for something with prestige, and I am open to anyone who you might know who is a male, over 40, and not divorced," Thomas said.

Monsignor Siffrin nodded. "I will make some calls," he said. He changed the subject, "Do you have an interest in the dialogue between the Eastern and Western parts of the church?"

"Absolutely I do," said Thomas.

Third Debate, MCRP HQ

The third debate had gone better than expected, Thomas thought. He was in a good mood. He also was wary of Dan Kavanagh and avoiding him all night long. Matt Harris kept shooting Thomas dirty looks.

The leader of the Japanese news team approached the volunteer from Indiana. "Hi Thomas," he said, polite as always. "Do you think, just tonight, that we could have one interview?"

Thomas had helped the four Japanese reporters for the past month, and given them behind-the-scenes information when he'd had it. They had seen him work and talk, but he had always refused to go on camera for an interview. It was a pity, because he was such a good speaker.

Thomas looked at the reporter, and then at the other three reporters. Several other people gathered around the camera and Japanese reporters.

Thomas held up a finger. "One more beer," he said.

Everyone burst into laughter. Dan Kavanagh was sitting holding his own beer a few feet away from the laughing crowd. There was hatred in his stare.

"I'll show you who you need to interview," Thomas said. He walked toward Dan, "This is our Director of the Board of Elections, Dan Kavanagh," he said. The reporters crowded around a surprised Dan Kavanagh and stuck a camera in his face while asking him questions. Thomas retreated to the kitchen.

Dan followed Thomas to the kitchen and blew smoke in his face. Several people in the kitchen were friends of Thomas, and the provocation didn't work. Kavanagh walked away, having tipped his hand to Thomas of what was about to happen. Thomas somehow knew that he had to wait to leave headquarters until the press left.

At midnight, the last of the press pulled away, and Thomas put on his sport coat and grabbed his backpack. He saw Dan talking to about twelve people standing outside of the door. Mark walked inside as Thomas approached the exit door.

"There is nothing wrong with the texts you sent," Mark said. Thomas realized that Dan was carrying out his plan now.

Thomas walked through the door and Dan used his body to push him against a pole. "You pervert, how dare you talk to my wife!"

"How drunk are you?" Thomas said. A few people laughed and the derisive sound sent Dan into a fury. Nothing had gone as planned. Kavanagh's rage was feigned a few seconds earlier, but now it was genuine. He backed away and hurled insults.

"What type of a man are you!" he said. "You pervert! I will destroy you! I know all the cops here, if you ever show up here again, if you ever show up to a South Range game, if you ever show up to St. Charles again, I will destroy you!" Dan continued to shout and curse. "Stay away from my father!" he said.

"I like talking to Jim," Thomas said. He was watching the scene carefully. Dan was using his belly again to push him against the pole. Thomas saw Matt Harris and Kyle Morrow ready to jump into a fistfight or worse. Thomas reached into his pocket and grabbed his keys. If punches were going to be thrown, he was going to disable two of the men as quickly as possible.

He knew his brain was increasing the consumption of glucose because he was thinking clearly. *This is what Dan Kavanagh wanted, he wanted a fight.* Thomas thought of the Kavanagh family: Jim, Melanie, Kayla, Katherine, the four boys. He held Dan Kavanagh's stare while he realized that no matter what he did at this moment, if he did anything, Dan Kavanagh would lose. Kavanagh would likely get fired, and the grandparents and kids would lose everything.

Kavanagh kept screaming. "Don't ever talk to my father again." His voice was shrill. "Don't ever talk to Katherine again," Dan said. He let another slew of curses fly. His voice reached a high pitch, "and Kayla!"

Mark Munroe stepped in between Kavanagh and Thomas. He looked up at Thomas and asked him to leave.

Thomas walked away when Mark cleared the space, and Dan Kavanagh chased after him. "It's not worth it," Matt Harris shouted. He made a spectacle of preventing Dan from fighting Thomas.

"Pervert!" Dan shouted.

Thomas made it to his car, opened the door, and drove away.

"I have never in my life seen something like that," Tracey said. She was not addressing anyone in particular.

"Thomas Ryan has no affiliation with the Republican Party," Chelsea said. She walked inside to fill out a report for Tony Russo and Justin Clarke of the incident at the MCRP HQ.

Several other people watching the incident expected the police to arrive any minute. Ed kept listening for sirens or watching for flashing lights.

They never came.

CHAPTER 44

Wednesday night, 19 October 2016, 20 Days
North Lima

Thomas walked slowly up and down the sidewalk and street edge in North Lima for hours. He felt sadness come over him. He walked back to the motel at 2:00 am and went to sleep.

He felt a presence touching the room and reaching up through the ceiling. He did not understand what was happening. Images from ten years earlier in Spain flashed before his eyes. The presence told him that the injustices were bundled together, and then the apparition vanished.

Thomas sat up in bed. It was 5:30 am. He got out of bed and started to work on an email and police report.

CHAPTER 45

Thursday, 20 October 2016, 19 Days
Mark Munroe's House, Canfield

Mark read Thomas' email and dialed his number.

"Hi Thomas, this is Mark Munroe."

"Hi Mark, thanks for calling me," Thomas said.

"Listen Thomas, I've known Dan for a long time," Mark said. "I don't know what the problem is, but I will talk to him this afternoon. If you could just hang tight for a few hours, I would appreciate it," Mark said.

"I was taken completely off-guard, and I have been nothing but kind to his entire family. I was over at their farm," Thomas said. He tried to keep his messaging simple.

"I know you have, I have seen how you act. Let me see what I can find out and call you back," Mark said.

Board of Elections

"Dan," Mark started. He smiled broadly. "What happened?" Mark was not accusatory in his tone, but rather he sounded like a father who was attempting to bring in a wayward child with gentle reassurance.

"Listen, I had a lot to drink last night, I'm not going to deny it," Dan said. He was over-enunciating his words. Mark thought this was a sign that he had rehearsed his answer. Dan continued, "But who is this guy anyway? Does anybody know who he is or where he came from, really?"

Mark stared and listened.

"This guy," Dan refused to use his name, "shows up out of nowhere, starts talking to my wife. Did you know that he was trying to get her phone number last week?" Dan grunted in disgust. "I asked him to leave my daughters alone and he would not." Dan squinted to see Mark's reaction.

Mark showed no emotion and continued to listen.

"That bastard threatened to kill my family and me," Dan said.

"What?" Mark blinked. He knew this was not true.

"Yeah, he got angry when I told him to stay away from my wife, and he threatened me. He threatened my family. I was angry."

Mark waited a moment to make sure Dan was done. "Well, listen, I don't think Thomas is going to bother you or your family, so I don't think you have anything to worry about." Mark said.

"That bastard," Dan said, looking away from Mark. He knew he had to keep the profanity to a minimum right now. He knew his plan had backfired. There was no fight, and there was no news coverage. There would be no embarrassing Trump in the Mahoning Valley.

Friday, 21 October 2016
Trip to Pittsburgh

Thomas needed this day off. It was the first day that he did no campaign work in three months. He was driving to Pittsburgh. He turned on the radio and scanned the stations. A Catholic station from Pennsylvania that he had not heard before, FM 106.7, filled the cabin.

"Hail Mary, full of grace, the Lord is with thee. Blessed art thou among women, and blessed is the fruit of thy womb Jesus," said a family, led by the father.

A small child read a scripture describing the passion of Christ. The family said another Hail Mary, then the sister read the next passage. This continued for the entirety of the hour-long drive.

FBI Headquarters, Washington DC

"They did what?" Director Comey said. He gripped the phone. "Can you come to my office?"

The head of the Office of Professional Responsibility put the handset down and walked out of his office, up one floor, and to the executive hallway.

"He'll see you now," said an executive assistant, barely looking up from her crossword puzzle.

Comey sat grim-faced as his top man for internal security explained to him that within a week he was likely to face the resignation of up to two hundred special agents, and that many of them had vowed to go to the press if Comey did not release key facts about the Hillary Clinton email scandal.

Saturday, 22 October 2016, 17 Days
YSU Music Room

Thomas played two works of Chopin and then pulled up his MacBook. Mike was sending him nightly reports of the absentee voters, and he could see a pattern emerging. "Trump is going to win," he spoke aloud. The evidence was undeniable.

St. Elizabeth's Hospital

"I'm terribly sorry, but your husband did die," said the doctor. A social worker stood by Mary and grabbed her when the doctor told her the news. She covered her face with her hands and wept.

An hour later she walked the half-mile up Market Street from St. Elizabeth's Hospital to her apartment.

Tuesday

Ring

"Hello?" Thomas answered.

"Hi Thomas, you told me to call you if something happened to my husband. He died on Saturday," she said.

Thomas offered to visit the next day.

Wednesday

Mary's apartment was perfectly kept, and was nicely decorated. A cat peered around the hallway and blinked at Thomas, and then approached him, zigzagging. Mary walked from the front door to the kitchen. She made something for her guest to eat and poked her head into the living room where he stood.

"Take a seat on the couch," she said. He did.

Mary walked into the living room from the kitchen and sat on a chair next to the couch. The cat rubbed against her leg and jumped into her lap.

On the kitchen counter sat a plate full of nuts and grapes while Mary talked for two hours.

Friday, 28 October 2016, 11 Days
FBI Headquarters

Director Comey sighed and hit Send. He was not about to have a coup of FBI agents on his hands. If the special agents who had threatened to resign en masse had done so, it would have been a political nightmare for the bureau and the country. *That's two hundred special agents, most of whom are former Marine officers, leading two hundred battalions in the next civil war,* he thought.

He sent a letter discussing Hillary's emails to the congressional oversight committee.

Washington DC

The staffer received the director's email first. "Holy shit!" he said. His drinking buddy looked at him.

"I have to go, right now," the staffer said. He walked out of the M Street bar and called his boss.

Ten minutes later the congressman tweeted Comey's email for the world to see. The Friday night bad news dump no longer worked, and r/the_donald frothed the Internet waters like piranhas as they led the meme annihilation of Hillary. Blood filled the water.

Trump Headquarters, New York, New York

Kellyanne Conway reacted to the tweets by laughing. She read the hot takes and knew this was great news. "Thank goodness for the FBI!" she said.

She hung up the phone with a donor and put up her feet on her large desk in her fourteenth-floor office. She picked up a glass of Kentucky Bourbon and sipped it. *Trump is going to win.*

CHAPTER 46

Final Week

Next on Thomas' to-do list was to call Deacon Murphy of St. Rose Catholic Church near his newly rented house in Girard, Ohio so that he could finish his RCIA process. He used the story that he was moving into the area and he had recently rented a house and moved out of his "executive short-term housing." The deacon made an appointment to talk to him the next morning.

The meeting with Deacon Murphy went smoother than expected, and the Deacon assured Thomas that he would call Deacon Dan of St. Charles to move him to St. Rose. Thomas knew that Deacon Dan would not make trouble, as the entire leadership team wanted Thomas out of their parish.

Tuesday, 2 November 2016, 7 Days

Two days later, Thomas walked down the stairs of the auxiliary building at the St. Rose grounds in Girard, Ohio. Deacon Murphy met him there.

"Let me introduce you to Pete, your new sponsor," he said.

"Welcome Thomas," Pete said. He gave a genuine smile.

Election Eve, 7 November 2016
Back Room, MCRP HQ

Thomas Ryan pushed send one last time on his phone. Over fifty local, national, and international reporters had his predictions on the Trump race in Mahoning County and the State of Ohio. He looked at the time.

11:48 pm

New York City

Stephanie heard her phone buzz. The *Bloomberg* reporter set the glass of red wine on the small stool near her bathtub and picked up her phone.

Expect Trump to receive 48% of the vote in Mahoning County with a two standard deviation error of +/-1.5%. The previous record high for a Republican candidate in Mahoning County is 40% Republican during Reagan's first election. Business Insider predicts a 42% Trump vote for Mahoning County. Anything higher than 40% in Mahoning County and Trump will win Ohio based on other projections. I am using daily absentee voting records to make this analysis. Trump is highly likely to win Ohio and likely to win Michigan.

"How is he getting absentee voter results?" Stephanie asked. Her cat stared at the twenty-eight-year-old blonde now sitting upright, splashing water on the marble floor.

Back Room, MCRP HQ

Thomas was not getting absentee-voter-specific vote results, but he was getting *who* voted, and their previous Republican, Democratic, or Independent voter registrations. Over the past two weeks he had used this voter data and past voter data available on the Mahoning County Board of Elections website to build a model that he used to make his predictions.

Two weeks earlier he had learned from congressman Bill Johnson that 83% of Republican voters who said that they would vote for the Republican US Senate Candidate Rob Portman said that they also would vote for Trump. Thomas figured that an additional six to eight percent of these people would secretly vote for Trump while denying their true intentions to any pollster. Ohio Republicans rejected Hillary Clinton too strongly to do anything else. If Trump could earn enough crossover voters in Northeast Ohio, he would win Ohio. Michigan was a similar story, particularly in the population heavy Southeast Michigan region, which shared many similarities to Northeast Ohio.

Thomas' work showed that Trump was well exceeding expectations in the blue-collar region. Northeast Ohio and Northwest Pennsylvania were going to be much more Republican than they had been in elections for the past several decades. Pennsylvania was so large it probably was a lost cause even with the Western Trump bump, Thomas thought. He did not talk about it to Party leaders or to the press.

Bing

Thomas looked at his phone and saw that the tall, beautiful, and no-nonsense German reporter who had visited Youngstown during the campaign, walked doors with him, and screamed her heart out at the Struthers-Poland football match had sent him a text.

No one in New York City expects Trump to win. Interesting.

Thomas smiled. The Kool-Aid was strong. He remembered when he had run for state representative years earlier. It is almost impossible to see anything resembling truth in the midst of a political campaign, whether politician, volunteer, party official, or reporter. The daily grind of the campaign somehow pushed out truth on every side. *Maybe I am drinking the other Kool-Aid,* Thomas thought. He laughed loudly.

Bing….Bing…Bing…

Other reporters were texting him back to thank him for his work throughout the campaign. No one really believed his predictions. No one understood the data.

Except for one person.

She understood everything.

CHAPTER 47

Tuesday, 8 November 2016
6:00 AM, Regional NPR Studio, WKSU Kent, Ohio

M.L. Schultze never bought Thomas' story that he was a volunteer on the campaign from the first time she interviewed him back in August. She was impressed by his calm, organized thoughts during that interview, and she liked the regular updates that he sent throughout the campaign. *What was Thomas doing here?* Maybe Thomas was building relationships with reporters for a future congressional run of his own. *But why Youngstown?* That part did not make sense.

Schultze studied the text that Thomas had sent last night. She was at the WKSU regional studio preparing for Election Day interviews. She planned to visit the poll lines this morning to hear what voters had to say and maybe get a read on the most bizarre election that she had ever covered.

She checked her hair and makeup in the mirror, more ritual than anything else. She smiled. She looked the part of a serious journalist, and at least ten years younger than her age, even with the gray hair. Good bone structure and a pursuit of truth kept the years at bay.

With one motion she gathered her phone and recorder and put them into her purse. She stepped into the parking lot and then into her car.

- THOMAS RYAN -

6:45 AM, Davis Motel

"Well, I am checking out today," Thomas said. "I found a house in Girard," he continued. He wore a shirt and tie under a fleece jacket.

Doug took his keys and leaned on the counter. "I wish you the best of luck. Girard is a good place; it's blue-collar, but it's safe. Your kind of town," Doug said. "This has been really interesting, the whole campaign season. You guys work really hard." Doug referred to his belief that Thomas was a national staffer who had come to Youngstown to keep things under control. Thomas had told him that he was from Indiana, but Doug noticed Thomas did not have a Hoosier accent.

"Thanks again, by the way, your beds are nice," Thomas said.

"Hey, one more thing, would you mind writing a review online? We just had a woman complain and it would help us out."

"Complain? This is a great place. I loved it here. Sure, I will write you a review," Thomas said. He reached to shake the owner's hand across the counter.

Doug watched Thomas walk out the door and drive away in his grey sedan. *Nice kid, but too bad Trump isn't going to make it. Who knows, I guess.* Doug thought.

7:00 am Polling Location, Akron, Ohio

A line of voters snaked from the locked front doors of the Ukrainian Byzantine Catholic Church at 7:00 am, and M.L. Schultze thought that this was the longest line she had ever seen here in Akron precinct number eight. She walked up to a young blonde woman.

"Hi, my name is M.L. Schultze, I am a reporter with NPR. Do you mind if I ask you a few questions for the NPR morning show?" Schultze asked.

"Oh, hi. No, I don't mind," the woman said. She felt butterflies.

Schultze turned on her recorder and put it close to the voter's face.

"Could you say and spell your name for me?

"Sure, Tammy Debarto, D-e-b-a-r-t-o." Tammy said.

Schultze realized that this woman was not a natural blonde. "So, whom are you voting for?" the reporter asked, annunciating her words in a neutral accent.

"Too be honest, I don't really like either candidate, but I don't like where our country is headed. We have to do something," she said. The woman continued and emphasized the next words. "I am voting for Trump."

Schultze thanked the woman and moved up the line to an older man. He gave a one-word answer, "Trump." That was a waste. She talked to three more people and no one admitted to voting for Hillary Clinton. It matched the prediction from the text message she read that morning.

Schultze then spoke into the recorder and gave a brief commentary on the strong showing Trump was making at the beginning of Election Day in Northeast Ohio.

Twenty minutes later the national NPR office in Washington DC produced her report, and scheduled it to play in the 7:30 am news cycle.

7:30 am, Thomas Car I-80, Near Akron

Thomas smiled at the early report of Trump's strength in Northeast Ohio. *Schultze is reporting against the grain! Wow, she has a great voice*, he thought. He reached down and turned the radio to a music station, missing NPR breaking to the first of a daylong string of reporters who directly contradicted M.L. Schultze's reporting out of Ohio. Thomas listened to classic rock for an hour before he drove out of range of the station. The next station he found had a much worse music selection.

Board of Elections, Mahoning County

A retired steelworker walked into the old hospital on Oak Street. Ann welcomed him and directed him to an empty voting booth in the main room. It was just before the lunchtime rush.

The man used a black pen to fill in the circle next to his choice for President, Donald Trump. Further down the ballot he switched parties and filled in the circles for the Democrat candidates. He did not turn the ballot over to fill in the non-partisan races.

Grimacing from arthritis but smiling because of his ballot, the man wearing the Pittsburgh Steelers hat walked to Ann. She pointed to a box and he deposited his ballot. Ann smiled, and he smiled back at her. He walked out the automatic doors and looked up at the blue sky.

The Lakes, Columbus, Indiana

Thomas pulled down the cul-de-sac to the brown lake house a few minutes before 2:00 pm. Two young men wearing white shirts and dark trousers were knocking at the front door. He pulled up the driveway and they turned to face him. "Hey guys, why don't you come inside for a minute?" he said. It was hot in Southern Indiana. Thomas fumbled through his backpack for the house key and led the two men around back to the kitchen door.

"Don't worry about your shoes," he said. "Listen, I just got back from Ohio and I am starving, so I am going to eat. Would you like me to fix you anything?" Thomas asked. "It's no problem," he added. He had already opened the refrigerator door and popped two dark cherries into his mouth. *These are delicious.*

"Oh no, we are fine," one nineteen-year-old said.

Thomas got out three glasses and gave them water before bringing over a sandwich for himself. The three men talked about the election. The conversation drifted after a few minutes.

Nearly an hour later Thomas said, "That's because young men like you are the hope of everyone, just as the Apostle John says," He had been talking theology and philosophy with a platonic bent. The two young men smiled and Thomas stood up. He shook each of their hands sincerely.

They left the house and walked up the cul-de-sac, talking about what they had learned.

Thomas walked up the stairs and across the bridge to his bedroom. He lay down on the Japanese mat and relaxed.

An hour later, Boots licked his face. He bumped her head with his own and held her. Thomas took a shower and put on his suit for the election night watch parties. He raided the kitchen one more time.

Hotel, Bartholomew County Republican Party Watch Party

A staffer at the front desk pointed Thomas down a long hall to the grand ballroom where the Bartholomew County Republicans were holding their election night party. He saw his neighbor and state representative and thanked him for making connections to the Trump campaign earlier in the year.

"Have you met our chairwoman?" the state representative asked. He motioned Thomas to follow him, and they made their way to a table near the front platform.

A few minutes later, at the Party Chair's insistence, Thomas stepped on the stage to address the hundred people in the room. "Ladies and gentleman," Thomas said, "I have returned from Northeast Ohio today where I have worked during the general election." He paused and then emphasized his next sentence. All eyes were on him. "Trump has a good chance of winning the presidency tonight." He could tell the audience didn't believe him.

"Throughout this campaign I have worked in Ohio, and I guarantee you that Trump will win the state of Ohio. The polls do not reflect the enormous support he has, especially among Democratic crossover voters, and voters who have not voted in multiple presidential cycles," Thomas said. He looked around the room with confidence and broke into a smile.

"Trump will win Ohio," he said. "The question will be if he wins Michigan, Pennsylvania, or another state with a similar demographic makeup. For example, Southeast Michigan has several counties that look a lot like Mahoning and Trumbull Counties of Northeast Ohio." Thomas sounded like a favorite teacher. He enunciated his words in perfect international English and with a kind tone.

"I expect Trump and Pence to win at least one other Midwest state. If they do, they will win the national election." Thomas stopped speaking, and once again looked at several faces in separate parts of the ballroom. The crowd began to clap, and the noise grew louder as he walked off stage. He handed the microphone to the party chair. She stared at him. *Who is this guy?*

The state representative slapped Thomas on the back when he walked back to him. "Great speech!" he said. He grinned from ear to ear. Thomas shook his hand, and walked out the main doors. He made his way outside, where a drizzle of rain had covered his car.

MCRP HQ

By 8:01 pm every local Republican candidate in Mahoning County had lost his or her race, and not by small margins. Several people left the MCRP HQ before Dan Kavanagh and Matt Harris arrived. There was no reason for them to come to headquarters except to watch the national election and drink from the well-stocked cabinets.

Dan had promised his wife that he would cut down on the drinking, but there was no evidence of temperance. He and Matt each sipped whisky out of brown bottles while watching the election night coverage in the back conference room. They made fun of the local candidates who had walked out of the headquarters building thirty minutes earlier. They watched and waited for the clown Trump to be humiliated in front of the entire the world.

St. Charles Catholic Church

Deacon Dan and Deacon Bob were preparing for a teen life event that would take place the following evening, and they had the flat-screen TV in the conference room turned to ABC news. A blonde anchor predicted that Trump had no path to victory. Deacon Dan twisted his waist while making a dancing move with his arms. He pointed his fingers like pistols. "I am glad this nonsense is over," he said.

Deacon Bob turned the TV off while celebrating with Deacon Dan. *It's time a woman was in charge,* Deacon Bob thought. He smirked and hit the lights. The two left the building.

- WINNING OHIO -

The Westin, Indiana Republican Watch Party, Indianapolis, Indiana

Thomas received his lanyard from the cheerful man at the check-in desk shortly before 10:00 pm at the Indiana Republican Party Watch Party at the Westin Hotel. He walked into the ballroom. *There must be a thousand people here,* he thought.

The state elections had been called and the new governor and senator took turns making their victory speeches.

11:00 pm

At the front of the ballroom on the left side a giant red Wisconsin state filled the vinyl screen from floor to ceiling. Thomas turned his head. "We are calling Wisconsin for Trump," the anchor said.

Thomas looked at his new friend, an accountant from Indianapolis. "Wow, this is big," he said. No one had expected Wisconsin to go for Trump.

2:00 am

"Bloomberg has called Pennsylvania for Trump," the anchor said.

Thomas yelled a full-throated primal scream. The accountant joined him. Several hundred people shouted. Thomas was unprepared for the emotion that washed over him. He kept shouting to tamp down a surge of feeling.

The night manager heard the screaming and promptly kicked the remaining Trump supporters out of the hotel. He had promised his wife that he would vote for Hillary.

Thomas walked out to the street and climbed in his car. He drove south to Columbus and turned on the radio. Vice President Elect Mike Pence was the first to speak.

Thomas knew there was an enormous split in the country now.

Trump walked to the podium to loud cheers. "USA! USA! USA!"

He motioned with his hands. "Thank you, thank you very much everybody. Sorry to keep you waiting, complicated business."

ABOUT THE AUTHOR

Thomas Ryan lives in Youngstown with his dog. When he is not writing, he loves to hike the hills of Western Pennsylvania. Earlier in his career, Thomas worked as an expert on Caspian Sea and Central Asian geopolitics, focusing in particular on energy politics of the Former Soviet Union.

If you have enjoyed this book, please leave an excellent review on Amazon or Goodreads. Also, to find out about upcoming book releases or other news, sign up for the Thomas Ryan author newsletter at winningohio.com.

You can reach the author at thomasryan@winningohio.com with your comments or questions. Thank you.

www.ingramcontent.com/pod-product-compliance
Lightning Source LLC
Chambersburg PA
CBHW030302080526
44584CB00012B/412